MONEY IN ART

David Trigg

MONEY IN ART

FROM COINAGE TO ÇRYPTO

David Trigg

HENI Publishing, London

Cover: Cornelia Parker, *Embryo Money,* 1996, ten pence pieces
in the earliest stage of production and bag, dimensions variable,
*c.*25 × 30 cm (*c.*9⅞ × 11¾ in.) Courtesy of the artist and Frith
Street Gallery, London. Special thanks to the Royal Mint.

ISBN 978-1-1912122-96-7

A catalogue record for this book is available
from The British Library.

Commissioned and edited by Rebecca Morrill
Picture Research by Annalaura Palma
Proofread by Catalina Imizcoz
Designed by Sylvia Ugga
Production by Sarah McLaughlin
Printed by GPS Group in Bosnia and Herzegovina
Typeface: Suisse Int'l, Söhne

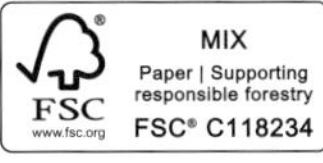

CONTENTS

FOREWORD by Mark Carney

During my 2021 HENI Talks with Damien Hirst on his *The Currency* project, we reflected on the complicated relationship between art and money. While artists, like everyone else, need to make a living from their profession, they occupy peculiar positions, in which financial success (in their lifetimes) is often treated with suspicion. The nineteenth-century European Romantic ideal of the 'starving artist' who sacrifices material comforts for creative pursuits once became the embodiment of virtue and still underpins some of the critical value systems in today's art world. Historically, money in art was usually represented as 'filthy lucre' – from Caravaggio's *The Cardsharps* (*c.*1594) to various Renaissance paintings of *Jesus and the Money Changers* (see pp.13–14).

Yet money and art are not always in opposition – there is also a fusion between them. Both are 'stores of value' intended to be worth more than the sum of their physical parts. A painting traditionally comprises a wooden frame, stretched canvas and layers of pigment. Banknotes are small sheets of printed cotton paper or polymer – materials that are worth a mere fraction of the face value of the note. In both cases, value is a social construct. We value a Jane Austen £5 banknote because others do, and such fiat money holds its value because of the institutions, such as central banks, that back it. The value of an object of art is not institutionally anchored but wholly subjective. Art's value is in the eye of the beholder, and as such, may fluctuate with time, fashion and scarcity.

During our conversation, Damien identified an important aspect of money in its tangible form, remarking that: 'coins are like sculptures and notes are like etchings'. Indeed, physical money serves as a collective memory for a country and its people, with cultural as well as economic value. One reason why the Bank of England chose J. M. W. Turner's *The Fighting Temeraire* (1839) to be represented on its £20 banknote was because it beautifully captures the disruptive poignancy of technological progress. A lesson all too relevant for us today, including artists.

Instead of shying away from the subject of money, the artists in this book tackle it head on, using their unique perspectives and aesthetics to explore the concept from multiple angles. Many use physical currency as a medium, exploiting the tension between money (perceived by users to have a stable value underpinned by financial institutions) and art (perceived to have more volatile worth, driven by the changing tastes and fashions of an unregulated art market). The invention of NFTs as a means to introduce ownership and provenance into the virtual realm has kickstarted a new branch of money-related art.

Taken together, this collection of artworks from the Pop art of the 1960s to the virtual art of today demonstrates the breadth of ways in which visual artists have explored forms of money and its histories, demonstrating that art can be money and money can be art.

INTRODUCTION: Money in Western Art History

It is often said that money makes the world go round. Indeed, it is hard to conceive how life would function without it. Money is so integral to human existence that it is no surprise to find that artists through the ages have consistently engaged with what is undoubtedly one of humanity's greatest and most troublesome of inventions. As the following overview demonstrates, the history of Western art – the shorthand term for work rooted in European and American traditions – is rich with artworks reflecting the complex role that money plays in society. From ancient Greek ceramics and medieval engravings, to biblically-inspired paintings and Dutch genre scenes of everyday life, to American trompe l'oeil, Dada photomontages and the multifarious works of contemporary artists; each conveys something about the attitudes towards money in the time and culture in which it was created.

Pennies from heaven

Unexpected financial gains, such as a surprise windfall or tax rebate, are sometimes likened to receiving 'pennies from heaven'. The phrase likely originated in a 1936 song that was popularised by Bing Crosby in an eponymous film released the same year. However, the motif of 'coinage raining down from on high' is much older, finding its origins in ancient Greek mythology. As told in Ovid's *Metamorphoses* (8 CE), Danaë was a princess of Argos, the daughter of King Acrisius. An oracle had prophesied that she would bear a son who would kill her father, and so the King had her imprisoned to prevent her encountering men. However, this confinement did not hinder Zeus (Jupiter in Roman mythology), the god of sky and thunder, who transformed himself into a shower of gold that rained upon her and impregnated her.

One of the earliest representations of this myth on a Boeotian bell-krater (**fig. 1**) dating to the fifth century BCE shows Danaë reclining on a *kline* (daybed) as

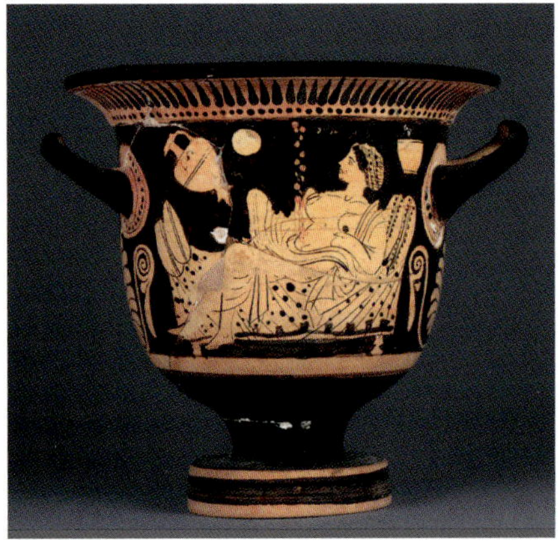

fig. 1 *Boeotian bell-krater*, *c.* 430 BCE, painted clay, red-figure technique, 23 × 25 × 22.8 cm (9 × 9⅞ × 9 in.), Musée du Louvre, Paris

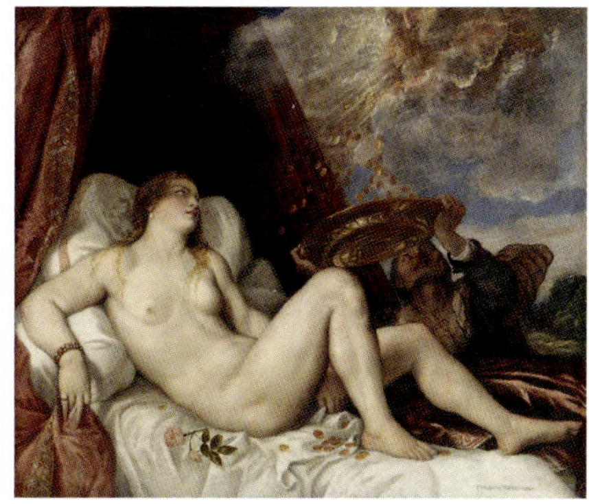

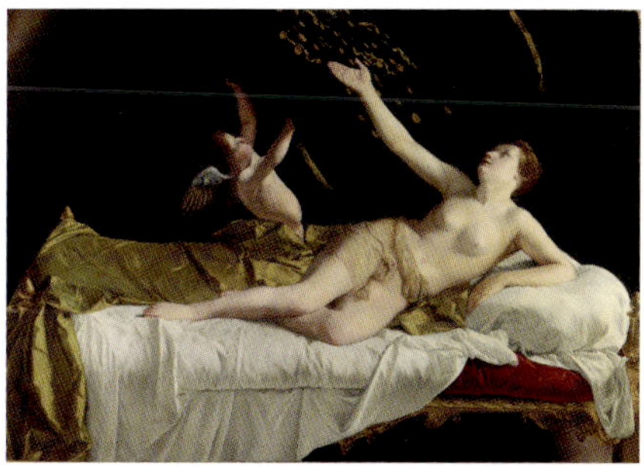

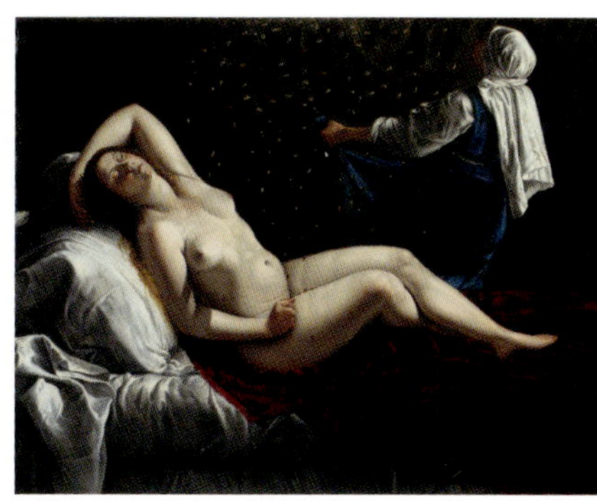

Zeus's stream of golden rain pours onto her exposed belly and into her womb. Some of the fertile droplets appear like flakes of gold, while others are more rounded and coin-like, their form reflected in the patterned fabric on which she lies. The Greek drachma was typically minted in silver, although as a result of the Peloponnesian War (431–404 BCE) and the depletion of silver to pay for it, the traditional silver coin changed to gold for a time. Regardless of whether the creator of the bell-krater had actual coins in mind, gold is presented in the design as a material of seduction. In later centuries, Roman poets portrayed Danaë as a venal woman, selling her love for money, and it is this interpretation that forms the subtext of many of the more erotic representations that followed.

In Renaissance Europe, the Italian humanist movement emphasised the value of studying ancient Greco-Roman culture. Titian (*c.*1485/90–1576) and his workshop painted several versions of the Danaë myth, including one made in 1551–3 for King Philip II of Spain as part of a cycle of seven mythologically themed compositions that the artist called his 'poesie' ('poems'). In this version, Titian paints the shower of gold as raindrops, whereas in a variant made after 1554 (**fig. 2**), gold coins spill down from a cloud, landing on Danaë's bedsheet.

In all Titian's compositions, the princess is depicted naked, reclining provocatively on her bed with knees raised and legs slightly apart. She gazes dreamily at the gold, offering no resistance to Zeus. Her handmaid, in contrast, stares agog, desperately collecting the gold in her smock or, in the after 1554 version, a large dish. Money is also the focus of a monumental depiction (**fig. 3**) of Danaë by Orazio Gentileschi (1563–1639). Here, cupid pulls back a dark green curtain while golden coins and ribbons rain down. This work was created around a decade after his daughter, Artemisia, (1593–*c.*1653), tackled the same subject (**fig. 4**) but with some notable differences in mood. In her composition, Danaë sends mixed messages: is she basking in post-coital bliss or has she crossed her legs in an attempt to resist the advances of the amorous god?

This moment in the Danaë myth has continued to be depicted by artists of the modern era, one of the most famous being Gustav Klimt (1862–1918). Eroticism was certainly the focus of his 1907 painting (**fig. 5**) depicting a naked, red-haired woman seemingly in the throes of ecstasy as a stream of gold pours between her legs. The flow of sperm-like coins is mirrored by the pattern of circular forms that cover the billowing purple chiffon in the bottom right of the composition – a design that the Austrian artist based on blastocysts, the clusters of embryonic cells from which a baby potentially grows. Danaë is thus reimagined as a mystical symbol of fertility.

Avarice: the all-consuming greed

In thirteenth-century Europe, trade was burgeoning like never before. The preceding two hundred years had seen towns established across the continent, many of which grew exponentially as they were enriched by profitable local commodities. Markets became increasingly integrated, banks were opened and coinage proliferated, allowing more and more people to participate in the growing monetary economy. The widespread presence of money in medieval society, and the tidy fortunes being amassed by burghers (middle class citizens), aroused considerable anxiety among Christian theologians. Avarice, the insatiable desire to gain and hoard wealth, is one the seven deadly sins of the Roman Catholic church and many thinkers obsessed over the dangers that money posed to the human heart. The debates around money and morality were also reflected in the works of artists, especially in the late medieval period.

In his panel painting *Death and the Miser* (**fig. 6**), the Dutch artist Hieronymus Bosch (*c.* 1450–1516) depicts Death as an emaciated skeletal figure clutching an arrow. Peering into the miser's bedchamber, he looks to see if the old man will accept the sack of coins offered to him by a crouching demon, or listen to the angel by his side who gestures upwards to the crucifix in the window, urging him to turn to Christ. At the foot of the bed, Bosch transports the viewer back in time, showing the man earlier in his life. His hypocrisy is evident to all:

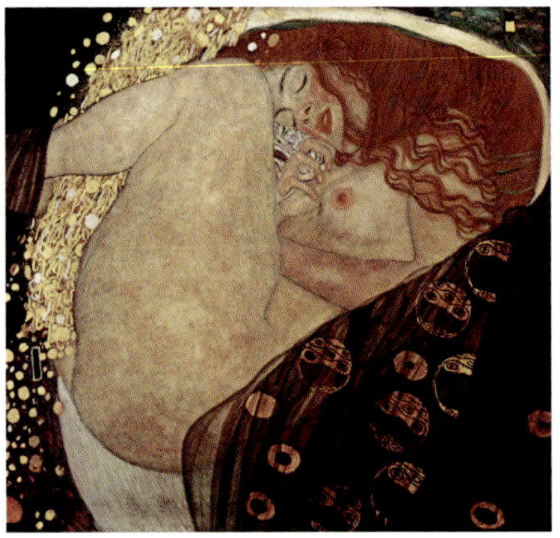

fig. 5 **Gustav Klimt**, *Danaë*, 1907, oil on canvas, 77 × 83 cm (30¼ × 33¾ in.), Galerie Würthle, Vienna

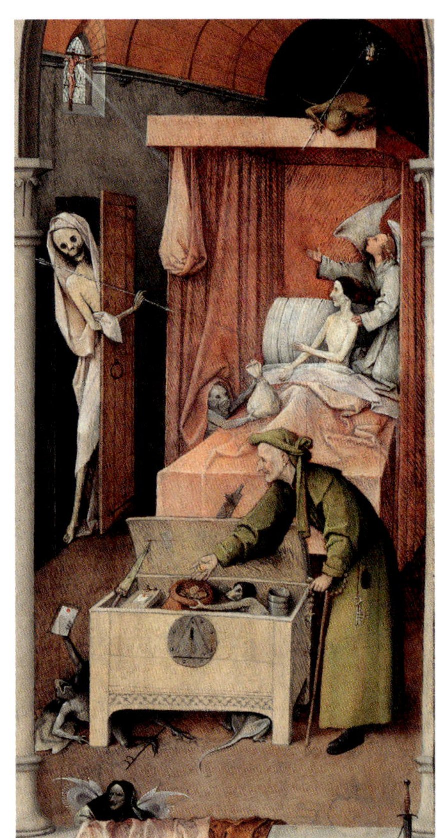

fig. 6 **Hieronymus Bosch**, *Death and the Miser* (detail), *c.* 1485–90, oil on oak, 93 × 31 cm (36⅝ × 12¼ in.), National Gallery of Art, Washington D.C.

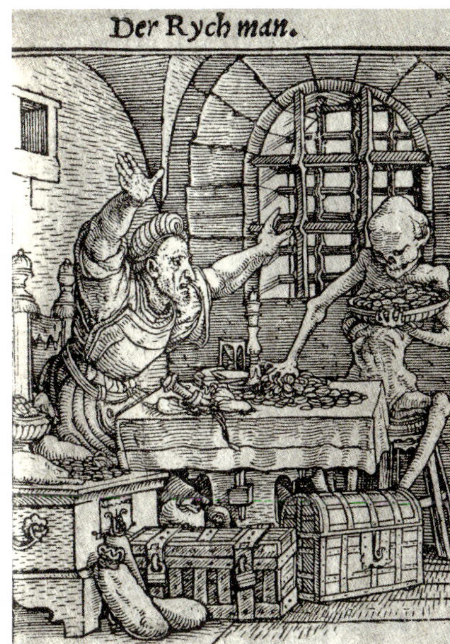

fig. 7 **Hans Holbein the Younger**, *Der Rychman (The Rich Man / The Miser)*, from the series 'The Dance of Death', *c.*1523–26, woodcut (by Hans Lützelburger), 6.5 × 4.9 cm (2½ × 1⅞ in.), Cleveland Museum of Art, Ohio

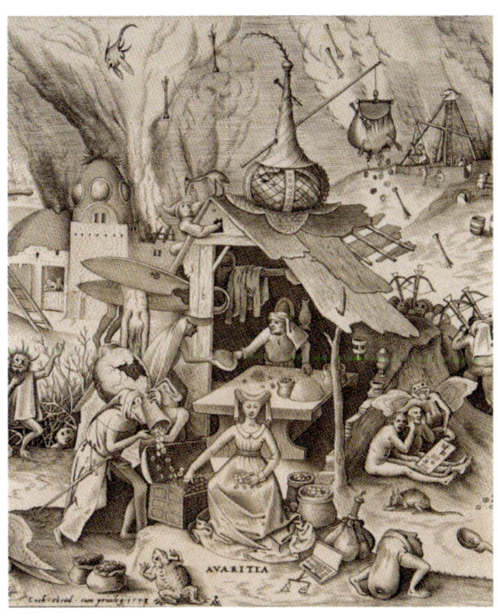

fig. 8 **Pieter Bruegel the Elder**, *Avarice* (detail), 1558, from 'The Seven Deadly Sins', engraving (by Pieter van der Heyden), 22.5 × 29.7 cm (8⅞ × 11¾ in.), The Metropolitan Museum of Art, New York

with one hand he tosses coins into a large jar held by a rat-like demon, and with the other he clutches a rosary, attempting the impossible feat of serving both God and Mammon. With the miser's fate hanging in the balance, will he inherit eternal life or eternal damnation?

Another avaricious man confronts death in the small woodcut *Der Rychman* (*The Rich Man / The Miser,* **fig. 7**), from 'The Dance of Death', an influential print series designed by the German artist Hans Holbein the Younger (1497–1543) to remind viewers of their mortality. Across 41 plates, Death surprises people at all levels of society, from king to physician to ploughman, leading – or in some cases dragging – each to their destiny. The rich miser has hoarded great wealth, filling a vaulted room with money chests, bags of cash and piles of coins. Flinging his arms up indignantly, he looks on in horror as Death gleefully grabs large handfuls of his money, adding it to his own brimming bowl. The scene recalls Jesus's Parable of the Rich Fool (Luke 12:13–21) in which a man selfishly stores away his surplus grain and goods, hoarding them for his future comfort, only to have God say: 'You fool! This very night your life will be demanded from you.' Similarly, the hourglass and extinguished candle on the table indicate that the miser's end has come.

Over time, artists began to personify Avarice as a woman because the Latin noun *avaritia* is feminine. In the series 'The Seven Deadly Sins' by Pieter Bruegel the Elder (*c.*1525–69), which was then engraved by Pieter van der Heyden (*c.*1495–1526), a fashionably dressed woman is depicted sitting at the centre of a hellish landscape populated by demonic figures and animals (**fig. 8**). Surrounded by baskets and bags of cash, she mindlessly gathers coins in her lap from a chest that is replenished by a beak-nosed figure. Greedy behaviour and its consequences are seen all around, and the surreal characters and fantastical setting recall the imagery of Bosch. In the complementary series 'The Seven Virtues' (1559–60), Bruegel sets the scenes in contemporary times, portraying Avarice's opposite number, Charity, as a humbly dressed woman in a town square, surrounded by acts of giving and sharing.

Artists of the Low Countries took up the theme with characteristic realism in the seventeenth century, a period in which avarice was thought to intensify in old age. In *Old Woman Examining a Coin by a Lantern* (**fig. 9**) by Dutch artist Gerrit van Honthorst (1592–1656), an aged woman, her facial wrinkles emphasised by the candle-light, intently studies a coin while grasping a bulging money bag. A second bag, overflowing with glistening coins, pokes out from from her bosom – this is a woman who keeps her money close to her heart.

A similar treatment of the theme is seen in the seventeenth-century painting *L'avarice* (**fig. 10**) by Matthias Stom (*c.*1600–after 1652). Again the anonymous figure is alone, counting her money by night, consumed and isolated by greed that is represented by the three coins on her palm. The candle motif was used again by David Teniers the Younger in *The Covetous Man* (**fig. 11**), a painting inspired by Christ's aforementioned Parable of the Rich Fool and which has echoes of Holbein's *Der Rychman.* Here, we see a grim-faced couple surrounded by sacks of money in a dark and shabby room. The woman, who is weighing coins on her handheld scales, glances at the man, who stares blankly into space; perhaps having noticed that the candle on the window ledge has burned right down and extinguished, signifying that his days are at an end. In all of these admonishments against avarice, the message is consistent: no matter how much wealth you accumulate on earth, none can be taken with you after death.

Christ and Currency: New Testament imagery

Jesus Christ had much to say about money. The four Gospels of Matthew, Mark, Luke and John record his teachings on the subject as well as dramatic episodes where currency plays a significant role. In one incident – (found in Matthew 22, Mark 12 and Luke 20) – Jesus is approached by a group of Herodians and Pharisees who, after flattering their way into conversation with him, ask him about taxes in an attempt to force him into aligning either with Rome or with Jewish law. 'Is it right to pay the imperial tax to Caesar or not?', they inquire,

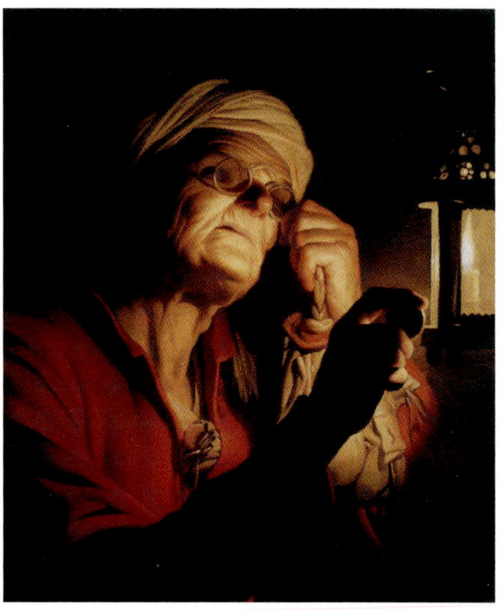

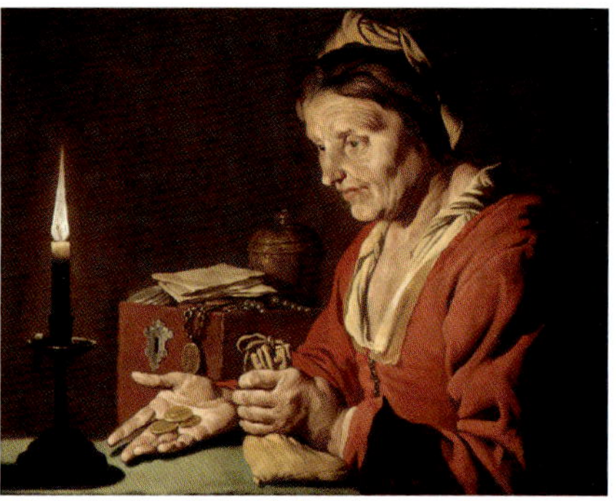

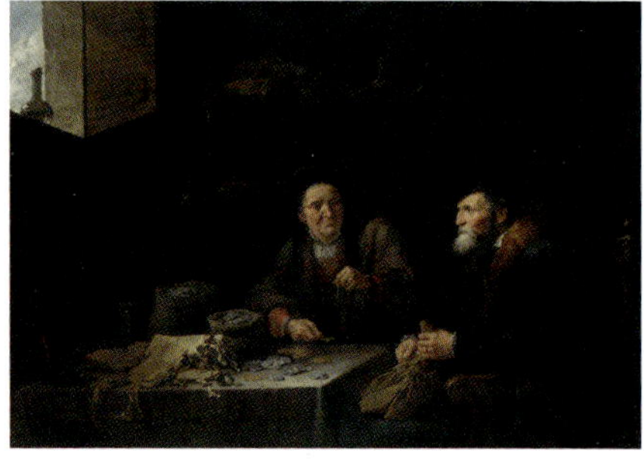

fig. 9 **Gerrit van Honthorst**, *Old Woman Examining a Coin by a Lantern*, 1623, oil on canvas, 75 × 60 cm (29½ × 23⅝ in.), The Kremer Collection
fig. 10 **Matthias Stom**, *L'avarice*, *c.*1625–50, oil on canvas, 66 × 81 cm (26 × 31⅞ in.), Musée de Grenoble
fig. 11 **David Teniers the Younger**, *The Covetous Man*, 1648, oil on canvas, 62.5 × 85 cm (24⅝ × 33½ in.), National Gallery, London

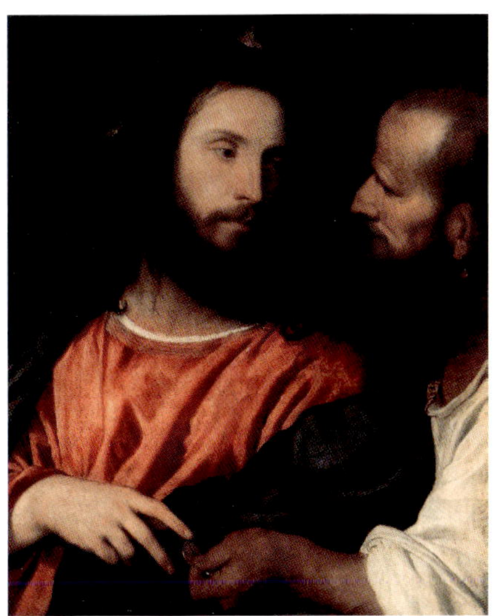

fig.12 **Titian**, *The Tribute Money*, c.1516, oil on poplar panel, 75 × 56 cm (29½ × 22 in.), Staatliche Kunstsammlungen Dresden

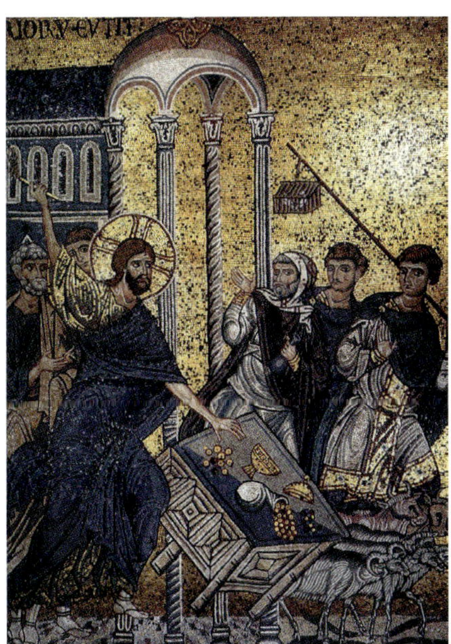

fig.13 **Byzantine school**, *Christ Banishes the Money Changers*, late 12th–mid 13th century, mosaic, Cathedral of Monreale, Sicily

reasoning that if he replied 'no', the Herodians (who supported the Roman occupation of Palestine) would report him to the governor and have him executed for treason, while if he answered 'yes', the Pharisees (a staunchly nationalist religious sect) would denounce him as disloyal to his people and discredit his ministry. Sensing their duplicity, Christ asked them to bring him a denarius, the coin used for paying the tax. When it was presented, he asked whose likeness is depicted on it, to which came the reply 'Caesar's'. His response then stunned them all: 'Therefore pay unto Caesar the things that are Caesar's and unto God the things that are God's'.

One of the earliest representations of this scene is Titian's work *The Tribute Money* (**fig.12**), a panel painting commissioned by Alfonso I d'Este, Duke of Ferrara, for the door of a cabinet containing the Italian nobleman's collection of ancient medals and coins. Titian shows us Christ meeting the eyes of the questioning Pharisee; the tightly cropped composition with the figures in close proximity heightening the drama. Christ's serene expression confirms the gesture of his hand, which points to the denarius. Titian revisited the subject around 1560 for King Philip II of Spain, adding a bespectacled scribe in the background and altering the composition so that Christ points not to the coin but to heaven, emphasising that one should focus attention on serving God rather than oneself.

Another story recounted in all four Gospels is that of Christ driving the money changers from the temple in Jerusalem. Christ had travelled to the temple to celebrate Passover, but found that it had been turned into a marketplace filled with dishonest traders and moneylenders. Incensed at their corruption, he angrily drove out all who were buying and selling there, knocking over tables and benches and accusing them of turning the house of God into 'a den of thieves'. A standout medieval treatment of the subject is found in northwestern Sicily, in the Cathedral of Monreale, Palermo (**fig.13**), as part of an extensive cycle of Byzantine style golden mosaics on biblical themes created between the late twelfth and mid-thirteenth centuries. The glistening scene depicts a haloed Christ brandishing a whip (as per John 2:15) as he scatters coins, people and animals alike. The bright gold coins jump out against the subdued blue and grey hues in the rest of the mosaic, emphasising the theme of financial wrongdoing.

During Europe's Counter Reformation, the subject of Christ driving out the money changers gained a new significance in painting as an allegory for the expulsion of Protestant heresy from the Catholic Church but to that end, the depiction of physical money became less of a focus. Notable exceptions include *The Purification of the Temple* (**fig. 14**), by Marcello Venusti (1512/15–79). Set in a grand architectural space, a central figure of Christ holds a whip aloft, ready to strike, while simultaneously pulling up one end of the money changers' table so that gold and silver coins scatter onto the floor. The greed of the money changers is highlighted by Nicolas Colombel (1644–1717) in his dramatic painting *Christ Expelling the Money-Changers from the Temple* (**fig. 15**), which shows one man desperately scrabbling around on the floor, trying to pick up the coins that have just been sent flying, while another, lying on the ground in shock, clutches his money bag as the chaos unfolds around him.

Another important episode in the life of Christ involving money is that of Judas Iscariot's betrayal of Jesus for thirty pieces of silver (Matthew 26). The duplicitous disciple leads an armed band of soldiers and officials to arrest Jesus on behalf of the chief priests, famously identifying him with a kiss. Later, seized with remorse, he returns the money, though his repentance is met with indifference. One of the few artists to portray his sorrow is Rembrandt, whose painting *Judas Repentant, Returning the Pieces of Silver* (**fig. 16**), shows the betrayer as a wretched man, distraught and fallen to his knees. With a tortured expression, he wrings his hands while looking towards the coins on the floor (most likely Tyrian shekels used for paying the Temple tribute). The high priest dramatically turns away from him while the others stare in astonishment.

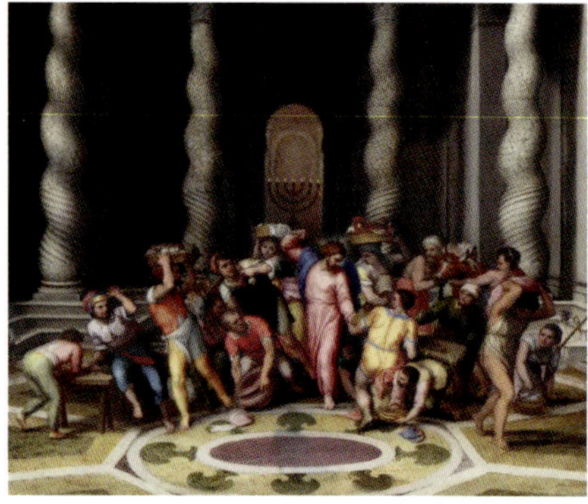

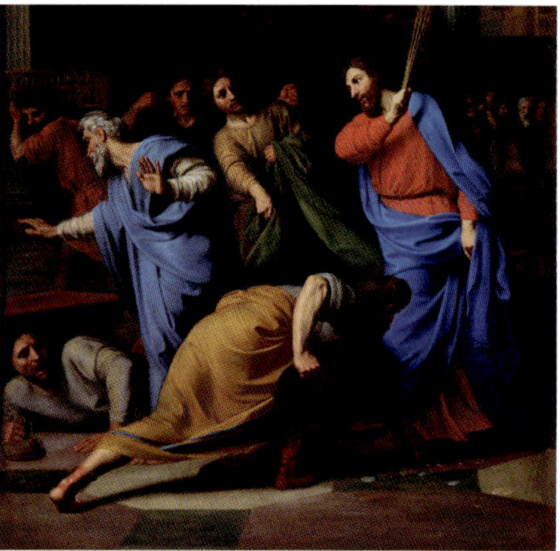

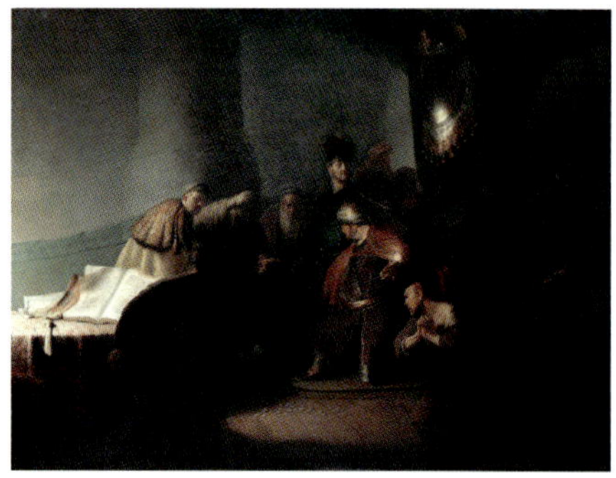

fig. 14 Marcello Venusti, *The Purification of the Temple* (detail) after 1550, oil on wood, 61 × 40 cm (24 × 15 ¾ in.), National Gallery, London

fig. 15 Nicolas Colombel, *Christ Expelling the Money-Changers from the Temple* (detail), 1682, oil on canvas, 119.4 × 88.3 cm (47 × 34 ¾ in.) St Louis Museum of Art

fig. 16 Rembrandt, *Judas Repentant, Returning the Pieces of Silver*, 1629, oil on wood, 79 × 102 cm (31 × 40 in.), Mulgrave Castle

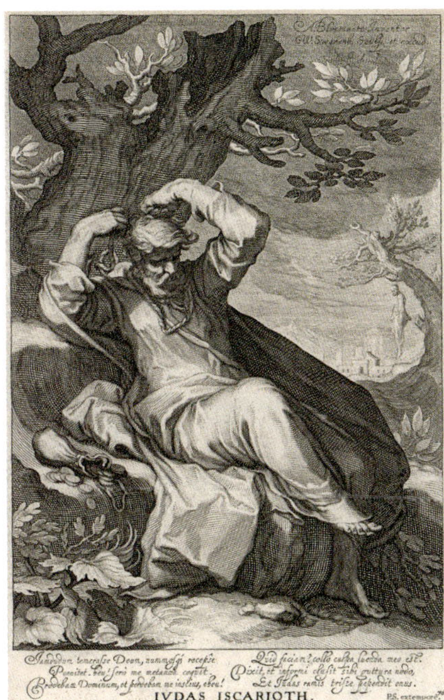

fig.17 **Willem van Swanenburg** after **Abraham Bloemaert**, *Judas Iscariot Hangs Himself*, 1611, engraving, 27.3 × 17.1 cm (10¾ × 6¾ in.)

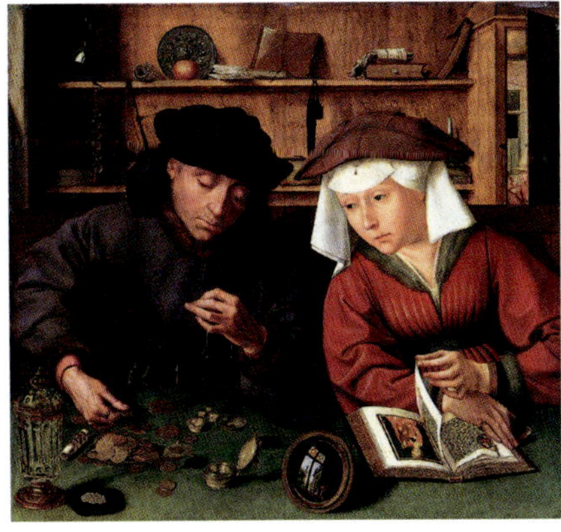

fig.18 **Quentin Massys**, *The Moneychanger and His Wife*, 1514, oil on panel, 71 × 68 cm (28 × 26¾ in.), Louvre Abu Dhabi

According to Matthew's Gospel, Judas left the priests and committed suicide, a subject represented by Willem van Swanenburg (*c.*1581/82–1612) in his haunting engraving after Abraham Bloemaert (1564–1651), *Judas Iscariot Hangs Himself* (**fig.17**). Sitting alone beneath a tree, Judas ties a rope around his neck. His face is downcast, wrought with anguish as he considers the weight of his actions. Although St Matthew tells us that Judas returned the thirty pieces of silver, here a money pouch is placed by his side as a symbol of his greed (according to John 12:6, as treasurer for the twelve disciples, Judas would regularly help himself to what was put into the bag). Coins spill out onto the ground but Judas, once motivated by money, either doesn't notice or no longer cares.

Today, the phrase 'thirty pieces of silver' continues to be used pejoratively against anyone who has compromised their integrity by taking money in exchange for betraying a person, principle or cause.

Lucifer's Evangelists: Flemish Money Professionals

In the early sixteenth century, Antwerp (in what is now Belgium) became recognised as the de facto commercial metropolis of western Europe. Facilitated by the opening of new trade routes, the city experienced a remarkable economic surge. It was amid this mercantile context that Quentin Massys (*c.*1465–1530) painted *The Moneychanger and His Wife* (**fig.18**), a portrait-like genre painting in which all eyes are on the money. The moneychanger, whose job was to exchange currencies, is carefully checking the weight of the various coins before him. His wife, distracted from her prayer book, gazes at the pile. A third character is ingeniously concealed as a reflection in the small convex mirror in the foreground. He cares not for the coins but is engrossed in a book and stands by a window that forms the shape of the Christian cross.

The painting has frequently been interpreted as an attack on money, a warning against becoming seduced by its allure. Certainly, its first viewers, upon seeing the tension that Massys sets up between devotion to spiritual matters and those of material wealth, would have recalled Christ's words from Luke's Gospel (16:13): 'You cannot serve God and money'. Yet the woman has not completely abandoned her prayer book, nor have the couple's faces become twisted and distorted by their greed, as we see in later pictures by Massys. On the painting's original frame (now lost) was an Old Testament inscription based on Leviticus 19:36 that read, 'Just balances, just weights … shall ye have' underscoring the heart of the painting's message that, in a world increasingly dominated by commerce, it was one's duty to ensure that money was handled in a just and morally responsible way.

In the following decade, Massys turned his attention to the subject of tax collecting and in so doing he launched a trend for unflattering paintings of money professionals. Such was the social antipathy towards tax collectors at the time that they were described in a Netherlandish proverb as one of 'Lucifer's four evangelists,' alongside usurers, millers and money-changers. *The Tax Collectors* (**fig. 19**) depicts two gnarled men pouring over an account book at a table strewn with coins and jewels. One, bespectacled and wearing an archaic red headdress, is busy writing while the other, gazing out from the composition, draws our attention to the accounts book with a finger pointing downwards.

In contrast to *The Moneychanger and His Wife*, this scene is secular with no overt religion reference. The man with the pen is most likely a city treasurer who is auditing the tax collector. Clasping a small stack of coins in his hand, he carefully sets them out in a line as he tots up the sum. The inscriptions in the accounts book show itemised excise receipts for wine, beer, fish and other items, and reveal that the man wearing the green headgear was involved in the business of tax farming, a practice in which a specified amount of tax was paid in advance to the government, leaving the tax collector free to collect revenues and keep the surplus. The tax collector's expression is ambiguous, somewhere between an uncomfortable grimace and a greedy smirk; sidling up to the treasurer, he is keen

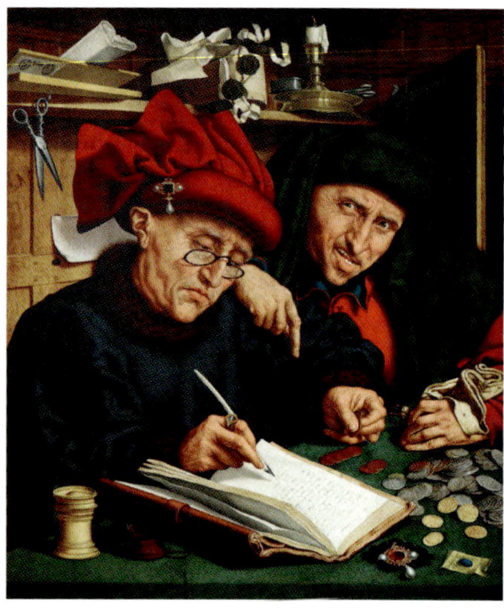

fig. 19 **Quentin Massys**, *The Tax Collectors*, c.1525–30, oil on panel, 86.4 × 71.2 cm (34 × 28 in.), Kunstmuseum Liechtenstein

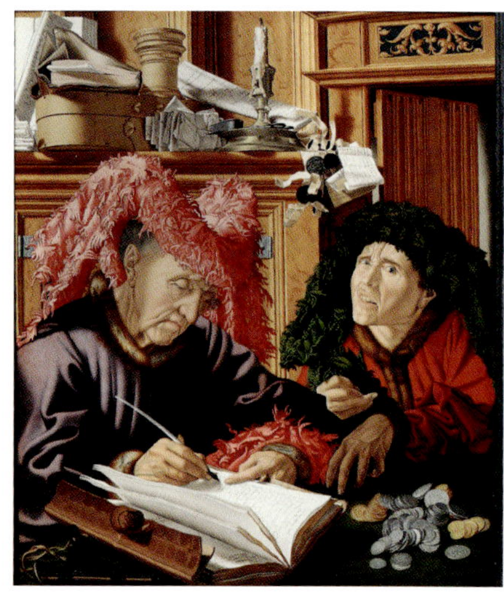

fig. 20 **Workshop of Marinus van Reymerswale**, *Two Tax-Gatherers*, 1540s, oil on oak, 92 × 74.6 cm (36 ¼ × 29 ⅜ in.), National Gallery, London

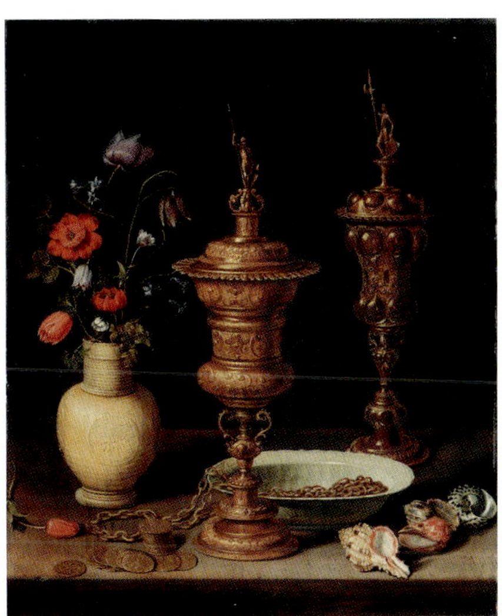

fig. 21 **Clara Peeters**, *Still Life with Flowers and Goblets*, 1612, oil on panel, 59.5 × 49 cm (23 ⅜ × 19 ¼ in.), Staatliche Kunsthalle Karlsruhe

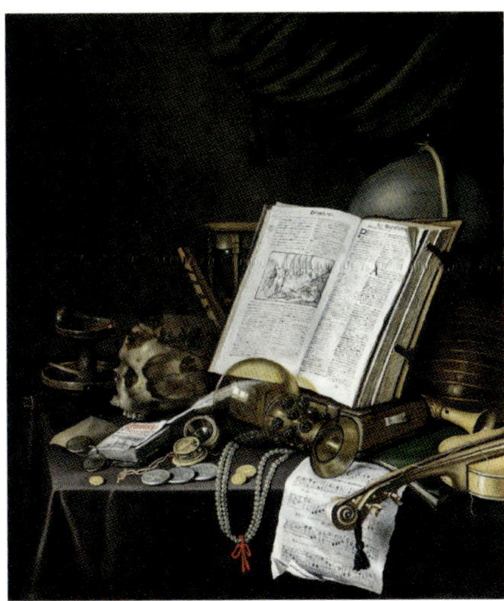

fig. 22 **Edwaert Collier**, *Vanitas Still Life*, 1661, oil on canvas, 91 × 76 cm (35 ⅞ × 30 in.), private collection

to stay close to his money, which includes gold double ducats, an English angel coin (featuring the archangel Michael slaying a dragon) and two unidentifiable gold German coins.

Massys's attack on avarice proved incredibly popular and inspired numerous copies and variants, including several by Marinus van Reymerswale (1490–1546). One of these, *Two Tax-Gatherers* (**fig. 20**), similarly depicts two men seated at a table covered in coins. Here, though, the second man has a pained expression, his contorted features suggestive of the corrupting influence of money. Indeed, his claw-like hand seems poised, ready to grab the coins in front of him. The two men's extraordinary clothing is anachronistic and intended to ridicule their greed: the pink heart-shaped hat is similar to those worn by fashionable women in the mid-fifteenth century, while the green wig-like headdress accentuates the tax collector's hideous appearance.

In all these pictures we see cluttered shelves filled with books, manuscripts, boxes and other everyday objects, which foreshadow still life becoming its own category of painting. These works of Massys and Marinus prominently feature an extinguished candle, a sobering metaphor for the brevity of life. This became a central motif of *vanitas* paintings, which flourished in Flemish and Dutch art during the 1600s. Literally meaning 'emptiness', *vanitas* referenced the vanity of clinging onto worldly pleasures and goods in the face of mortality. Artists working in this style include Clara Peeters (*c.* 1587–after 1636) whose compositions, such as *Still Life with Flowers and Goblets* (**fig. 21**), depict ephemeral natural objects — flowers and seashells empty of life — but also items representing wealth: intricate goblets, a gold chain and, in the bottom left corner, coins. Edwaert Collier (1642–1707) in a painting of 1661 (**fig. 22**) foregrounded money and pearls, alongside reading glasses, musical instruments and books, to emphasise that no matter how many earthly riches or skills you acquire, death cannot be avoided: as the looming presence of an empty candleholder and human skull make plain.

Painting the Almighty Dollar

In years that followed the American Civil War (1861–5) the United States experienced rapid industrialisation and economic expansion. Dubbed by historians as the 'Gilded Age', the period was characterised by materialistic excess and political corruption as money became a major preoccupation of American life. The nation's new found obsession found its way into art, and from the late 1870s, paintings of currency emerged as a distinct category. Although these painters drew from the European tradition of ultra-realistic trompe l'oeil (French for 'deceives the eye'), their subject was uniquely American.

The first illusionistic money painting was produced by William Harnett (1848–92) whose *Still Life – Five-Dollar Bill* (**fig. 23**) depicts a solitary bill on a brown, nondescript background. The well-worn note features the seventh US president Andrew Jackson and a pioneer family. Recalling popular trophy paintings of the period, the image invites viewers to consider the true worth of this tatty specimen. Harnett's painstakingly accurate technique made him famous in the field of still life painting, but in an era when forgers were growing rich it also attracted the attention of the Treasury Department's Secret Service. In 1886 they seized this work from the New York saloon where it was hanging, and threatened the artist with arrest for counterfeiting. Harnett duly abandoned money painting but other artists, including John Haberle (1856–1933) and Victor Dubreuil (1842–*c*. 1900s) flagrantly ignored the injunction and continued the genre.

Having exhibited an astoundingly realistic collection of coins, stamps and paper bills entitled *Imitation* at New York's National Academy of Design in 1887, Haberle's work of the following year *The Changes of Time* (**fig. 24**), makes clear the link between money and power. Portraying paper money dating from the colonial era to the present day, as well as coins and stamps (used as currency during the Civil War) the printed material is surrounded by a depiction of a wooden frame carved in relief with portraits of every US president to date. Displayed prominently atop the pile of bills, the recently issued five dollar silver certificate bears the image of

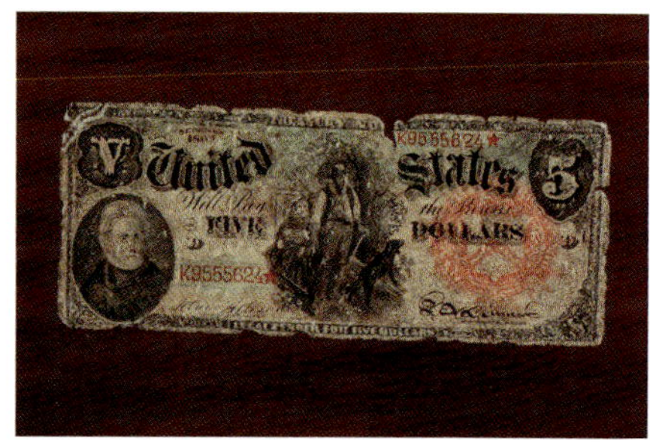

fig. 23 **William Harnett**, *Still Life – Five-Dollar Bill* (detail), 1877, oil on canvas, 20.3 × 30.8 cm (8 × 12 ⅛ in.), Philadelphia Museum of Art

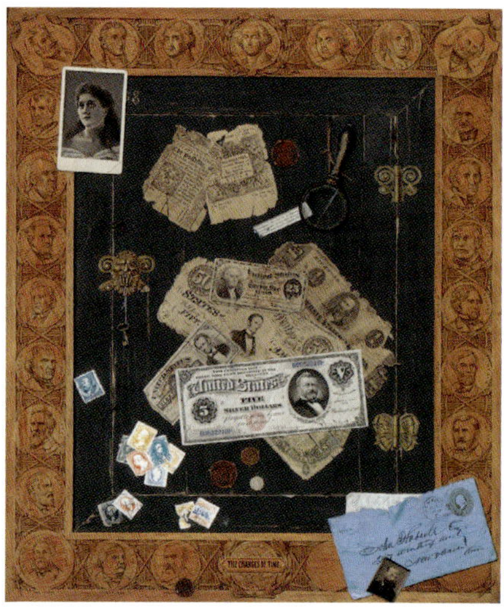

fig. 24 **John Haberle**, *The Changes of Time*, 1888, oil on canvas, 62 × 51.4 cm (24 ⅜ × 20 ¼ in.), Manoogian Collection, New York

President Ulysses S. Grant, whose administration was plagued by corruption. Money, the painting suggests, is at the heart of the American political system, but even presidents are not immune to its corrupting influence.

In some sections of society, attitudes toward the pursuit of money and material wealth were changing. The seemingly boundless financial power of wealthy industrialists and growing divisions between rich and poor became cause for concern. Money as a corrupting influence is reflected by French–American artist Dubreuil. Some of his paintings recall those of Haberle, showing single or multiple overlapping notes, while others, however, feature wads of cash, stacked on tabletops or hanging bundled in ribbon. Among his most striking paintings are those of overflowing, money-filled barrels such as *Money to Burn* (**fig. 25**). The oak casks recede beyond the picture plane, suggesting limitless wealth and calling attention to human greed. The stash of unused money in a range of denominations invites viewers to consider the morality of selfishly accumulating earthly treasures.

After the early 1900s, as forgery laws became stricter, the trend for painting currency mainly disappeared, with the exception of Otis Kaye (1885–1974). Ignoring a move towards abstraction in international painting trends, Kaye adopted the theme with aplomb in the 1920s, producing simple trompe l'oeil compositions of cash. But when the artist's financial circumstances deteriorated due to the Wall Street Crash of 1929, his works became more complex and cryptic. In *Holding the Bag* (1929), he included, alongside banknotes, a precisely-rendered document on which is written: 'Otis Kaye, Dec. 2 1929, your account is closed. $102,635.12 Due IMM Utility Securities Company, 230 S. LaSalle St. Chicago'. In 1937, Kaye also took on the precarious nature of investing. *D'JIA VU?* (**fig. 26**) arranges bonds and various denominations of US currency into the form of a graph showing the trajectory of the US stock market from 1929 to 1937 (when the economy was again sliding towards recession). Beneath, suggesting that gains may go up in smoke, are several tobacco products, while dice, playing

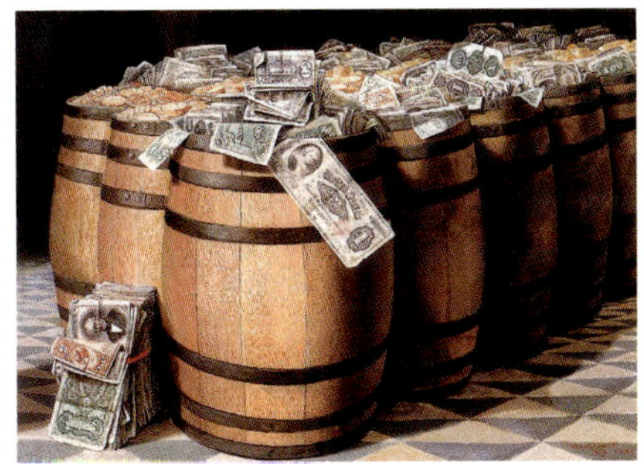

fig. 25 **Victor Dubreuil**, *Money to Burn*, *c.* 1893, oil on canvas, 61 × 81.3 cm (24 × 32 in.), private collection

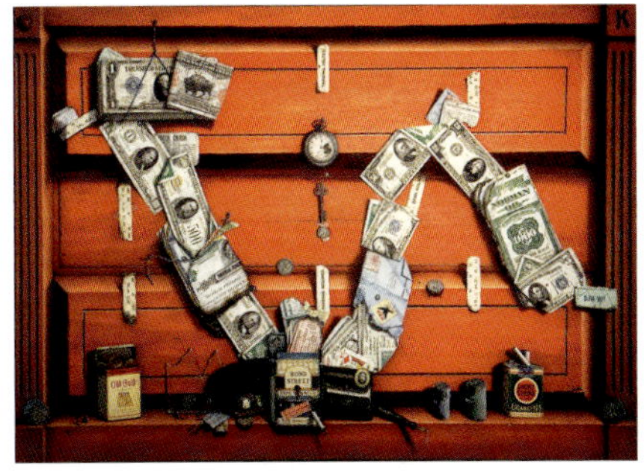

fig. 26 **Otis Kaye**, *D'JIA VU?*, 1937, oil on board, 68.6 × 100.3 cm (27 × 39 ½ in.), private collection

cards and poker chips make the connection between investing and gambling. The work's title is a cynical pun on the phrase 'déjà vu' (French for 'already seen'), while also referring to the Dow Jones Industrial Average (DJIA). Born from Kaye's bitter experience, the painting is a complex critique of a money-driven culture ruled by capitalism, greed and chance, where fortunes are made and lost in the blink of an eye.

Money as Material: interwar Germany

While the First World War was still ravaging Europe, a group of artists led by the German poet and philosopher Hugo Ball (1886–1927) expressed their disgust at the conflict by forming a reactionary movement known as Dada. The art produced by the movement was satirical and often nonsensical, calling into question the values of a capitalist society that could allow such a horrific war to occur. Dada artists worked in a range of mediums, but collage and photomontage were especially effective for expressing political critique.

Raoul Hausmann (1886–1971), a founding member of the Berlin Dada group, created *The Art Critic* (**fig. 27**) to express his anguish at the bias of conservative critics in the Weimar Republic towards bourgeois forms of art and culture. Comprising collaged imagery cut from newspapers and magazines, the deliberately chaotic composition depicts the critic as suited figure with an oversized head. His cartoonish eyes and mouth are drawn with coloured pencil, suggesting that what he sees and what he says serve only high society (represented by the coiffured woman). As with many Dada artists, Hausmann was also highly critical of money's dominant influence and here he includes a triangular fragment of an actual German banknote sticking into the critic's neck: with money always in the back of his mind, he is a slave to capitalist forces.

Kurt Schwitters (1887–1948) – a peer rather than a direct participant in Berlin Dada – employed many of the group's ideas and worked extensively with collage. Physical money is surprisingly rare as a material in his oeuvre, though a notable example is *Das Kotsbild*

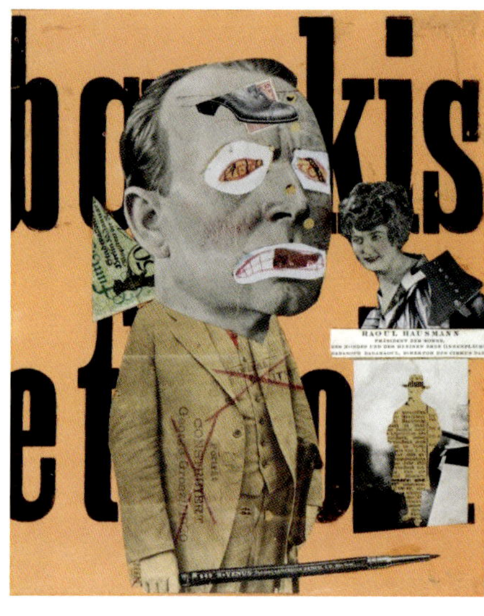

fig. 27 **Raoul Hausmann**, *The Art Critic,* 1919–20, lithograph and printed paper on paper, 31.8 × 25.4 cm (80 ¾ × 64 ½ in.) Tate, London

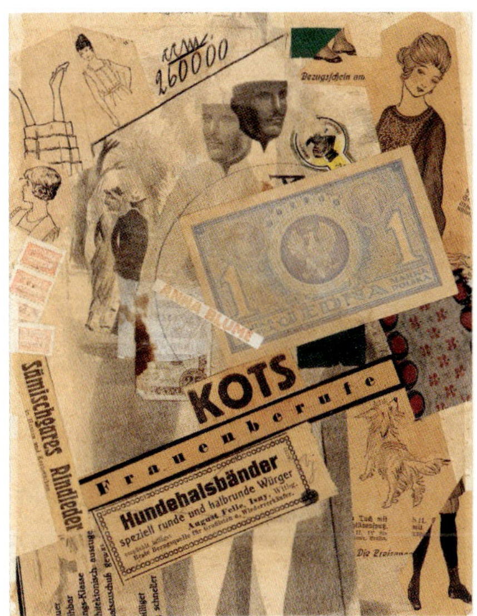

fig. 28 **Kurt Schwitters**, *Das Kotsbild*
(*The Vomit Picture*), 1920, collage,
27 × 19.5 cm (10 ⅝ × 7 ⅝ in.)

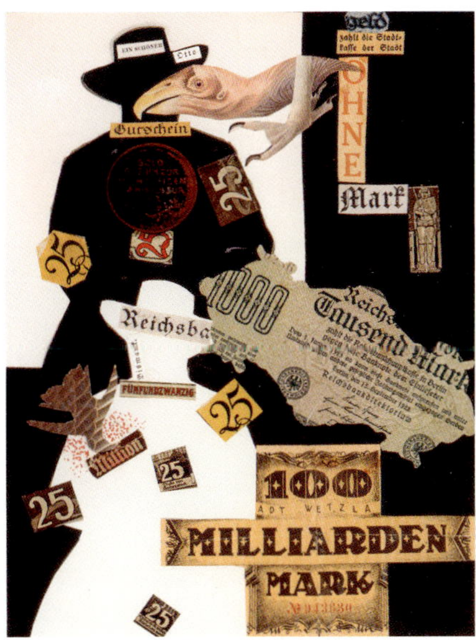

fig. 29 **László Moholy-Nagy**, *25 Pleitegeier*
('*25 Bankruptcy Vultures*'), 1922–23, collage,
30 × 23 cm (11 ¾ × 9 in.), Israel Museum

(**fig. 28**), a complex work featuring multiple images of fashionable young women that addresses the theme of women's emancipation. Women had gained suffrage with the birth of the Weimar Republic, but public opinion about their role in the new society was ambivalent. The nonsense word 'kots' at the centre of the collage has homonymic similarities with 'kotz' ('vomit'). When juxtaposed with 'frauenberufe' ('women's professions') he draws attention to the restricted (and often literally vomit-filled) range of jobs available to women at the time, such as nursing, childcare and domestic services. The prominent inclusion of two pieces of paper money (a devalued Polish one-mark note and a worthless torn Notgeld note) further emphasise the raw economic deal experienced by women working in essential, yet undervalued, roles.

From 1921 to 1923, Germany experienced one of the greatest economic disasters in its history: hyperinflation. The Papiermark, the currency of the Weimar Republic, lost nearly all of its value. Prices increased until essential goods cost billions of marks. During the crisis, László Moholy-Nagy (1895–1946) was sharing a freezing cold studio with Schwitters. He could no longer afford paint or canvas and so, at Schwitters' suggestion, turned to paper currency as a material. Made almost entirely from worthless high-denomination banknotes, the collage *25 Pleitegeier* ('*25 Bankruptcy Vultures*', **fig. 29**) relates directly to hyperinflation. Amid the fragments of 100 billion mark notes, two shadowy, silhouetted figures suggest those who lurk like vultures – businessmen, landowners and bankers ready to ruthlessly profit from people suffering financial hardship.

By 1932, Adolf Hitler was well on the way to becoming Chancellor of Germany, having exploited the 1929 Wall Street Crash (which had brought the German economy to a standstill) to garner support from business leaders fearful of a communist takeover. Sensing the danger that Hitler posed, the Berlin Dada artist John Heartfield (born Helmut Herzfeld, 1891–1968) used photomontage as a political weapon, fearlessly criticising and exposing Nazi propaganda.

One of his most famous photomontages, *Adolf, Der Übermensch* ('*Adolf the Superman*', **fig. 30**), took a widely published photograph of Hitler and superimposed it with an image of a chest X-ray, which reveals an oesophagus filled with coins descending to his stomach. The caption reads: 'Adolf the Superman: Swallows Gold and Spouts Junk', a reference to the contradiction between Hitler's anti-capitalist rhetoric and the large financial contributions that rich industrialists were making to the Nazi Party. The image was turned into a poster and pasted up all over Berlin, resulting in beatings of Heartfield by the Nazis and an assassination attempt, until he fled to Czechoslovakia in 1933. He eventually rose to number five on the Gestapo's most-wanted list: evidence of the political power that artists wielded to critique the dynamics of authority and economics through their work.

Postwar: from Pop to Cryptocurrency

In the immediate decades after the Second World War, money as a subject and material in art became increasingly prevalent, especially in the United States, which was experiencing an unprecedented economic boom. Consumer culture was flourishing, the art market was expanding and the dollar was becoming a symbol of prosperity and aspiration, both within the US and internationally.

It is here that the main body of this book begins. From early works of Pop art, which convey the seductive power of money while simultaneously exposing art as a commodity, the selection that follows traces a path through seventy years of modern and contemporary art.

It showcases examples of artists who, concerned by the commercialisation of the art market, have attempted to critique or disrupt its systems of value. Those who, as their predecessors in Weimar Germany did, have engaged with more recent instances of hyperinflation (particularly in Latin America and Zimbabwe), as well as other significant periods of severe economic instability: the global financial crisis of 2007–8 onwards, or the COVID-19 pandemic. It also highlights how artists have

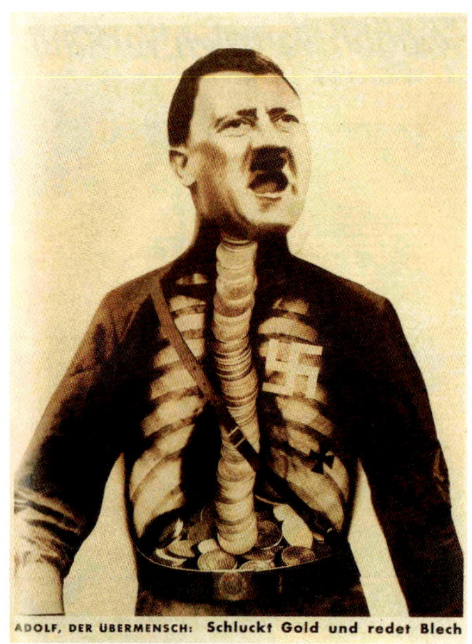

fig. 30 John Heartfield, *Adolf, Der Übermensch: Schulckt Gold und redet Blech* ('*Adolf the Superman: Swallows Gold and Spouts Junk*'), 1932, rotogravure, (38.1 × 27.9 cm (15 × 11 in.) from the Arbeiter-Illustrierten Zeitung (AIZ), Akademie der Künste, Berlin

used their work to expose economic inequalities, or to propose possible alternative systems of finance.

While some contemporary artists use coins and banknotes as found objects, incorporating them as part of installations and sculptures, others alter them in innovative ways to imbue them with new meanings. Still others create their own currencies, which may even be used to pay for goods and services (albeit sometimes with very real consequences in relation to counterfeiting laws).

Today, carrying cash and writing cheques are rapidly becoming consigned to the past. The way that finances are managed has changed significantly as digital payment methods become the norm. The advent of cryptocurrencies such as Bitcoin, and the blockchain technology that underpins them, has begun to revolutionise the world of finance and profoundly altered understandings of currencies as geographically defined. Artists have responded to these technologies and the accompanying societal changes in various ways: some critical and cautionary, others embracing the new possibilities, challenging perceptions of value and exploring the persistent notion that money and art are interchangeable.

The relationship between art and money remains notoriously complex and rarely a comfortable one. But when currency is the subject or even the substance of an artwork, it can become a lens through which to enhance our understanding of the social, political, economic and aesthetic issues relating to money, its function in the world and the many ways in which it affects our lives.

THE ARTWORKS

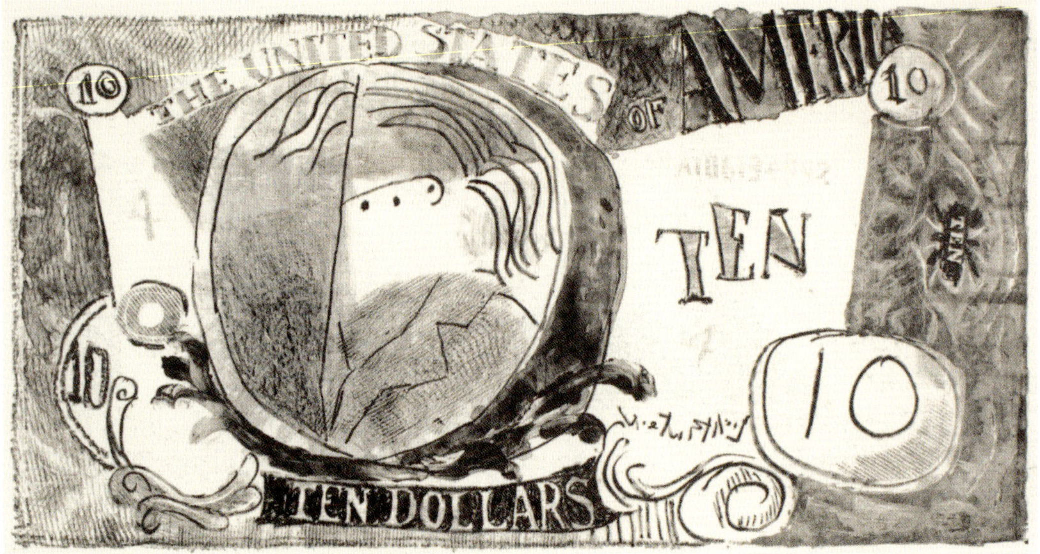

By reimagining the US ten-dollar bill as a light-hearted, Cubist-inflected abstraction, Roy Lichtenstein (1923–97) was among the first artists in postwar North America to make everyday currency the subject of high art. Although the print's proportions approximate those of a banknote, its off-kilter design bears little resemblance to real money: the text is imbalanced and erratic, while the familiar image of Founding Father Alexander Hamilton (first Secretary of the US Treasury between 1789 and 1795) is refashioned as an inchoate, Picasso-esque portrait with distorted features. This is far removed from the engraving of the eighteenth-century statesman used for Federal Reserve notes between 1928 and 1990, itself based on an 1806 painting by John Trumbull (1756–1843). Produced in a limited edition, Lichtenstein's work echoes the multiple nature of printed money and, just as each banknote carries a unique serial number, his lithographs are all individually signed and numbered. Made several years before his peer Andy Warhol (p. 30–1) started his now well-known representations of dollar bills, this playful parody of an iconic symbol of consumer culture is an important precursor to Lichtenstein's celebrated Pop art works of the 1960s, which appropriated the graphic language, imagery and Ben-day dot printing method of comic books, magazine advertisements and other mass media culture in colourful paintings and prints.

10 Dollar Bill, 1956
Lithograph in black
on Rives paper
25 × 47.7 cm
(9 7/8 × 18 3/4 in.)
Edition of 25

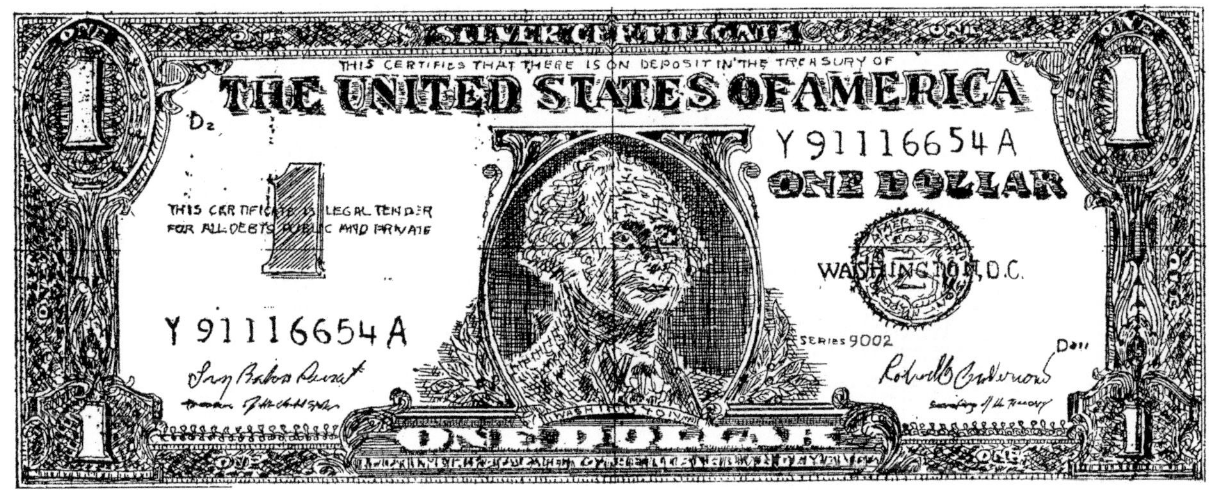

Robert Watts (1923–88) was a key member of Fluxus, an international network of anti-establishment artists active in the 1960s and 70s. In the same year that Andy Warhol began depicting US currency, Watts made a black-and-white sketch of a dollar bill. The similarities between this and the one Warhol produced as a template for his first silkscreen painting (p. 31) are striking, though Watts altered George Washington's portrait to imply decrepitude. *Dollar Bill* was first reproduced as a small edition of dry-point etchings by Arturo Schwarz, the Italian art historian, writer, poet and curator who ran Galleria Schwarz in Milan. But it was George Maciunas, the Lithuanian American artist and Fluxus founding member, who had the ambitious idea to reproduce large quantities as offset lithographs trimmed to actual dollar bill size, with which to infiltrate the local economy, thus devaluing both art and currency. Such a proposal typified Fluxus practice, which employed humour, confrontation, chance and audience participation to disrupt social norms and undermine the elitism of the commercial art world. However, the plan did not come to fruition and *Dollar Bill* was ultimately sold in FluxKits — small boxes containing cards and objects designed by artists such as Christo (1935–2020), Yoko Ono (b. 1933) and George Brecht (1926–2008) — and included in Watts's sculpture *Dollar Bills in Wood Chest* (1975), a plain wooden box brimming with the facsimile banknotes.

Dollar Bill, 1962
Offset printing
on card stock
6.5 × 15.5 cm
(2½ × 6⅛ in.)
Edition size unknown

Rendered with a playful and childlike quality, this invented currency is associated with a series of group performances organised by Claes Oldenburg (1929–2022) at the Judson Gallery in Greenwich Village, New York, in 1960. The carnivalesque events, known collectively as 'Ray Gun Spex', were inspired by the 'happenings' of Allan Kaprow (1927–2006) a pioneer of live art and conceived as a Dada-esque parody of American consumer culture. Leading the revolt was Oldenburg's alter-ego Ray Gun, a metamorphic character who assumed different identities, appearing as a person and also an object in the form of a child's toy gun. Oldenburg worked with fellow pop artist Jim Dine (b. 1935) to build the sets for his performances which, like most happenings, were characterised by a conspicuous lack of narrative. Using a mimeograph duplicating machine, he produced Ray Gun currency, distributing a million dollars' worth to each audience member to buy artworks used in the performances, most of which comprised detritus gathered from the surrounding streets. Although the money was intended to be ephemeral, a number of notes have since been circulated on the art market. The emergence of the Ray Gun character signalled Oldenburg's transition from painter to sculptor. In 1961, he continued to satirise the notion of art as commodity with The Store, a storefront on the Lower East Side of Manhattan that sold sculptures of cakes, burgers, underwear and other everyday objects made from plaster and paper maché that prefigured the large soft sculptures for which he is best known.

    Claes Oldenburg

Ray Gun Stuff (Money used in 'Ray Gun Spex' *performance)*, 1959
Black-and-white mimeograph on loose leaves, printed both sides
Each: 5.3 × 10.9 cm (2⅛ × 4¼ in.)

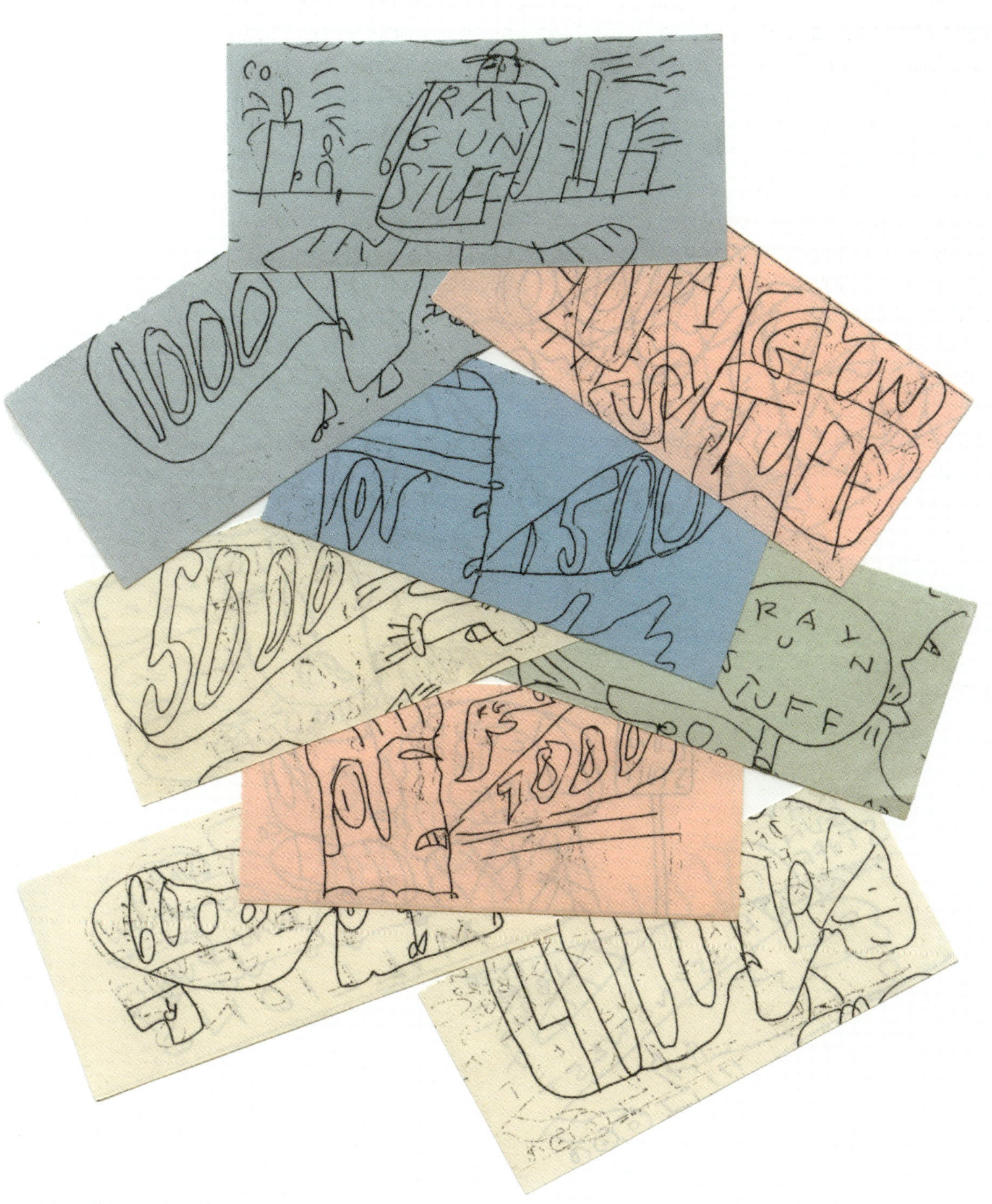

RAY
GUN
STUFF
1000
RAY GUN STUFF
500
5000
7000
RAY
GUN
STUFF
6000
4000

Filling the viewer's field of vision with a grid of US one-dollar bills, this large painting was among the first that Andy Warhol (1928–87) made using the silkscreen printing process that came to define his practice. Although he had previously created repeating imagery in his 32-panel *Campbell's Soup Cans* (1962), these used laboriously handmade stencils. Wanting to present the US dollar bill 200 times on a single canvas, silkscreening offered a more practical way to reproduce the images. As it would constitute forgery to use a photograph of a real dollar bill, Warhol based the work on his own drawing of a banknote which was not an exact copy: he omitted some details and simplified others, such as the blue seal and the portrait of George Washington, which, with plump cheeks and pursed lips, appears like a caricature. He also increased the size of his silk-screened notes, making them about 50 percent larger than an actual bill. Money is a recurring theme throughout Warhol's work, reflecting his fascination with consumerism, wealth and pop culture in postwar North America in particular. With the many pictures of dollar bills he produced in the 1960s, and his 'Dollar Sign' series of the 1980s, Warhol emphasised the potent potential of art as a commodity in and of itself.

200 One Dollar Bills, 1962
Silkscreen ink and pencil on canvas
203.8 × 234.3 cm (80¼ × 92¼ in.)

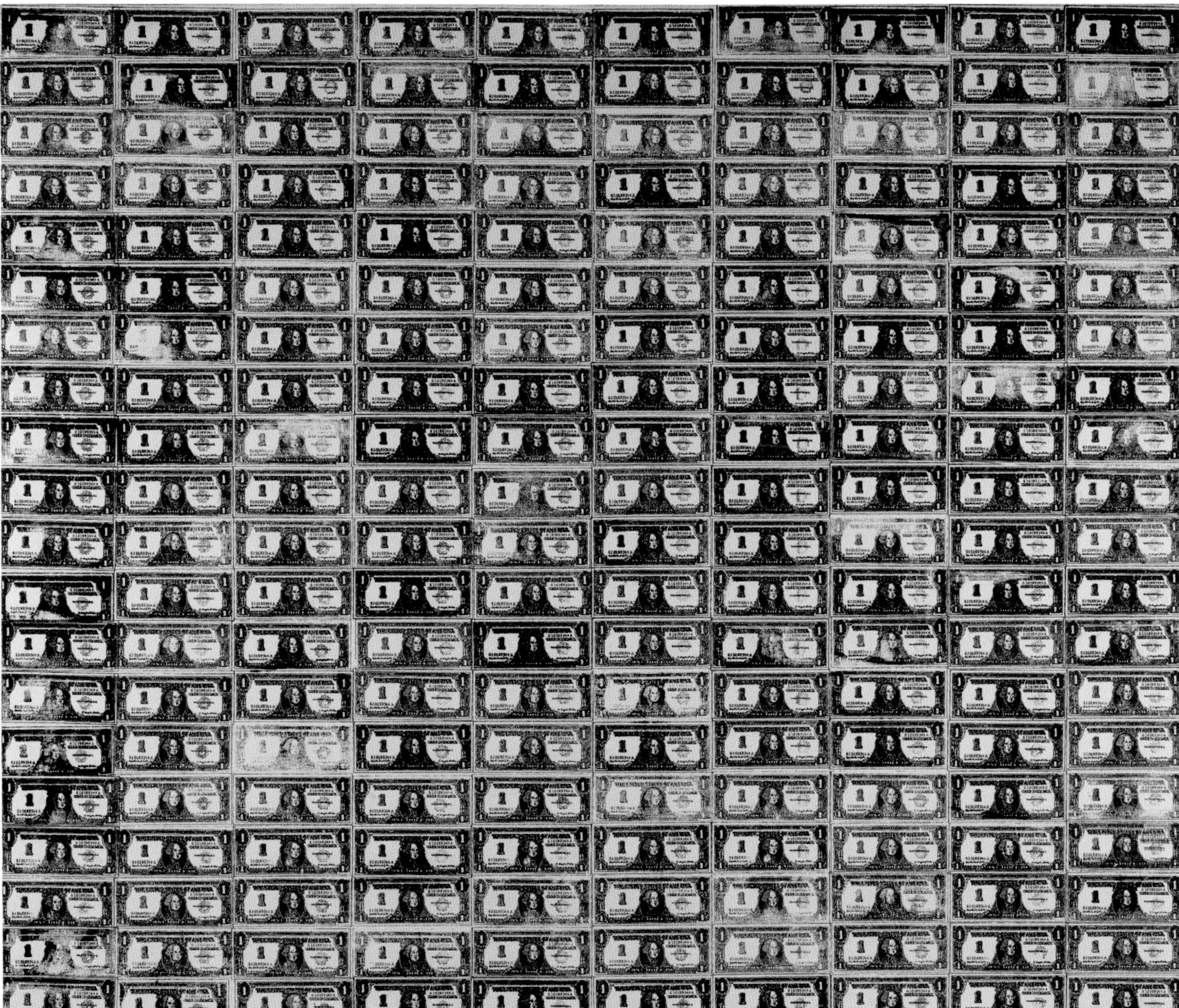

For its 50th anniversary edition, *Art in America* magazine commissioned seven American sculptors to reimagine the tired and old-fashioned coinage of the US as something fresh and modern. Each artist was assigned a different denomination, with Robert Indiana (1928–2018) invited to redesign the penny. His solution was this striking decagonal shaped coin with a red, white and blue design incorporating elements of the US flag: a star and stripes. Bright colours, bold numerals and letters, and geometric forms would come to define Indiana's output of paintings, prints and sculptures from the 1960s onwards — most notably the iconic *LOVE* (1964), a four-letter design with an oblique 'O', which became his most famous work. A dipytch painting, *New Glory Penny* (1963), featuring a slight variation of his coin design, was reproduced on *Art in America*'s front and back covers, and shown the same year in the Guggenheim Museum exhibition 'Coins Designed by Sculptors'. Of all the artists commissioned, Indiana was the only one to propose using plastic rather than metal, a choice which he noted 'would be a welcome change from the familiar copper coins long in use'. However, this material has never been adopted in the US because of concerns over durability and security: plastic would wear down much quicker than metal and be considerably easier to counterfeit. Nevertheless, in 2014, the tiny republic of Transnistria, near the Moldova-Ukraine border, introduced the world's first plastic composite coins with face values of 1, 3, 5 and 10 Transnistrian rubles, which, it claimed, would be long lasting and difficult to forge.

    Robert Indiana

New Glory Penny, 1963
Obverse and reverse design
for new penny commissioned
for *Art in America* magazine,
Vol. 51, No. 2, April 1963

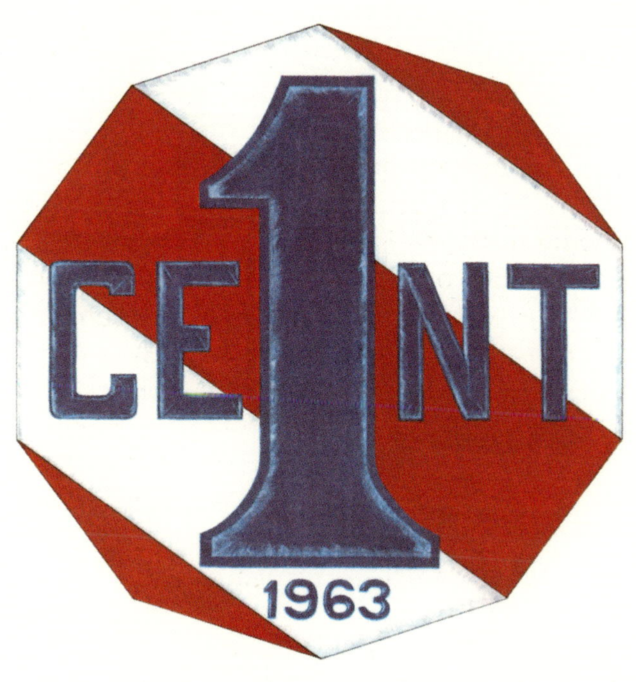
CE1NT
1963

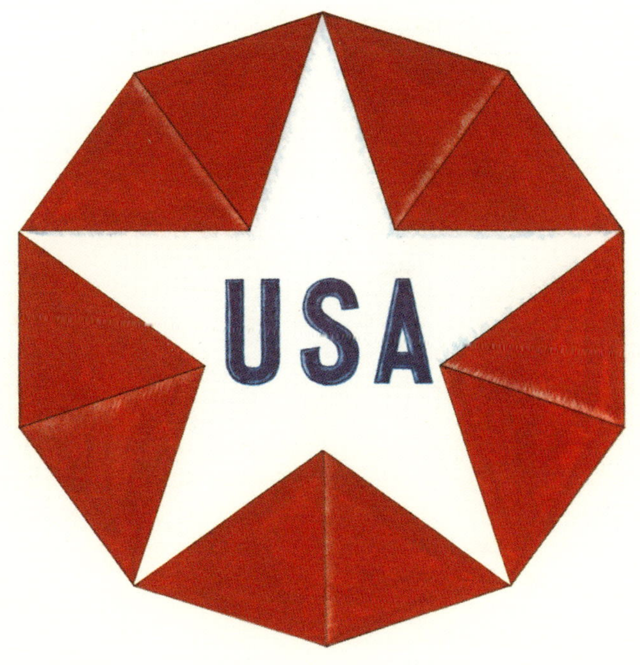
USA

In 1963, Japanese artist Genpei Akasegawa (1937–2014, born Katsuhiko Akasegawa) printed several hundred one-sided replicas of a thousand-yen note, using them as invitations to an exhibition by radical art collective Hi-Red Center, of which he was a founding member. Printing more fake notes, he then burned some in a performance and used others to wrap everyday objects, which he titled 'Packages'. The following year, the authorities launched a criminal investigation, leading to a high-profile counterfeiting trial. Although Akasegawa's currency was clearly unusable, and despite two appeals, he was convicted and sentenced to three months hard labour. Suspecting he had been targeted as part of a crackdown on leftist activists, he responded with this *Greater Japan Zero-Yen Note*, a self-declared valueless bill created as a political protest. The nineteenth-century Japanese statesman Iwakura Tomomi's face is erased — an act of iconoclasm against the state. Tomomi, whose portrait appeared on the obverse of the five hundred-yen banknote between 1951 and 1954, was credited with modernising Japan, including its financial systems. The reverse of the zero note includes a triple portrait of Johannes Gutenberg, his assistant Peter Schöffer and patron Johann Fust, in homage to the history of printing and freedom of the press.

          Genpei Akasegawa

Greater Japan Zero-Yen Note, 1967
Ink, paper, printed matter: offset lithograph, printed both sides, showing obverse and reverse
14.4 × 30.8 cm (5 ⅝ × 12 ⅛ in.)

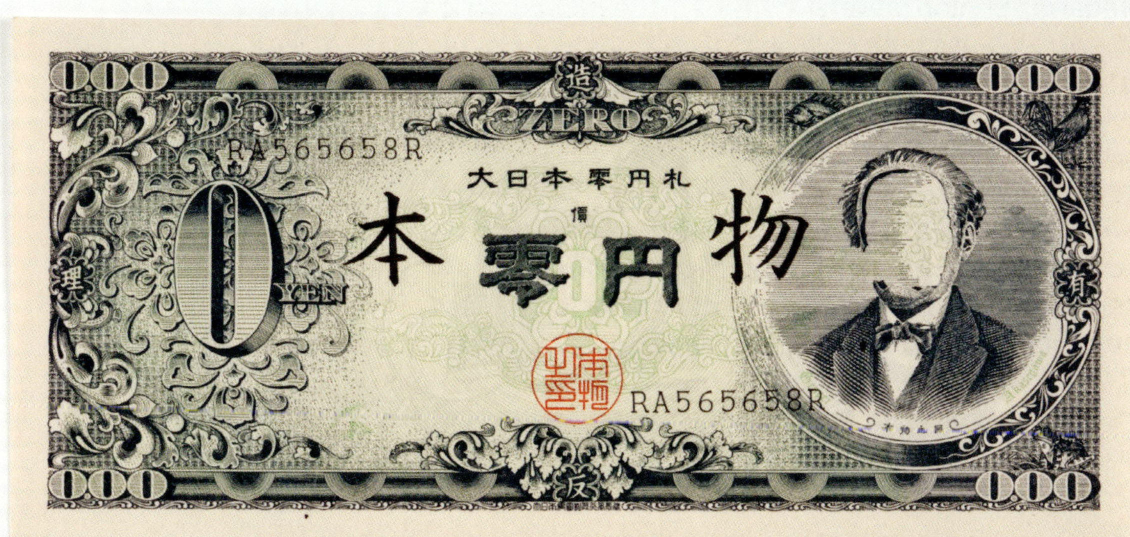

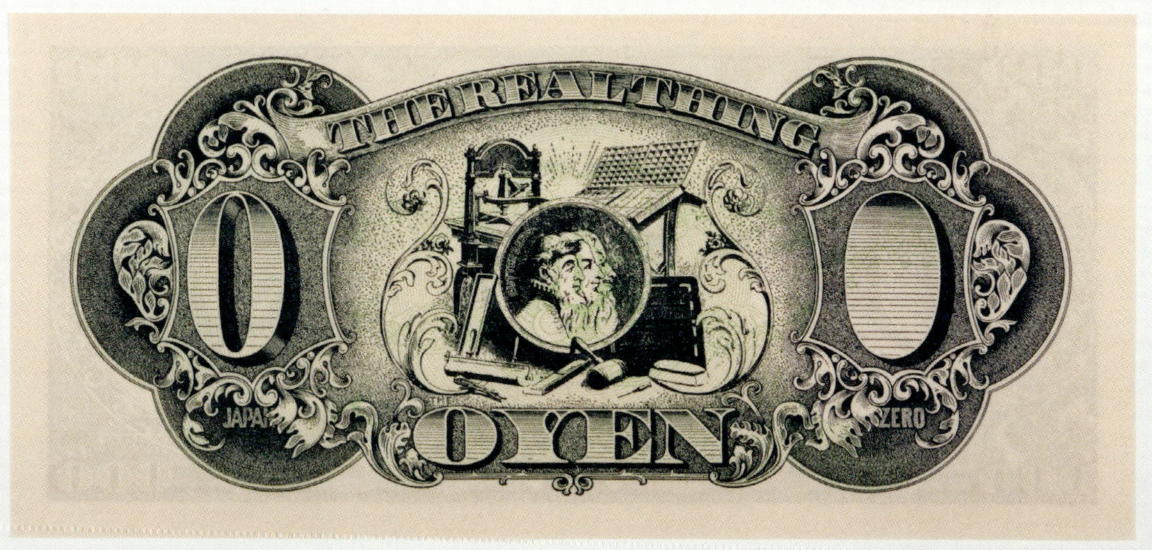

The prospect of unexpectedly receiving a large bundle of banknotes through the mail is at once exciting and fanciful. Imagine the disappointment, then, when what appeared to be a parcel packed with a wad of cash was revealed to be a single dollar bill wrapped up with multiple rectangular pieces of denim fabric. The New York based painter Ed Plunkett (1922–2011) was sent this tongue-in-cheek artwork by the pioneering mail artist Ray Johnson (1927–95), who from the 1950s began using the United States postal system to distribute his artworks — collages, drawings, objects and illustrated missives — as gifts to friends and strangers alike, often inviting them to 'add to' his work and either return it to him or forward it to another recipient. Plunkett, who coined the term New York Correspondence School to describe Johnson's activities, was a long term recipient of the artist's mail art, and especially enjoyed receiving bulky packages such as this one. The artwork was presented in an exhibition of collages featuring real one-dollar bills at Richard L. Feigen Gallery, Chicago, in 1970. Recalling the work of artists associated with Dada, the collages were densely filled with found imagery, text, drawings and photographs of movie stars and artists, offering an oblique commentary on the shallowness of America's money and celebrity-obsessed culture.

          Ray Johnson

One Dollar Bill Series, 1969
Dollar bills, fabric and denim
17.8 × 7.6 × 4.5 cm (7 × 3 × 1¾ in.)

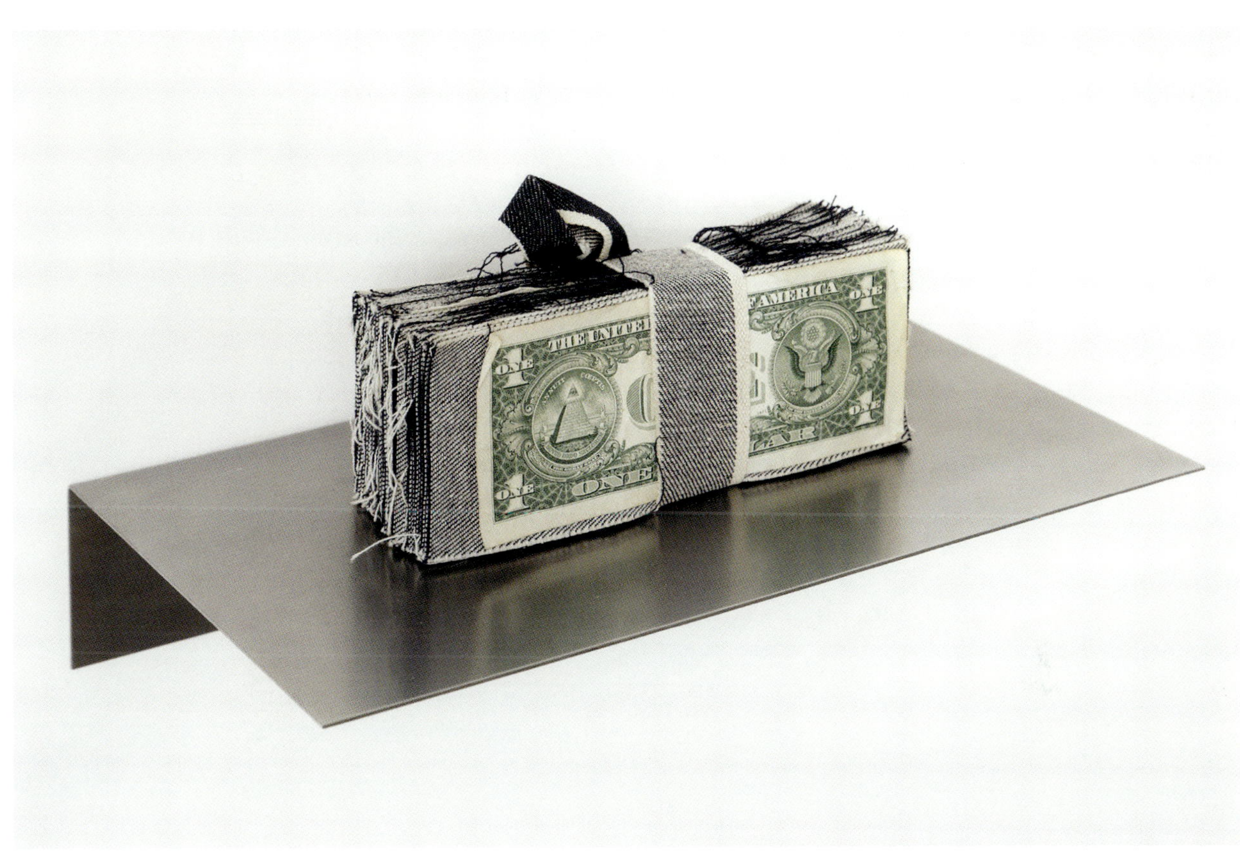

THE UNITED
F AMERICA ONE
ONE
ONE
ONE

Recalling a shop mannequin and a classical sculpture such as the *Venus de Milo*, this female torso contains US one-dollar bills suspended in disarray within transparent plastic. Operating at the intersection of high art and mass culture, the sculpture belongs to a wider body of work that Arman (1928–2005, born Armand Fernandez) called 'accumulations' — assemblages of a single type of mass-produced object, such as clocks, telephones, cutlery, electric toothbrushes and bottle tops, which he typically presented in Plexiglas cases, embedded in resin or, as here, inside a polyester figure. In elevating everyday objects to the status of art, the French-American artist took his cue from the Dada movement of the early twentieth century. By using seriality and repetition as a formal structure for these works, he laid bare the disposable nature of modern consumer culture. While many of the items selected for these works had been discarded, the dollar bills used here continue to signify value, although in removing them from circulation, Arman emphasized their potential for accumulation as wealth. Nevertheless, by associating the banknotes with the human body, *Venus aux Dollars* suggests money as the lifeblood of consumer culture, flowing through and sustaining systems of commerce.

Venus aux Dollars ('*Venus with Dollars*'), 1970
Accumulation of US currency in polyester
80 × 35 × 27.2 cm (31½ × 13¾ × 10¾ in.)
Edition of 20 + 4 AP

  Arman

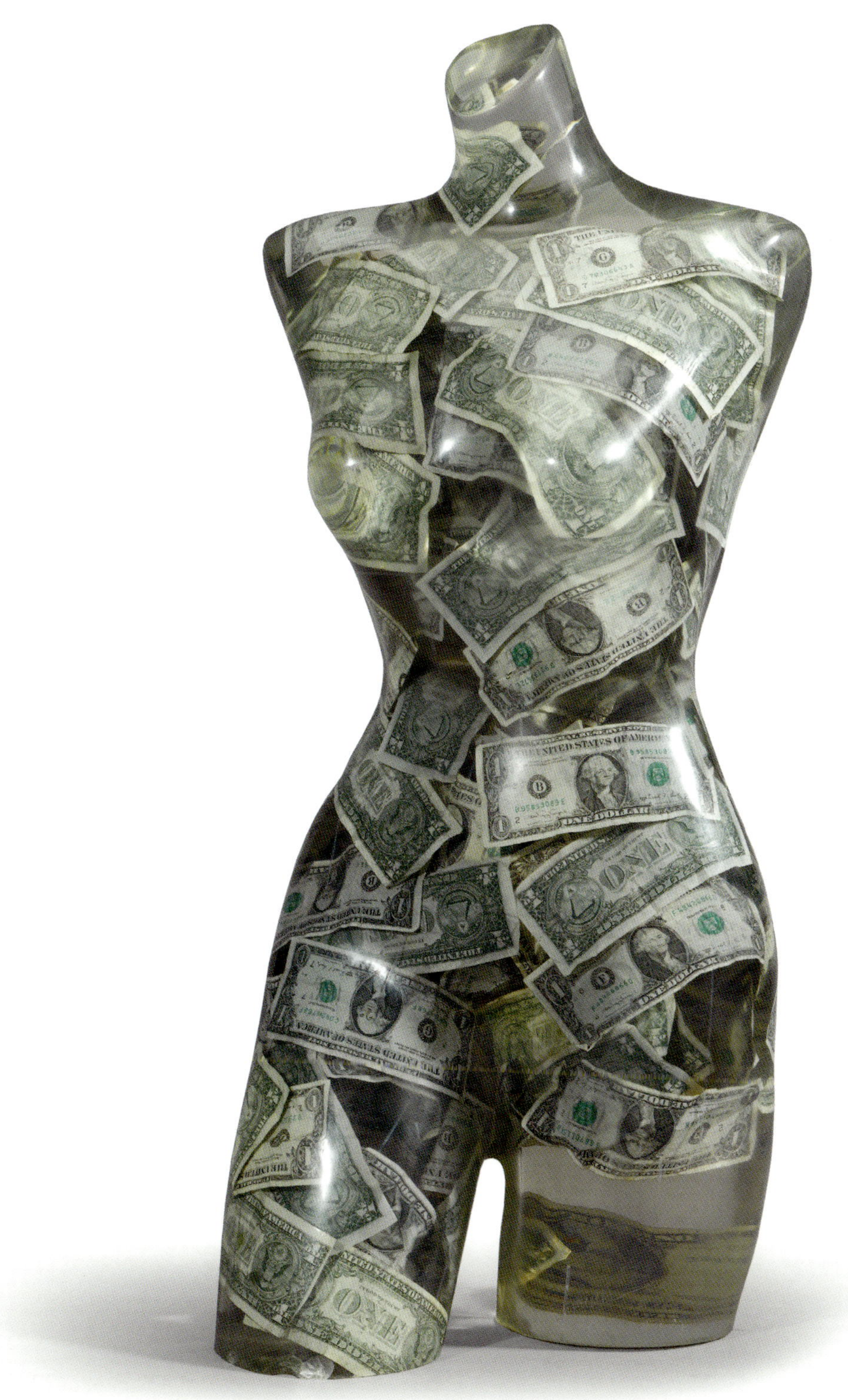

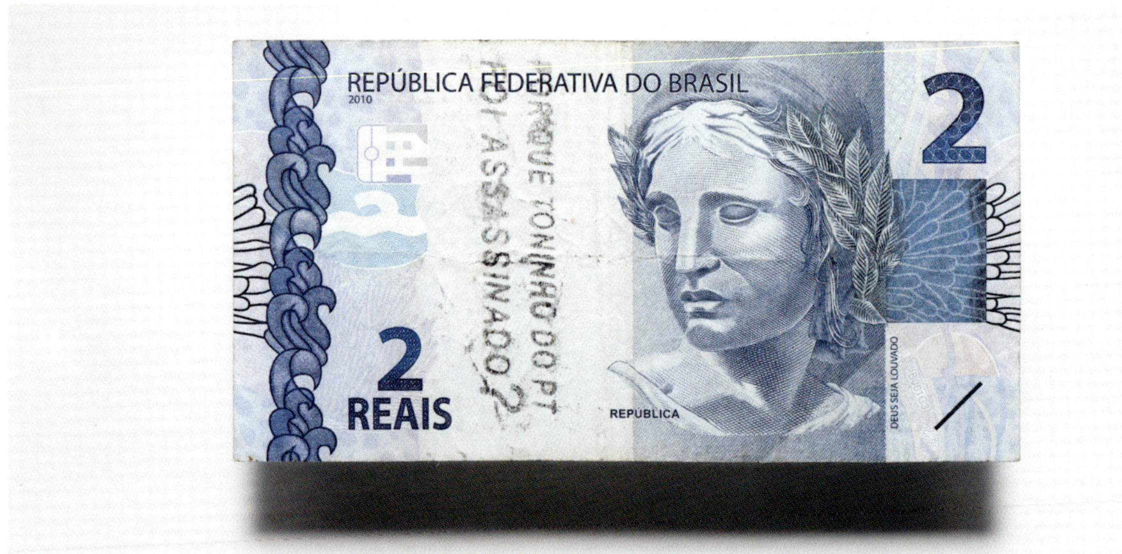

This Brazilian two-reais banknote has been stamped with a stark question: 'Why was Toninho do PT murdered?' It belongs to a series that the Brazilian artist Cildo Meireles (b.1948) began in 1970 while his home country was in the grip of a military dictatorship (1964–85). Faced with severe state censorship, he used rubber stamps to print subversive messages calling for democracy and political freedom onto banknotes before returning them to circulation. This enabled him to create a system for the dissemination and exchange of information away from any centralised control. Meireles continued the project long after military rule had given way to democracy. This example from 2013 denounces the murder of Antônio da Costa Santos, better known as Toninho do PT, who was a member of the Workers' Party (PT) and mayor of Campinas in southeast Brazil, when he was shot dead on 10 September 2001. As Meireles's inky text suggests, there are many uncertainties surrounding his death, which some believe was politically motivated because of his efforts to expose corruption. Many of Meireles's banknotes are now in museum collections but, because the artist insists that the work is only activated when the money is in use, they are only considered to be documentation.

Por que Toninho do PT foi assassinado? ('*Why was Toninho do PT murdered?*') from the series 'Inserções em Circuitos Ideológicos: 2 – Projeto Cédula' ('Insertions into Ideological Circuits: 2 – Ticket Project'), 1970/2013
Banknote
6.6 × 15.5 cm
(2⅜ × 5⅛ in.)

BREITMORE ACCOUNT
3007 JACKSON STREET
SAN FRANCISCO, CALIF. 94115

208

90-48
1211

19

PAY TO THE
ORDER OF

$

DOLLARS

BANK OF AMERICA NT&SA
BERKELEY MAIN OFFICE
2129 SHATTUCK AVENUE
BERKELEY, CALIF. 94704

MEMO

⑆ 1211 0048 ⑈ 208 01754 06430 ⑈

DELUXE CHECK PRINTERS – LH (1)

In 1973, the multimedia artist Lynn Hershman Leeson (b. 1941) transformed herself into the fictional character Roberta Breitmore for an expanded performance investigating selfhood, femininity and identity. For five years, Leeson worked, shopped and pursued other real-life activities as Breitmore in San Francisco, including opening a bank account, obtaining a credit card, checking into hotels and eventually renting an apartment and seeking roommates. Breitmore's image was carefully constructed; she had a wardrobe, a make-up routine, mannerisms and even handwriting style that were distinct to the artist's own. Upon use, each Bank of America cheque ('check' in US-English) was signed 'Roberta Breitmore,' and became one of 144 artefacts from Leeson's thoroughly documented project, including drawings, surveillance photos, psychiatric reports and a driver's licence. As far as official institutions were concerned, Breitmore was a real person; the fact that she could access financial services and credit cards (something that Leeson herself was unable to do due to bad credit) reveals the bank's lax security procedures and failure to carry out due diligence. For Leeson, it was a risky endeavour, leaving herself vulnerable to accusations of fraud, tax evasion and money laundering if she was ever caught. Nevertheless, the artist was never charged with any crime and, despite exhibiting the project in major museums, her actions apparently went undetected by the authorities.

Roberta's check, 1975
Bank cheque
7 × 15.2 cm
(2¾ × 6 in.)

In 1969, Edward Kienholz (1927–94) needed screwdrivers, but instead of simply buying a set with money, the American artist produced a small watercolour stamped with the words 'For Nine Screwdrivers,' which he offered to his neighbour in exchange for the tools. It was the first of his 'barter' works, paintings that could be acquired in return for whatever objects Kienholz had inscribed on them. From that series came another in 1974, of which these two are examples, that followed the same format but, instead of goods, each painting described a sum of money from one to ten-thousand US dollars. These were sold to collectors at literal face value. Signed with the artist's thumbprint, the works feature lettering with a serif typeface over pale watercolour washes; the more expensive (*For $501* and above) are streaked horizontally in blue, the median priced works in red, and the cheapest (*For $100* and below) in yellow or grey. As with real money, each piece comprises an image on paper with little material value, their worth being established by a consensus between artist, gallery and buyer. By essentially offering the 'same' piece at wildly different prices, Kienholz effectively satirised the art market and its systems of value that often appear arbitrary to those outside of the art world. He further emphasised his self-serving manipulation of the market by withholding *For $1.00*, which could only be bought together with *For $10,000*.

  Edward Kienholz

For $264.00 and *For $265.00*, 1974
Aquarelle and ink on paper
Each: 30.5 × 40.6 cm (12 × 16 in.)

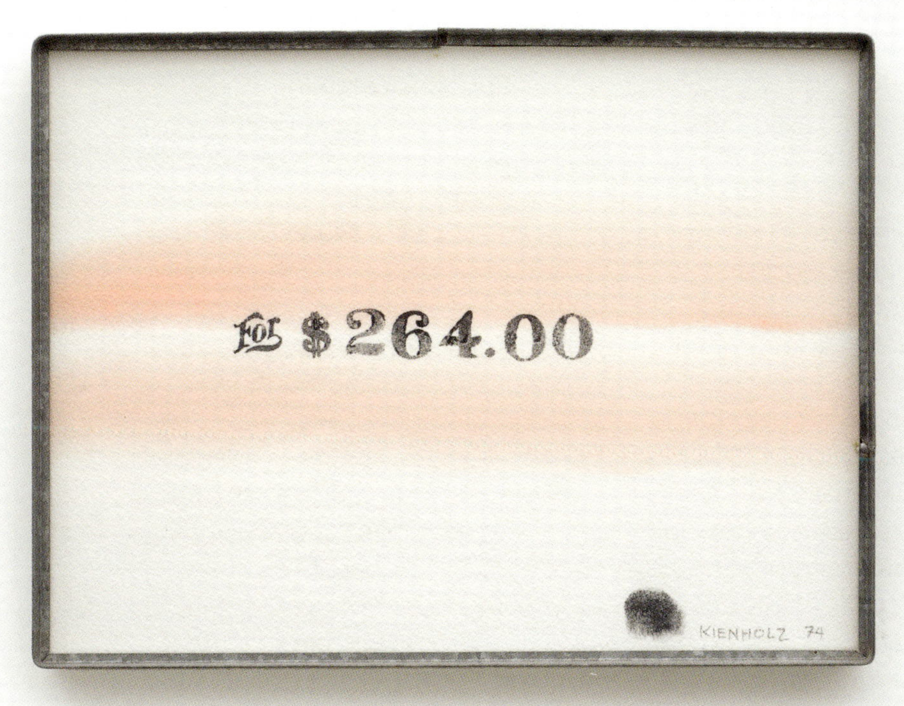
for $264.00
KIENHOLZ 74

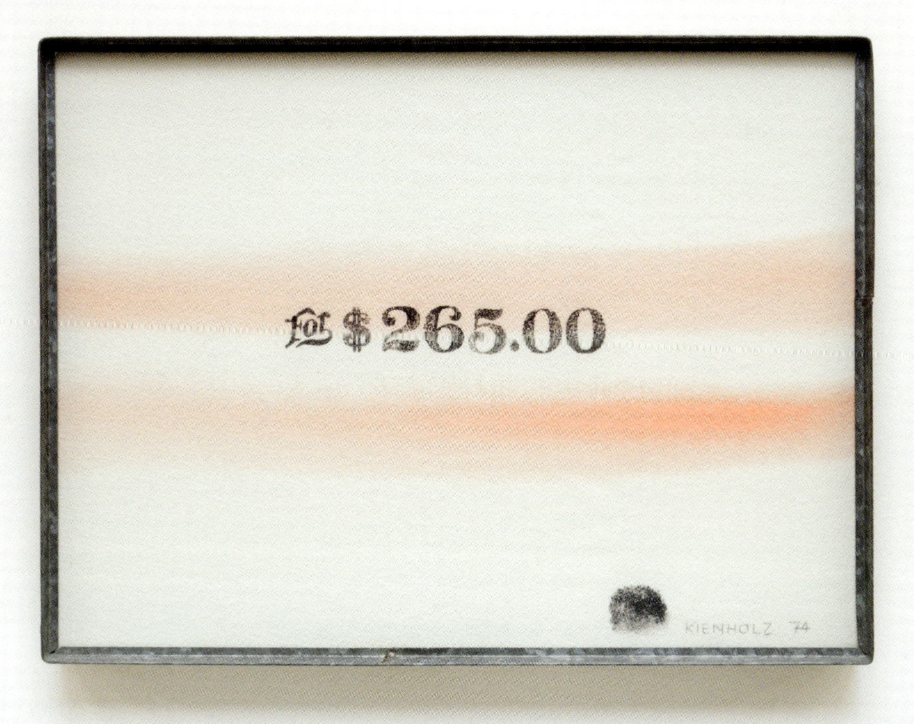
for $265.00
KIENHOLZ 74

Eleven cheques are neatly arranged in vertical columns and accompanied by small, typeset explanations; together, they represent Chris Burden's (1946–2015) expenditures for the month of November 1976. The American artist displayed this board and eleven others (one for each month), along with his bank statements and 1976 Income Tax forms, at Baum-Silverman Gallery in Los Angeles in September 1977. By doing so, he made a fully public financial disclosure, allowing visitors to track his fiscal transactions in detail over a twelve-month period. An accompanying booklet designed to resemble a chequebook detailed his earnings, including sales and lecture fees ($12,210), and grants ($5,000), as well as expenses: art materials ($3,416), travel ($4,309), studio expenses ($2,325) and television advertising ($6,106). His largest investment was the production and broadcast of a 30-second television commercial, which aired 30 times over a two week period. In it, he appeared sitting at a desk in front of a US flag and, in the manner of a politician running for office, declared his income, expenditures and net profit for the year ($1,054). The matter-of-fact project couldn't have been further from the provocative and often violent performances with which Burden made his name as a cutting-edge conceptual artist in the 1970s, which included being shot in the arm, nailed to a Volkswagen Beetle and kicked down a flight of stairs. *Full Financial Disclosure* laid to rest any notion that his artwork was earning him a fortune.

          Chris Burden

Full Financial Disclosure, 1977
Cheques and paper laid down on board
76.2 × 91.4 cm (30 × 36 in.)

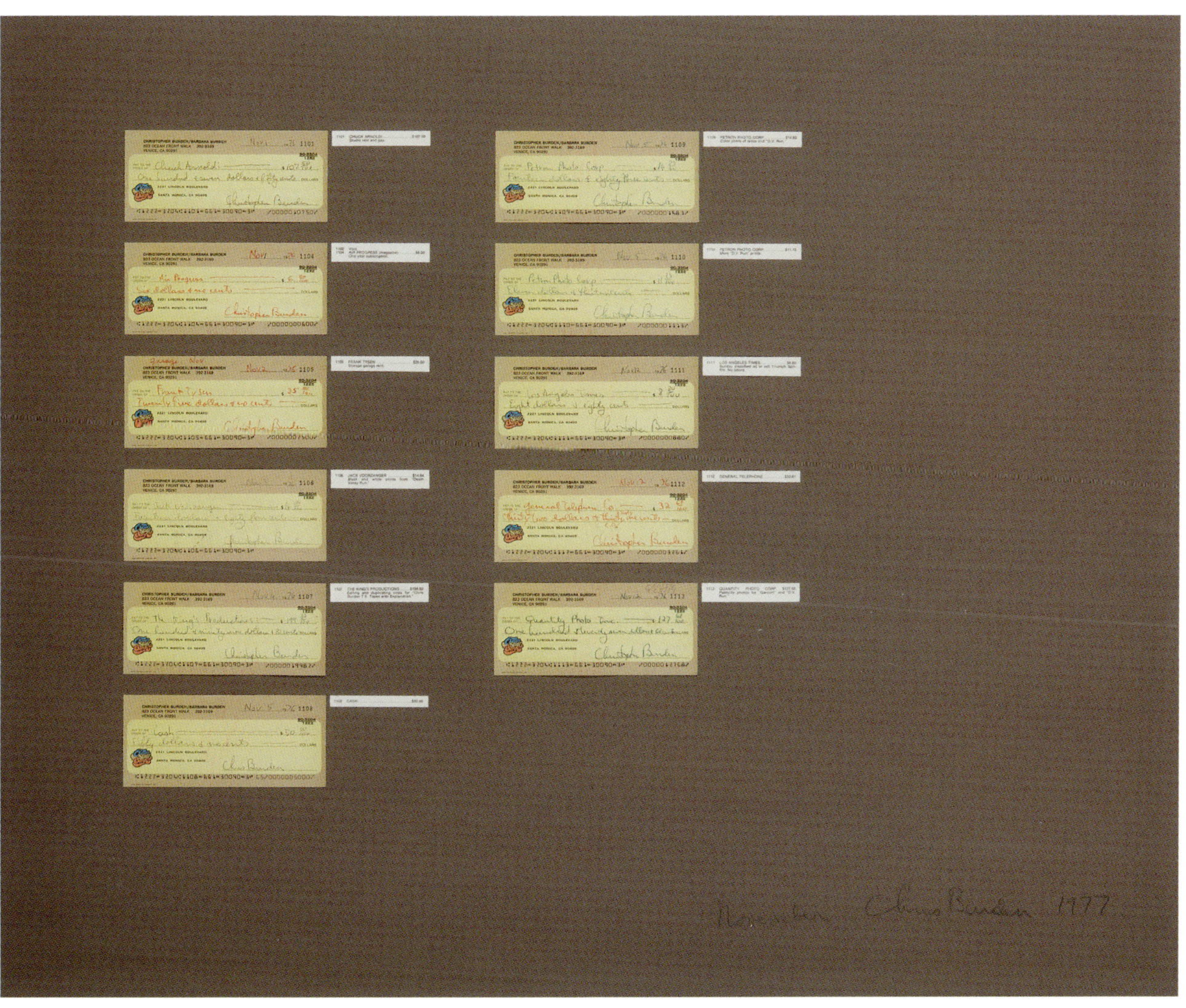

November Chris Burden 1977

When US banknotes reach the end of their life and are no longer deemed 'fit for commerce,' they are officially destroyed by shredding. Before 2010, these remains were simply burned or dumped in landfill, whereas today, the strips might be turned into compost, used to insulate houses or incinerated in power stations to generate electricity. One of the more unusual uses for shredded notes is seen here: as an art material. In 1979, the Dutch artist Jan Henderikse (b. 1937) persuaded the American Federal Reserve Bank to provide him with two 1.5-metre (50-foot) high bales of shredded money, each one estimated to contain ten million dollars of obsolete currency. One was exhibited as a sculpture titled *Shredded Value* (1979) while the second was divided up and used to create wall-based works, such as this frame stuffed with the straw-like material. So finely sliced are the bills that it is only their green and black colours that give any clue of their origin. Like some strange form of alchemy, Henderikse has taken worthless cash and given it value again by transforming it into art. As with the original notes, the piece has little intrinsic material worth, yet its market value is determined by an agreement between artist, gallery and collector. Using money as a material since the 1960s, Henderikse has made reliefs from one-cent coins, filled suitcases with counterfeit bills and produced gold jewellery from melted down coins. These and his many other projects question the nature of value, how it is created but also destroyed within the capitalist system.

    Jan Henderikse

Untitled (Shredded Value), c. 1979
Shredded dollar bills in artist's frame
102 × 68 cm (40⅛ × 26¾ in.)

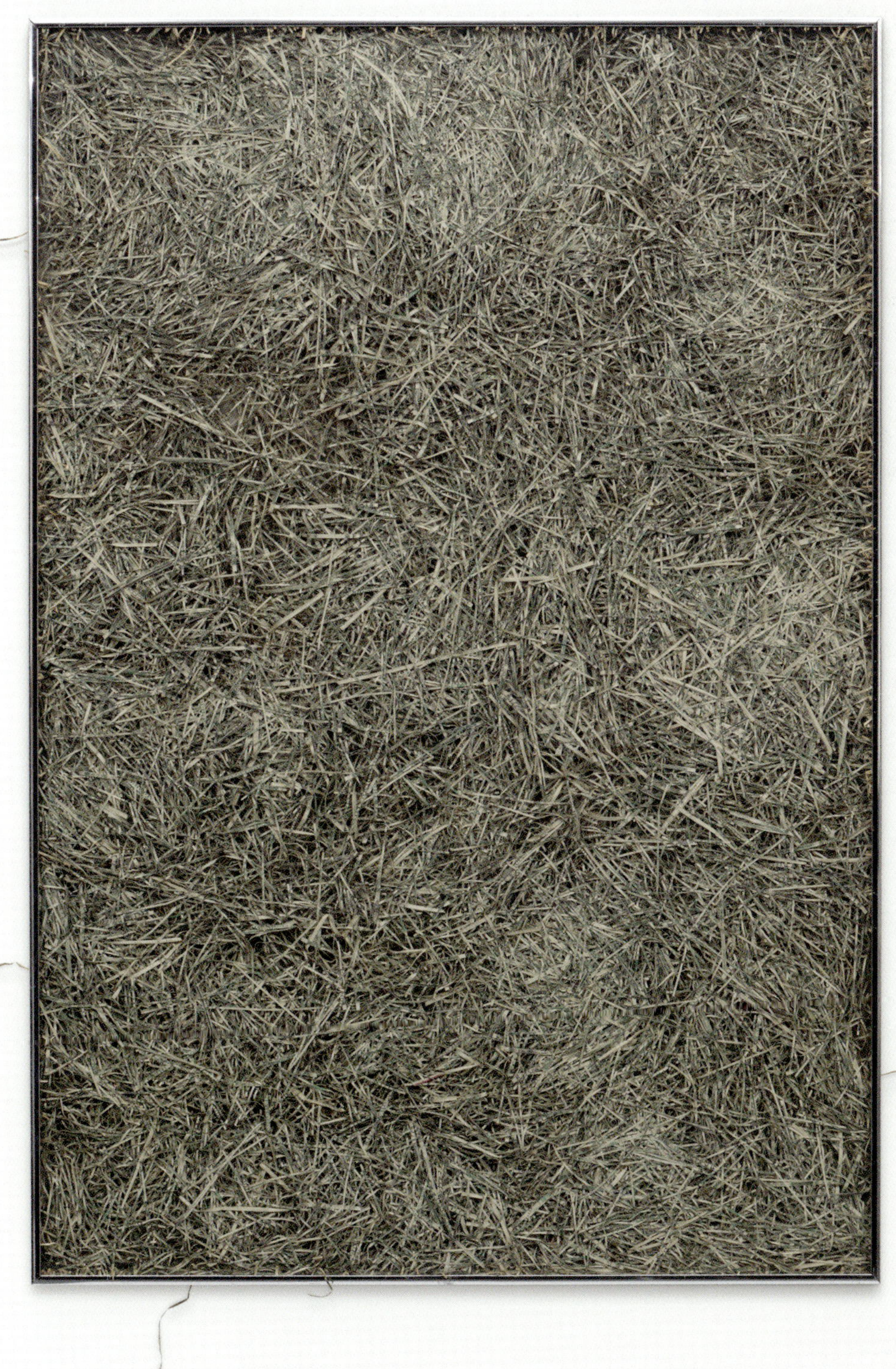

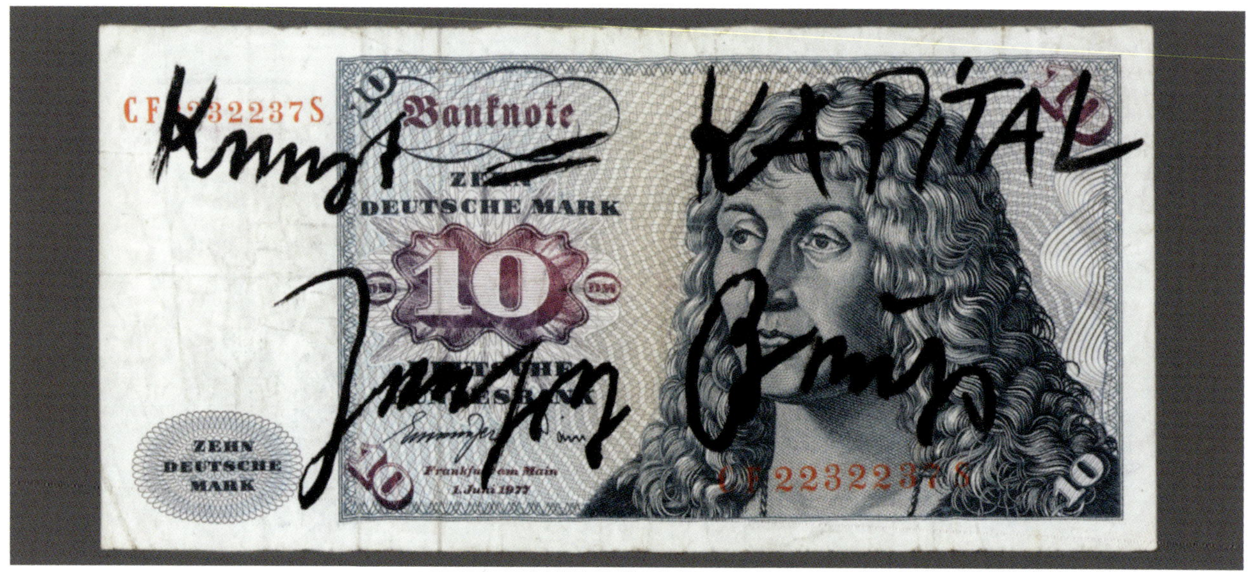

In the final decade of his life, the influential German artist Joseph Beuys (1921–86) began inscribing banknotes from different countries with the formula 'Kunst = Kapital' (Art = Capital), scrawling it along with his signature in pen or crayon before placing the money back into circulation. Using legal tender as a medium for political protest is a well established form of dissent; the coinage of Napoleon III was widely defaced after France suffered a major defeat at Sedan in 1870, and the British suffragette movement countermarked pennies with the legend 'votes for women' to promote their cause in the 1910s (see also p. 40). While Beuys's subversion of the West German Deutsche Mark might be seen as a reaction against the commodification of art in the 1970s, his intention was quite different. Believing that capitalism's commodification of labour degraded human dignity, he developed a theory of 'social sculpture' based on the notion that every aspect of life could be approached creatively. He redefined 'capital' as human creativity, while art, as an expression of that creativity, he considered as true work which, he said, could powerfully transform society by replacing 'degenerate' capitalism with a new economic system. His signing of bank notes concisely summarised his utopian proposal, hinting at an alternative monetary order.

Kunst = Kapital
('*Art = Capital*'), 1979
Banknote, titled and
signed in felt-tip pen
6.5 × 13 cm (2½ × 5⅛ in.)

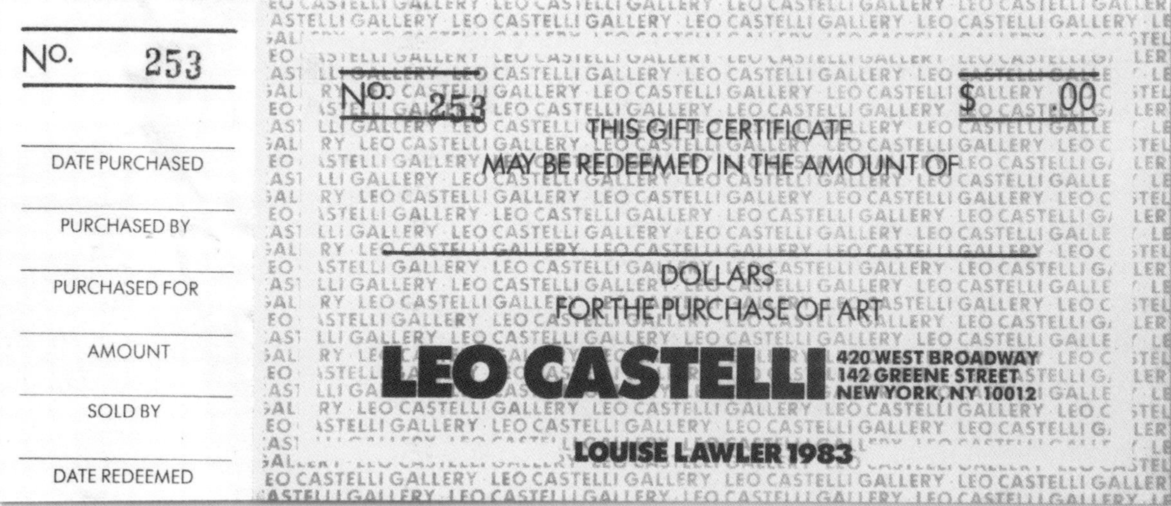

This artwork was first shown at the prestigious Leo Castelli Gallery, New York, in June 1983 in a group exhibition of works on paper — an art form that is typically less expensive than painting or sculpture. Presented behind Plexiglass, the design was based on the gift certificate of luxury fashion brand Brooks Brothers but using the gallery's typography, and it was accompanied by the simple statement 'Gift Certificates Are Available'. Although such vouchers are commonly issued by retail stores, often promoted next to the cash register, it is not standard practice for a major commercial gallery to purport to offer them. American artist Louise Lawler (b. 1947) typically questions the value, meaning and function of art in society through her work, and this print was not just an artwork posing as a gift certificate — it could actually be used towards the purchase of a work by Andy Warhol, Roy Lichtenstein or any other artist represented by Castelli. Whoever bought it, therefore, had the choice of keeping it as a work by Lawler, gifting it to a third party or spending it in order to acquire another artist's work. Produced in an edition of 500, the work reflects on the influence of economic and social conditions in determining the value of artworks. Within the context of the gallery, the work's value did not depend on the usual factors of edition size or artist signature, but solely on the amount for which it was originally purchased. On the open art market, however, its value would be as a Louise Lawler limited edition artwork.

Gift Certificate for Leo Castelli Gallery, 1983
Printed matter
9 × 16.5 cm (3½ × 6½ in.)

A black and white image of a US dollar bill, several times larger than life, is bisected by a line so as to mark two thirds and illustrate the stark message printed beneath it. This poster was created in 1985 by the provocative activist group Guerrilla Girls the year after the group was founded. As with many of the anonymous artists' early projects, it first appeared pasted on walls across SoHo and the East Village in New York City. Its design and content is typical of their graphic sensibility and feminist stance, revealing the salary gap in the art world between men and women to be far greater than that of the United States average. Since their inception in 1984, Guerrilla Girls have appropriated the visual language of advertising to expose gender and racial imbalances. Describing themselves as the 'conscience of the art world', they have targeted museums, dealers, curators, critics and artists that they believed were — wittingly or unwittingly — involved in exclusionary practices in relation to exhibitions, public and private collections and gallery representation. Members wear gorilla masks when representing the group in public and also assume the names of female artists from history — including Käthe Kollwitz (1867–1945) and Frida Kahlo (1907–54) — to foreground their shared concerns rather than their individual personalities. Aiming to inspire social change, the group state of this work on their website: 'Women have never gained economic equality by just working hard and being good girls. With this poster we wanted to make women artists angry as hell and not willing to take it anymore.'

     Guerrilla Girls

*Women in America Earn Only
2/3 of What Men Do*, 1985
Poster, offset print on paper
43.2 × 55.9 cm (17 × 22 in.)

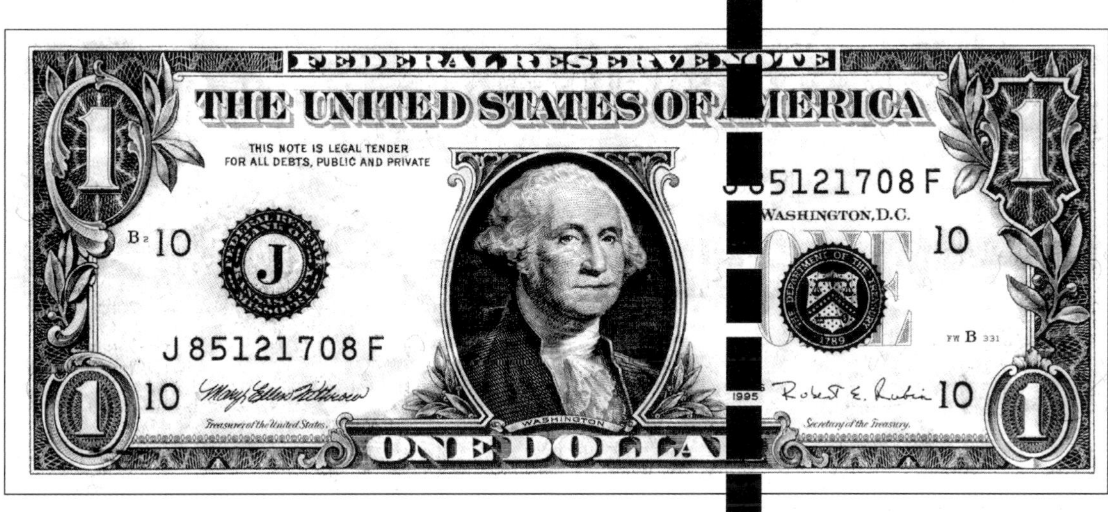

WOMEN IN AMERICA EARN ONLY 2/3 OF WHAT MEN DO.
WOMEN ARTISTS EARN ONLY 1/3 OF WHAT MEN ARTISTS DO.

A PUBLIC SERVICE MESSAGE FROM GUERRILLA GIRLS CONSCIENCE OF THE ART WORLD

In 1987, a sunflower painting by renowned artist Vincent van Gogh (1853–90) sold at auction for £24.75 million ($39.9 million), which at the time was the highest amount ever paid for a work of art. Inspired by the record-breaking sale, British artist Rose Finn-Kelcey (1945–2014) created *Bureau de Change*, an installation featuring a larger than life rendering of the iconic painting made from £1,000 worth of UK coinage laid out on temporary wooden flooring and lit by spotlights. The gold, silver and copper coins, which effectively approximated the tones of the original painting, showed signs of having been in circulation; some were quite dirty, having passed through multiple transactions. A uniformed guard patrolled the space while a video monitor suspended from the ceiling displayed a live feed of the coins as seen from directly overhead — elements designed to infer a far higher value on the work than the actual worth of the coins. The entire tableau could be surveyed from a raised platform, giving the viewer an almost voyeuristic vantage point. The title of the installation, which references the commonly-used French term for a place where foreign currencies can be bought and sold, encouraged reflection on the way that market forces can completely change the perception of artworks as they are transformed in the auction house from aesthetic objects to stores of value, instruments of wealth transfer and conduits of speculation.

     Rose Finn-Kelcey

Bureau de Change, 1987
£1,000 of loose change, wooden floor, surveillance camera and monitor, auctioneer's stand/viewing platform and security guard wearing full Tate uniform
Dimensions variable
Installation view, Matt's Gallery, London, 1988
Collection Tate, London

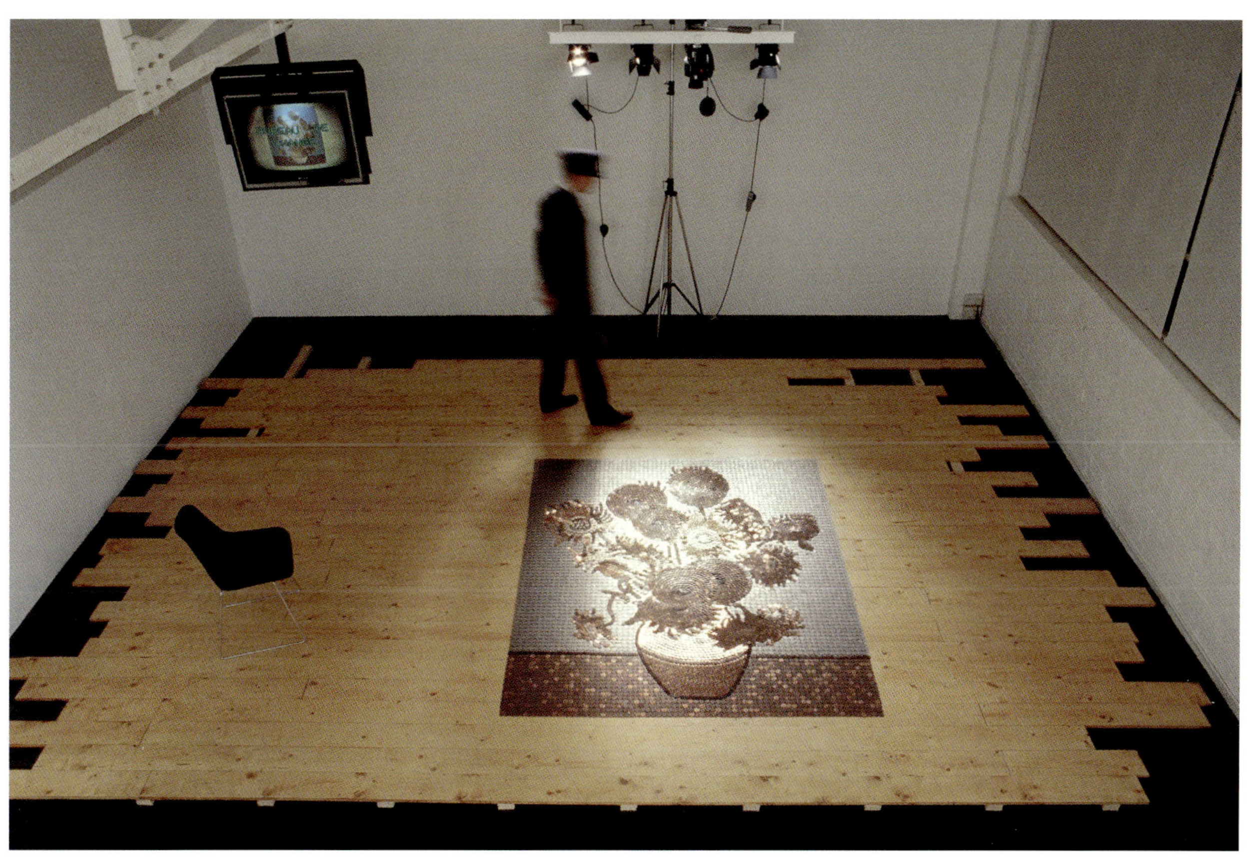

Described by the Guggenheim Museum as 'mesmerising and often inscrutable' the large, multi-sensory installations of American artist Ann Hamilton (b.1956), of which the site-specific *privation and excesses* is exemplary, engage viewers on physical, intellectual and emotional levels. Displayed at the not-for-profit Capp Street Project in downtown San Francisco, the installation responded to issues of wealth and need in the local neighbourhood, where Hamilton observed vagrants wandering the streets, circulating among commercial businesses and asking for money. Those visiting the project space, which was open to the street, encountered the glistening spectacle of 750,000 one-cent coins (a sum that represented the project's budget) arranged by hand in an undulating rectangle and held to the floor with honey. The performative work also featured a person (at times the artist herself) who sat silently dipping and wringing their hands into a felt hat brimming with honey (a greedy or perhaps despairing gesture), while three live sheep were penned in a smaller room overlooking the main space. On nearby shelves, two mechanical mortars and pestles were in motion: one grinding human and animal teeth, the other pennies. The whirring, clattering and crushing sounds combined with the pungent smell of honey and livestock to create a visceral environment. Each element was selected for its association with a different type of economy: from the use of animals and their products in pre-monetary exchange systems, to modern economies in which all exchange is organised through monetary currency. As a complex and poetic meditation on prosperity and lack, *privation and excesses* left viewers to draw their own conclusions from its multiple strands.

privation and excesses, 1989
750,000 pennies, honey, three sheep, two motorised mortar and pestles, human teeth, a felt hat, a gesture and hands wrung in honey
Rectangle of coins: 144.3 × 81.3 cm (45 × 32 in.)
Installation view, Capp Street Project, San Francisco, 1989

     Ann Hamilton

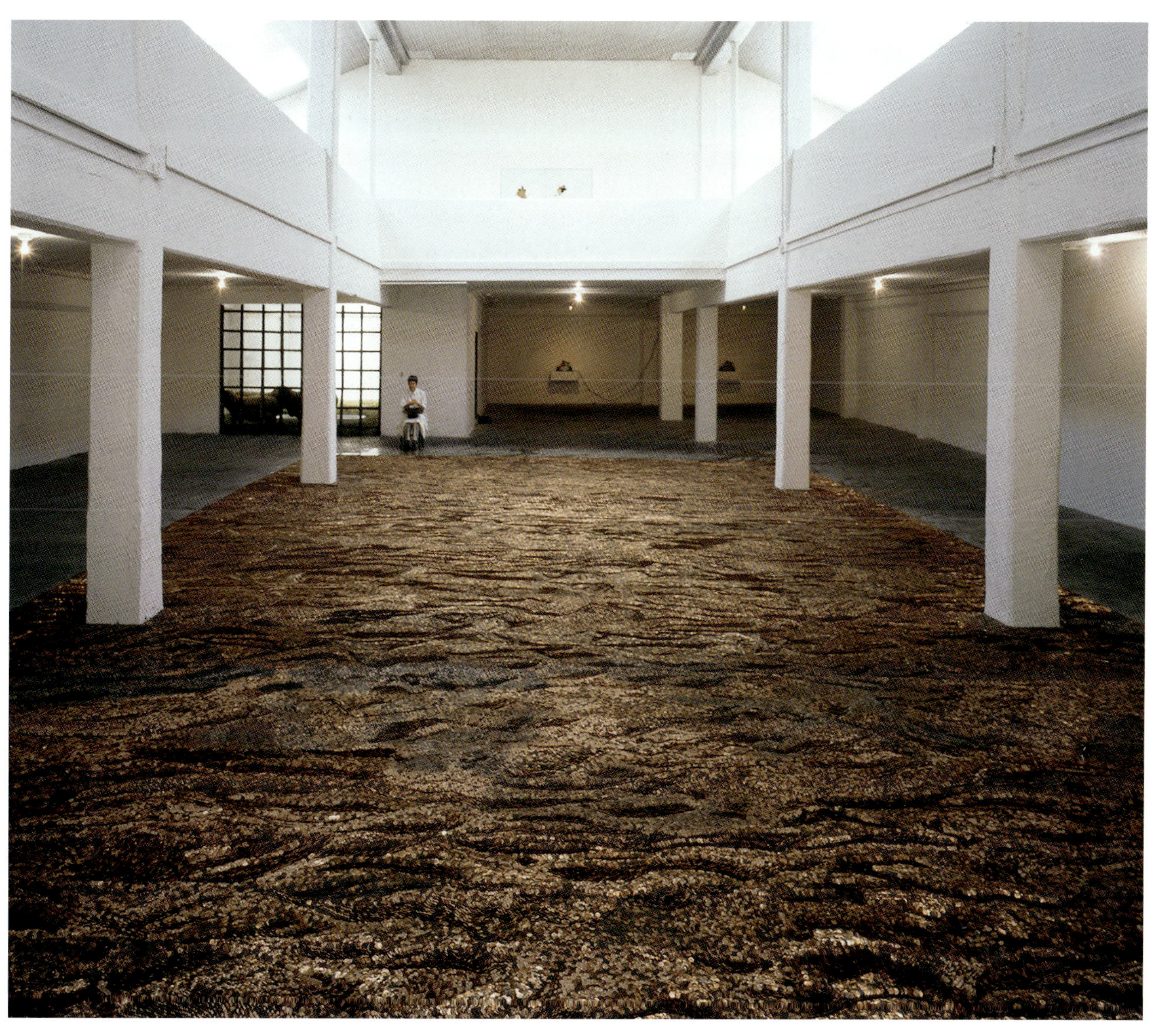

Close inspection of this hand-drawn English 50-pound note reveals several curious anomalies: the text flowing in a ribbon across its face reads 'Bank of Bohemia'; one of its pound symbols has been rendered in reverse; and the Chief Cashier is signed 'J.S.G. Boggs'– the name of the American artist who created the work and spent three decades drawing his own versions of local currencies and, where he could, spending them. Boggs (1955–2017) began his money drawings in 1984 when a waitress at a Chicago diner accepted his sketch of a dollar bill as payment for a coffee and doughnut. She also gave him 10 cents change and a receipt, thus conferring the status of tender on the drawing. Buoyed by this success, Boggs continued to offer his creations as payment for goods and services. If his 'Boggs Bills' were accepted, he requested a receipt and, where appropriate, change. Many receipts were sold to collectors who tracked down the business owners and negotiated the purchase of Boggs's drawings. Although the artist always insisted his banknotes were artworks, law enforcement agencies often disagreed. In 1986, he was arrested and had works seized from a London gallery. He was charged with violating the Forgery and Counterfeiting Act and taken to court, though the jury unanimously acquitted him. Between 1990 and 1992, the US Secret Service raided his apartment three times and took possession of more than 1,000 artworks, yet no legal case was brought against him. Boggs's pre-Bitcoin questioning of the status of fiat currency and reported involvement with a proposed digital currency in the early 2000s has led some to dub him the 'Patron Saint of Cryptocurrency'. Several of Boggs's artworks, including this drawing, have subsequently been made available as NFTs.

    J.S.G. Boggs

50 Pound Note #B10 888990, 1990
Ink and coloured pencil on paper
48.3 × 87.6 cm (19 × 34½ in.)

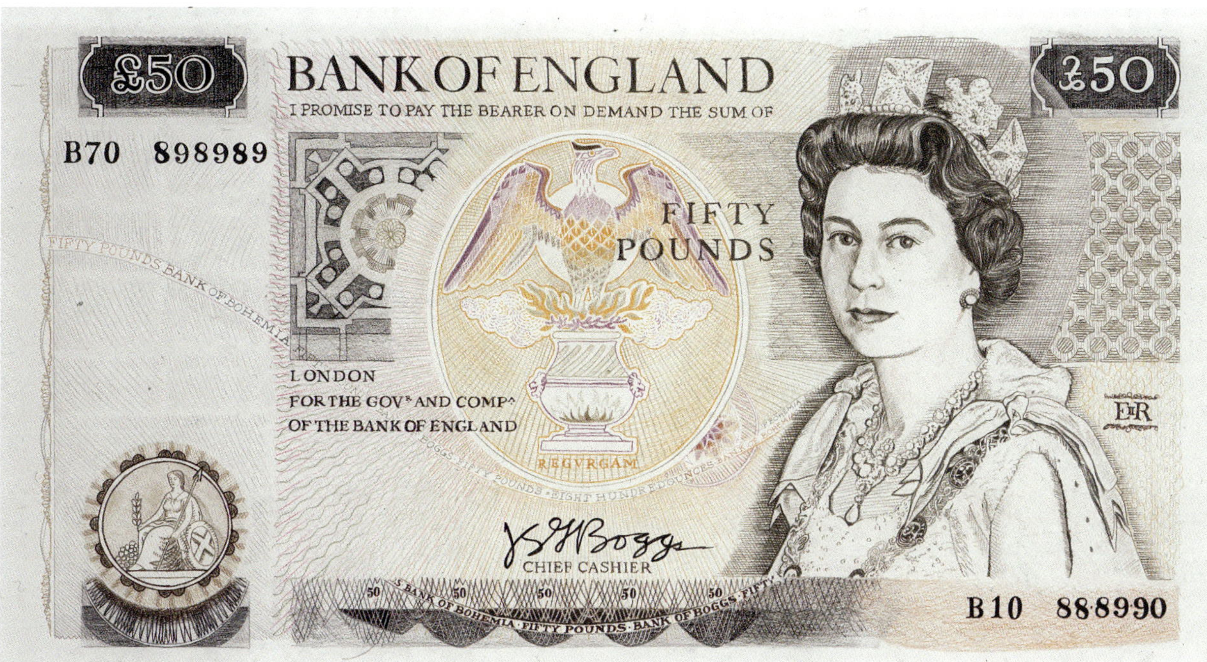
£50
BANK OF ENGLAND
I PROMISE TO PAY THE BEARER ON DEMAND THE SUM OF
B70 898989
FIFTY POUNDS
LONDON
FOR THE GOVᴿ AND COMPᴬ
OF THE BANK OF ENGLAND
REGVRGAM
CHIEF CASHIER
£50
ER
B10 888990
50 50 50 50
FIFTY POUNDS · BANK OF BOGGS FIFTY

On New Year's Day 1994, the Taiwanese-American artist Lee Mingwei (b.1964) visited a San Francisco cafe and began folding US ten-dollar bills into geometric origami shapes. He gave away nine of the small sculptures to passersby, all of whom agreed to stay in touch with him for a year. Lee took a photograph of each piece, documenting their fate after six and then twelve months in a series of photomontages. At the end of December, only five remained. Three had been unfolded and exchanged for goods — including footwear, a Paul Simon CD and groceries — and one had been stolen. The others had been kept intact by their owners, one of whom, a homeless man named John, stated that his held more value for him than anything he could have spent the money on. Lee's mixed-media installations bring people together for shared experiences; from the writing of letters to the sharing of food, each project stimulates contemplation and introspection. His strategy of inviting strangers to become participants draws from Chinese Ch'an Buddhism, which centres on the relational and experiential aspects of everyday life. Lee revisited *Money for Art* in 1997, this time in a gallery and using US one-dollar bills. Visitors could exchange the origami forms for any object they found equally valuable, along with a card stating their name and profession. Items left included antidepressants, a credit card (including PIN) and a condom; one visitor left only a first name and the word 'thief'. In both incarnations, Lee's project gently interrogated notions of giving and receiving, the obligation of reciprocity and the subjectivity of value.

Money for Art, 1994
Silver dye bleach prints (Ilfochrome)
3 from a set of 5, each: 27.9 × 35.6 cm (11 × 14 in.)
Collection Lee Studio

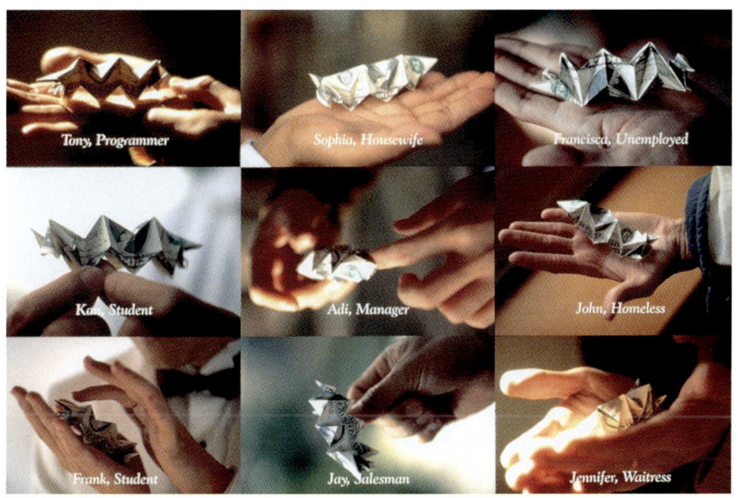

Tony, Programmer
Sophia, Housewife
Francisca, Unemployed
Ken, Student
Adi, Manager
John, Homeless
Frank, Student
Jay, Salesman
Jennifer, Waitress

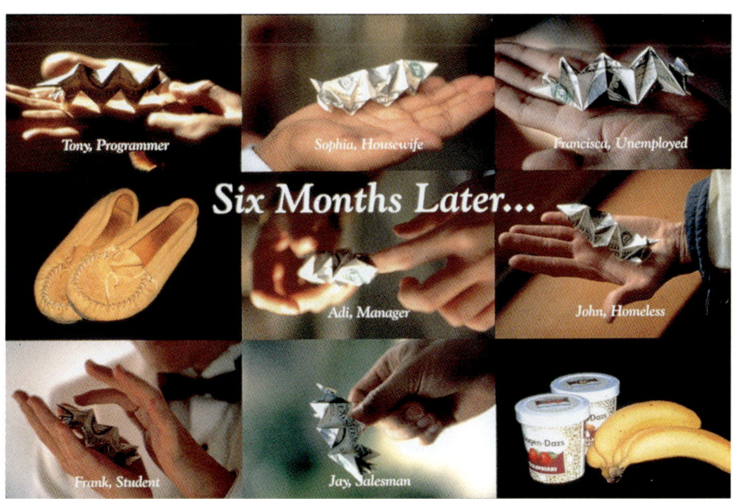

Tony, Programmer
Sophia, Housewife
Francisca, Unemployed
Six Months Later...
Adi, Manager
John, Homeless
Frank, Student
Jay, Salesman

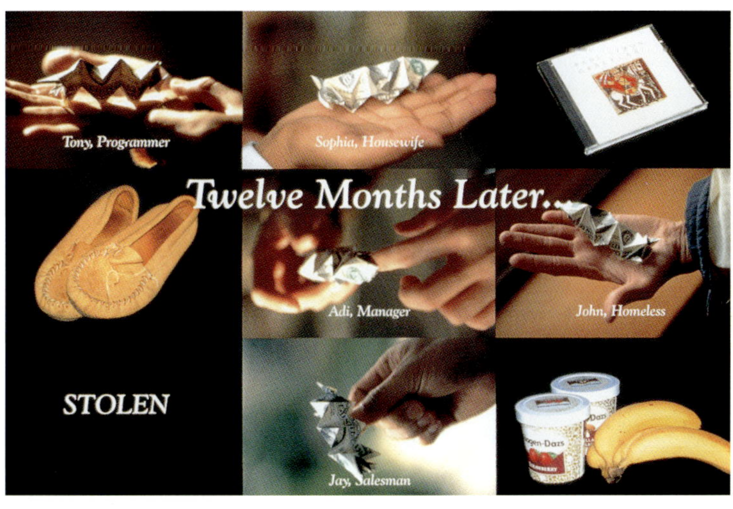

Tony, Programmer
Sophia, Housewife
Twelve Months Later...
Adi, Manager
John, Homeless
STOLEN
Jay, Salesman

In the early hours of 23 August 1994, an abandoned boathouse on the Scottish Isle of Jura played host to an audacious act of destruction, for it was here that Bill Drummond (b.1953) and Jimmy Cauty (b.1956), formerly of maverick electronic group The KLF and now operating as the K Foundation, burned one million pounds in cash. The money represented practically all that the chart-topping duo had left in their bank account, the proceeds from a string of critically-acclaimed hit singles and albums released between 1990 and 1992, which the pair, jaded with the music industry, had since removed from sale. The burning was witnessed by freelance journalist Jim Reid and was recorded on a Hi-8 video camera by KLF collaborator Alan Goodrick (aka Gimpo). A year later, the grainy film, in which the duo are seen tossing handfuls of 50-pound notes into the flames for just over an hour, was released as *Watch the K Foundation Burn a Million Quid* and screened at various locations around the UK, with Drummond and Cauty hosting debates about the meaning of the action. Audience reactions ranged from horror and shock to bewilderment and incredulity. To some it was a publicity stunt, to others a moral outrage, while to a few it represented a profound statement about our relationship with money and the desire to break free from its control. Although Drummond and Cauty have since acknowledged regret, they have never provided an explanation as to why they burnt the cash. All that physically remains of their iconoclastic action is a house brick made from some of the ashes.

Burning a Million Quid, 1994
Film stills from *Watch the K Foundation Burn a Million Quid, 1995,* and *The Brick* made from the ashes of the money burned by the K Foundation

  K Foundation

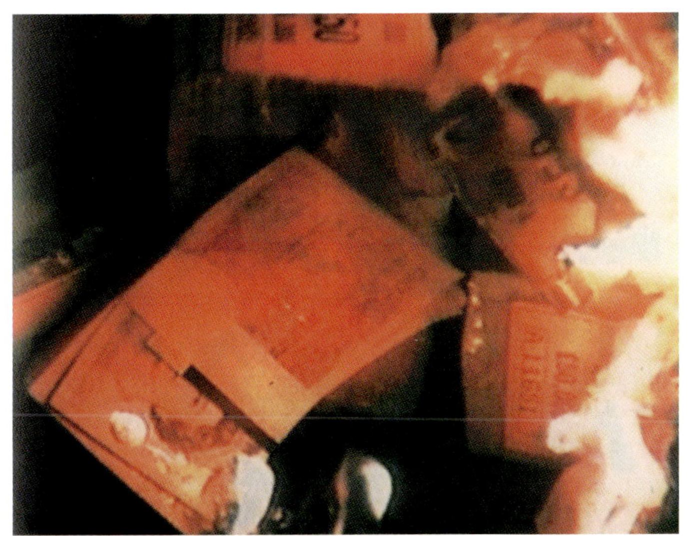

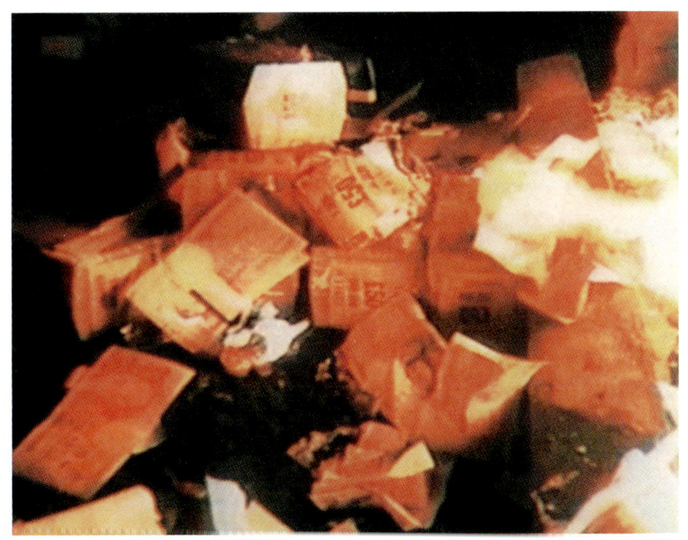

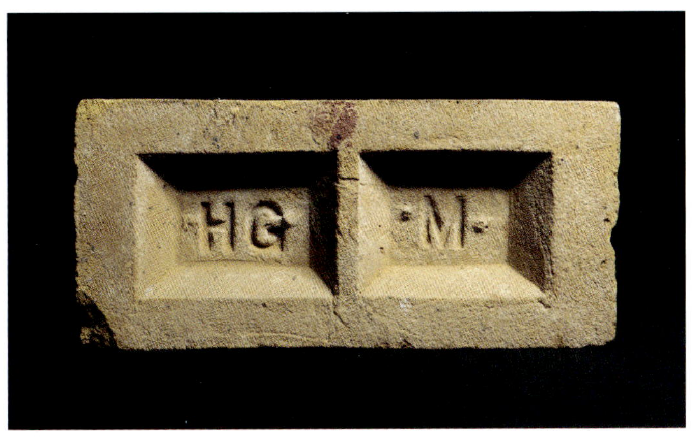

All UK coins are produced by the Royal Mint, a limited company wholly owned by His Majesty's Treasury that has been operating for more than 1,000 years. Located since 1968 in the town of Llantrisant, Wales, it also manufactures coins for around 60 countries annually, making it the world's leading export mint. In 1996, British conceptual artist Cornelia Parker (b. 1956) arranged a visit to the Royal Mint to see the production process. In her art, Parker explores the hidden meanings in objects, often altering them to create poignant sculptural works. Intrigued with the process by which metal can be transformed into powerful objects, in 1995 she made *Embryo Firearms,* a pair of cast steel Colt 45 guns in the earliest stage of production, when their form is barely recognisable. During her tour of the Mint, she became fascinated by piles of coin blanks — flat discs punched from long strips of copper-nickel alloy that would eventually become legal tender after being cleaned in acid, fed into a coin press, and struck with the appropriate design. After gaining permission, she removed a handful of ten pence blanks from the Mint and presented them spilling out of a sackcloth bag as a sculpture. Without the monarch's portrait, or any other indicator of value, these silvery-grey cupro-nickel discs represent potential currency, arrested before acquiring any power as money. A total of 118,738,000 UK ten pence coins were minted in 1996; *Embryo Money* prompts reflection on the process by which these simple pieces of metal transmute into symbols of economic value and social influence.

     Cornelia Parker

Embryo Money, 1996
Ten pence pieces in the earliest stage
of production and bag
Dimensions variable, *c.* 25 × 30 cm
(*c.* 9⅞ × 11¾ in.)

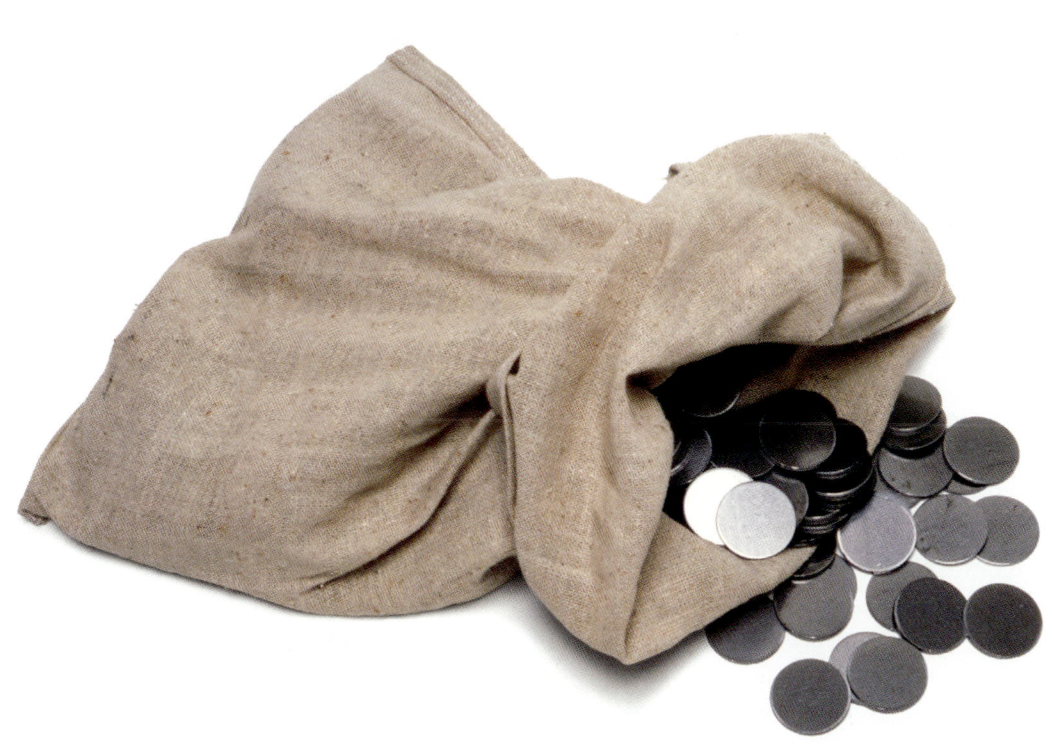

The Buddhist wheel of life, or *Bhavachakra*, is an ancient symbolic representation of the continuous cycle of life, death, and rebirth. By simplifying the wheel's form and exchanging its religious content for nine images of UK one pound coins, London-based artists Gilbert and George (b. 1943; b. 1942) allude to the unending cycle of money, a perpetual process of earning, spending, saving, investing, borrowing and repaying that underpins economies. Each of the coins in this multi-panelled work feature floral or heraldic emblems representing the United Kingdom and its four constituent nations. At the top of the circle we see a Northern Irish celtic cross with a pimpernel flower at its centre; the royal coat of arms of the United Kingdom appears next, followed by a thistle and royal diadem for Scotland. A less familiar coin from Gibraltar depicting a castle is seen on the lower right leg of the wheel, while at the bottom, Wales is represented by a dragon and then a leek sprouting from a royal diadem. Scotland is represented again by the heraldic lion rampant before the UK royal arms shield completes the circle. At the wheel's centre, reproduced on a smaller scale, is a 1988 Isle of Man pound featuring an antiquated mobile phone, which, just like these coins, has long passed into obsolescence. *Money Wheel of Life* thus captures a moment in UK monetary history. None of these coins are still legal tender, having been superseded by a new 12-sided coin in 2017, which, unlike the old round one pound, is significantly harder to counterfeit. While this work primarily refers to the flow of cash in society, it points to the fact that physical currency also has its own cycle of birth, death and renewal.

     Gilbert & George

Money Wheel of Life, 1997
Mixed media
190 × 226 cm (74 ¾ × 89 in.)

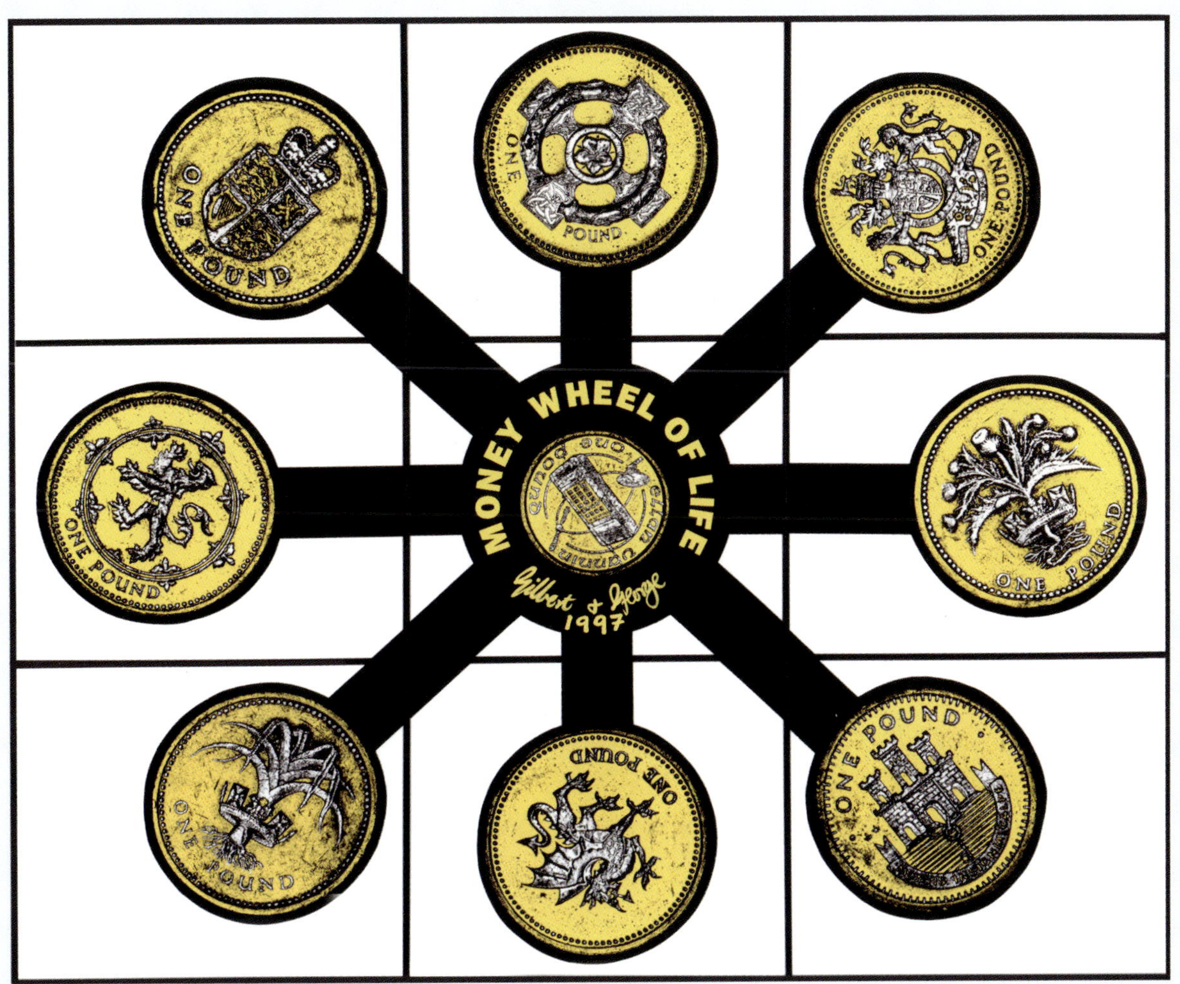

MONEY WHEEL OF LIFE
ONE POUND
ONE POUND
Gilbert & George
1997

In the 1980s, Brazil suffered a protracted period of high inflation, which in 1990 developed into hyperinflation. Its currency, the cruzeiro, was devalued several times before being replaced by the cruzado and then the cruzado novo, which both also failed. At the height of the crisis, the cruzeiro was reintroduced before finally being replaced by the real in 1995, which is still in use today. Fascinated by the phenomenon of worthless currency in her home country, Jac Leirner (b.1961) started collecting devalued banknotes to use as material for her artworks. Her earliest pieces, made with cruzeiros, are titled *Os Cem* ('The One Hundreds') — a pun in Portuguese for its similarity to 'os sem', meaning 'those without'. Some are sculptural, such as *Os Cem (Roda)* (1987), a wheel made from thousands of bills, while others take the form of collaged squares. Though nodding to Minimalism, many of these works highlight a more intimate relationship with money by using notes featuring inscriptions made while the bills were still circulating. The two squares comprising *Todos os Cem (Xingamentos)* contain expletive-laden graffiti, expressing the frustrations and grievances of those affected by the inflationary crisis. On one, the face of president Juscelino Kubitschek (1902–76) is defaced by the slur '*doido*' ('insane'), while others are scrawled with insults such as '*vagabunda galinha*' ('chicken slut'), '*filha da puta*' ('son of a whore') and the extremely disparaging '*vaca*' ('cow'). Leirner's works with cash speak to the life cycle of currencies, while giving new value to objects previously considered worthless.

     Jac Leirner

Todos os Cem (Xingamentos) ('*All the One Hundreds: Swearings*'), 1998
Brazilian banknotes
53 × 73.3 cm (20 × 28 in.)

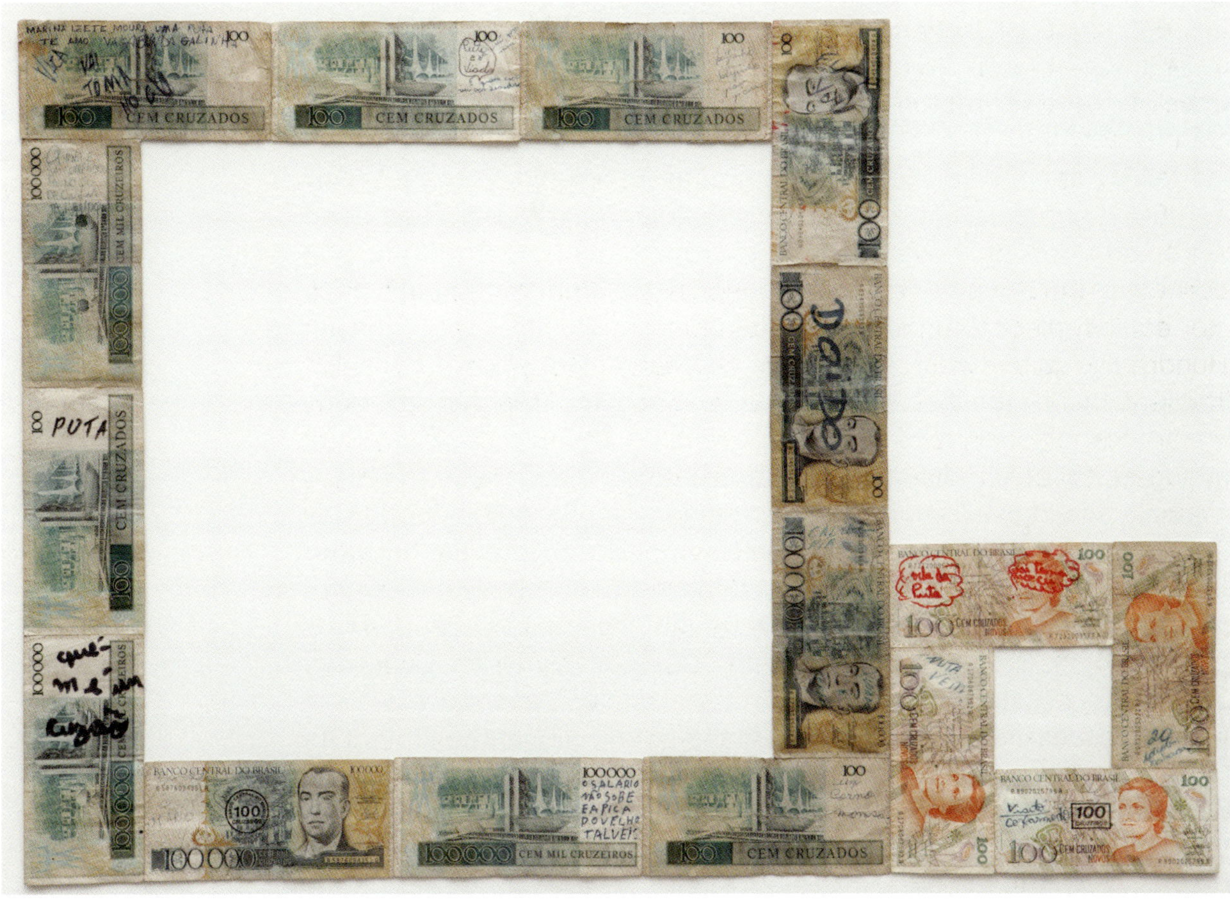

The high accumulated weight versus low aggregate value of small denomination coinage may result in its removal from a pocket or purse to be stored elsewhere for future use or exchange once a more substantial amount has been amassed. Upon arrival in Berlin in 1996 for the DAAD artist-in-residence programme, British artist Craig Wood (b. 1960) discovered that just such a jar of German pfennigs had been left behind by a previous resident. The abandonment of money by a fellow artist intrigued him — representing both a direct challenge to the stereotype of the 'penniless artist' and an invitation to consider the creative potential of the coins in aesthetic and conceptual terms. Inspired by the Italian Arte Povera artists, who transformed humble, non-traditional materials into artworks by simple means, Wood attached the coins together with double-sided sticky pads to create a coiled, snake-like form — a small change that offered a neat pun for the work's title. Exhibited on a plinth under spotlights like valuable jewellery (though the tarnished coins could equally be reminiscent of faeces), the sculpture was ultimately bought for the art collection of a German bank, a blunt demonstration of how art's market value can exceed its constituent parts. The work also had resonance in relation to discussions around funding of the arts which, at the time of its creation, was an acute issue in Berlin. After returning to the UK, Wood remade the piece using two-pence pieces, one of the largest British coins, which has not changed dimensions since it was introduced with decimalisation in 1971. Originally minted from bronze, in 1992 the tuppence was changed to copper-plated steel after the rising price of copper caused the bronze coins to become worth more than their face value.

    Craig Wood

Small Change, 1998
Two-pence coins and self-adhesive pads
12 × 35 × 35 cm (4 ¾ × 13 ¾ × 13 ¾ in.)

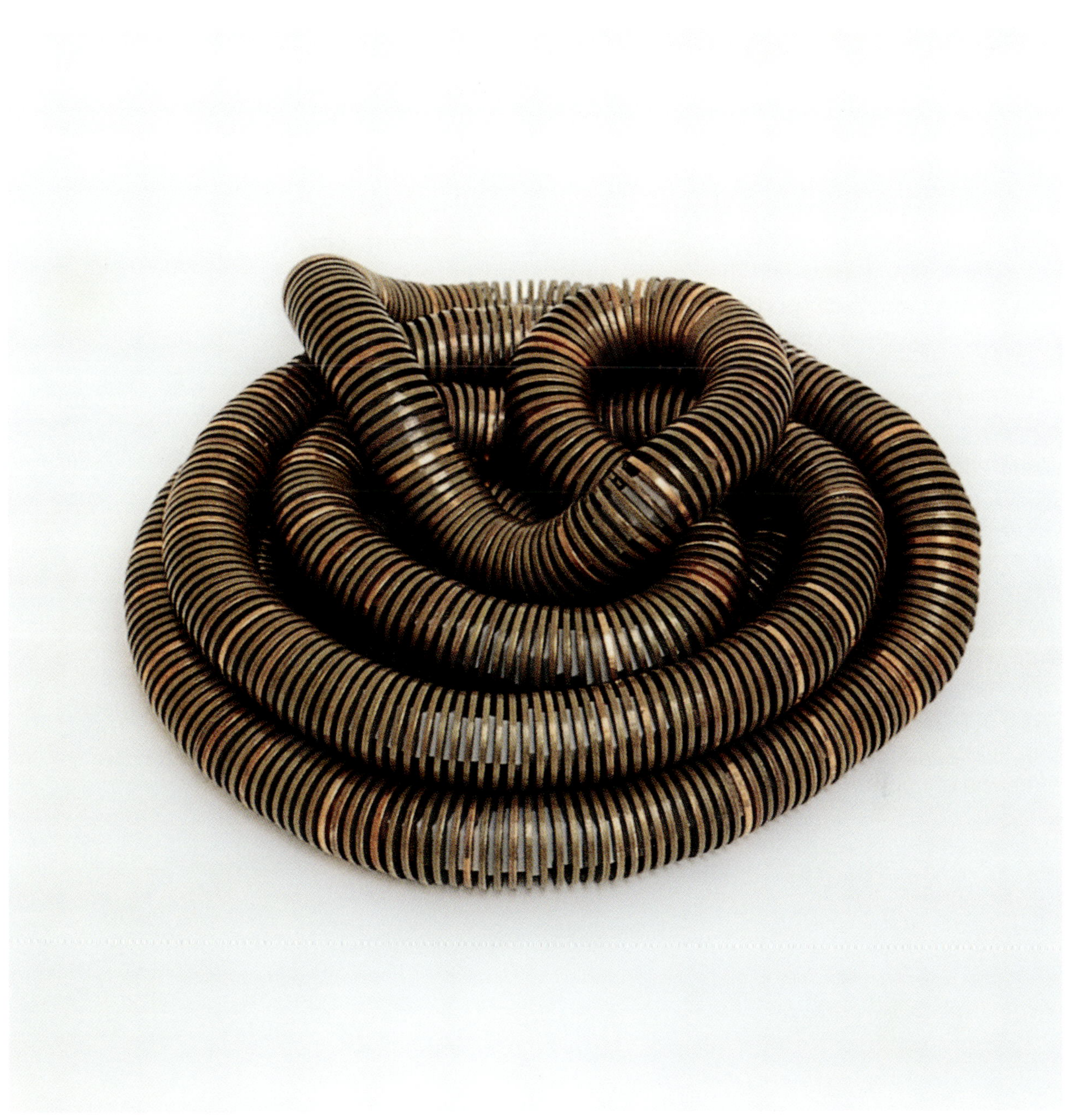

At first glance, this photograph recalls the type of public flaunting of wealth associated with the excesses of Wall Street in the 1980s: successful young traders flashing wads of cash and revelling in their newfound riches. In fact, as the title clarifies, the reason for the large amount of money has to do with the location on the French Caribbean island of Saint Barthélemy, a playground of the prosperous that at the time was largely a cash-based economy. The playful demeanour of the two Americans, posing with their credit cards stuck to their foreheads, also nods toward the overt displays of affluence that became cliched in 1990s hip-hop culture (where Russell Simmons, seen on the left, made his fortune). Photographer and filmmaker Lauren Greenfield (b.1966) took this photograph at the exclusive L'Iguane restaurant (just days after Simmons was married nearby) for her multi-platform project 'Generation Wealth' that encompasses a film, exhibition and photographic mono-graph. For two and a half decades, she travelled the world — from the US to Russia, to the United Arab Emirates to China — documenting the far-reaching obsession with prosperity. Touching on themes of consum-erism, narcissism and capitalism, her project tells eye-opening stories of the super rich and how they spend their money, those who lost fortunes during the global financial crisis of 2007–8, and people overwhelmed by unsustainable debt yet who persist in purchasing luxury goods in the hope of finding happiness. In laying bare the primal desire to become rich at any cost, Greenfield encourages reflection on the human costs of insatiable greed.

     Lauren Greenfield

Film director and producer Brett Ratner (right), 29, and Russell Simmons, 41, a businessman and co-founder of hip-hop label Def Jam, at L'Iguane restaurant, St. Barts, 1998. Few establishments on the island accepted credit cards, and visitors often carried large amounts of cash, December 29th 1998

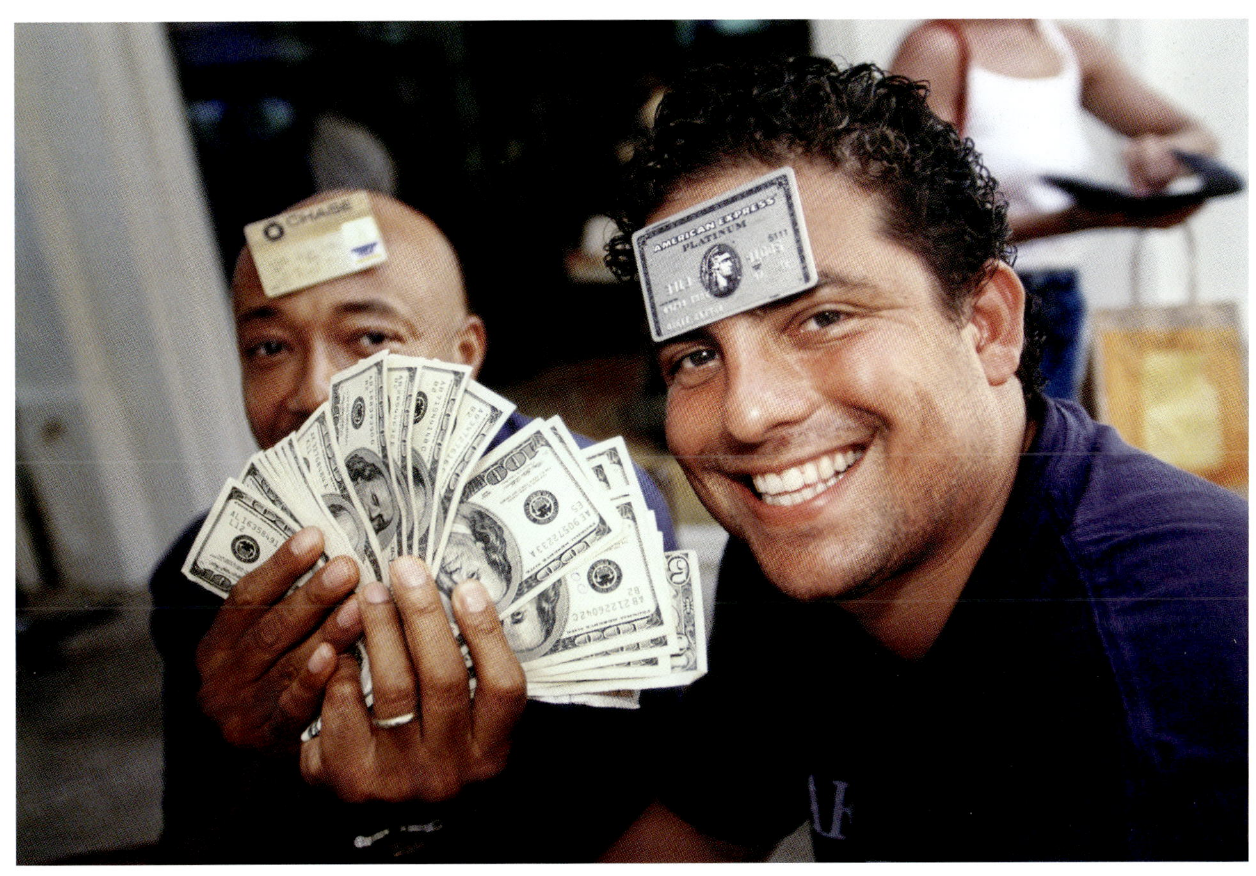

These spherical, hybrid coins have been created by fusing together Cuban pesos (CUP) and American quarters (USD) so that their faces are bisected at right angles. Words and images become jumbled up so that Cuban national hero José Martí now shares George Washington's hair and the Cuban legend 'Patria o Muerte' (Homeland or Death) is transformed into the politically-charged motto 'Homeland of America'. As with many of the works of Cuban artist Yoan Capote (b.1977), these pieces are deeply connected with the complex history of his home country and were created when Cuba was struggling for autonomy of its financial system. The island nation was economically dependent on subsidies from Moscow during the Cold War, but after the dissolution of the Soviet Union in 1991, Cuba's economy collapsed. With tourism the only stable sector delivering income to the country, Cuba's Communist government made the US dollar legal tender in 1993 to facilitate tourist spending, establishing a dual currency system. In 2004, the US dollar was replaced by the Cuban Convertible Currency (CUC), which was pegged to USD for stability. This was scrapped in 2021 and today Cuba again has a single currency: the Cuban peso. Capote's diminutive sculpture succinctly visualises the coming together of two very different ideological systems: capitalism and socialism, encapsulating the complex and contradictory economic reality that existed in Cuba at the start of the twenty-first century.

    Yoan Capote

Bilingual Money, 2002
US and Cuban coins
Each: 2.5 cm (1 in.) diam.
Private collection

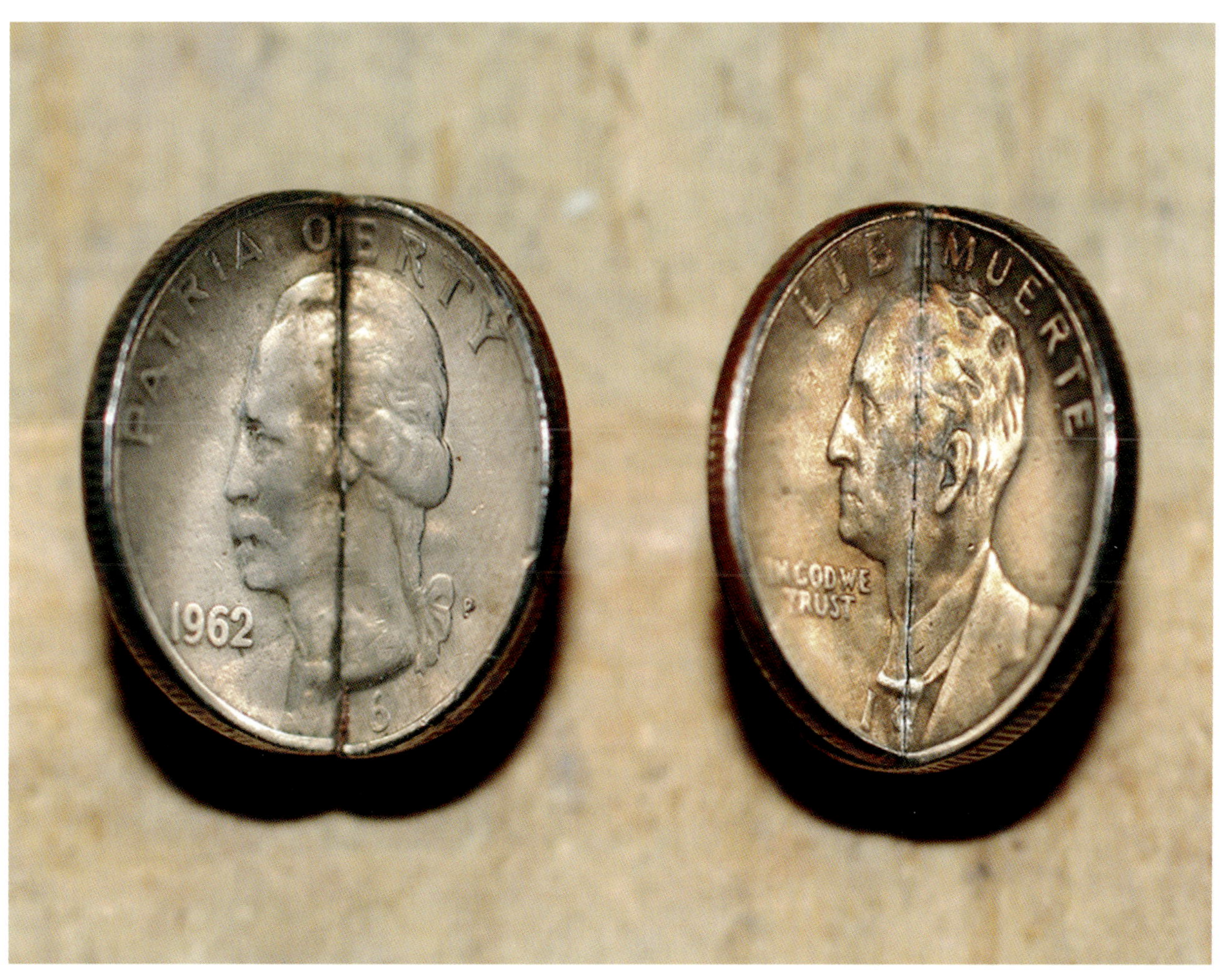

PATRIA OERTY
1962
LIB MUERTE
IN GOD WE TRUST

Evoking dreams of unlimited wealth, this sculpture by the Cuban artist Wilfredo Prieto (b.1978) uses the infinity mirror principle to create the illusion of countless banknotes receding into space. Using just two mirrors and a single US dollar bill, its simple economy of means belies its complex message regarding the nature of art, value and money in the twenty-first century. An integral aspect of this artwork, reflected in its title, is Prieto's claim that it has a market value of one million dollars. This is a comment on the dominance of the American dollar in the global economy (something that is acutely felt in Cuba where the dollar is often used in preference to the native peso, on account of its perceived superior stability) as well as on the art market's seemingly arbitrary system of valuation, in which the list price may not necessarily reflect the amount for which it would sell. *One Million Dollar* typifies the understated simplicity of Prieto's sculptures and installations, which employ everyday materials to explore social and political issues with humour, satire and subversion. Although this sculpture was created before the global financial crisis of 2007–8, its seemingly limitless supply of cash also raises the spectre of quantitative easing, a monetary policy of essentially printing money that many countries adopted in order to stimulate their troubled economies and mitigate economic recession. In this way, *One Million Dollar* can be considered a multilayered critique of late capitalism.

    Wilfredo Prieto

One Million Dollar, 2002
One US dollar bill and mirrors
35.4 × 15.6 × 7.4 cm (13⅞ × 6⅛ × 2⅞ in.)

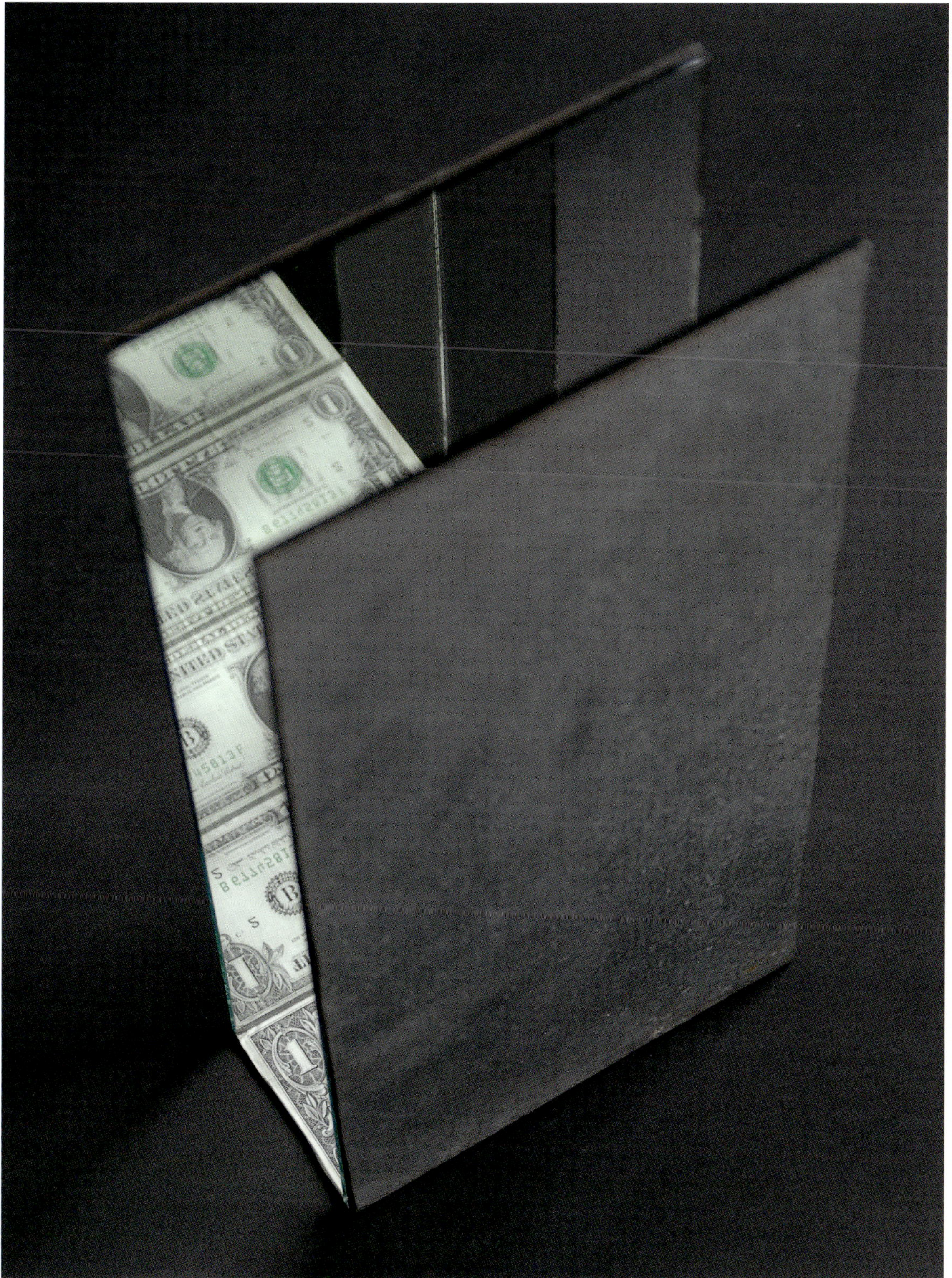

Delicately crafted from layers of coloured sand and encased in Perspex, this ten-thousand-yen note has been defaced by a colony of ants that has tunnelled and scuttled through its grainy structure. *Yukichi* — titled after Fukuzawa Yukichi (1835–1901) a prominent Japanese intellectual, educator, writer and founder of Keio University, whose portrait this denomination features — belongs to Yukinori Yanagi's (b.1959) 'Money' series (1999–2002). In it, larger-than-life pictures of US dollars, Chinese yuan and European currencies are variously marred by the burrowing insects — a metaphor for the vulnerability of fiat currencies to economic and geopolitical shocks, among other threats. For Yanagi, currencies and national flags are symbols of the barriers that separate nations, something that was particularly apparent to him in the period in which he lived in the USA while undertaking an MFA at Yale University. Indeed, the Japanese artist has also made several 'ant farm' works based on flags, initially motivated by the fall of the Berlin Wall in 1989, which came to signify a key moment in the collapse of Communism in Eastern Europe and the Soviet Union and the end of the Cold War. One such example is *Pacific* (1996), which comprises a grid of 49 interconnecting sand-filled boxes, each depicting the flag of a country bordering the Pacific Ocean. Such works convey Yanagi's rejection of borders and his longing for the unification of the world's nations, where barriers to the free movement of goods, people and capital are removed.

     Yukinori Yanagi

Yukichi US268635Y, 2002
Ants, coloured sand and plastic box
53 × 103 cm (20⅞ × 40½ in.)

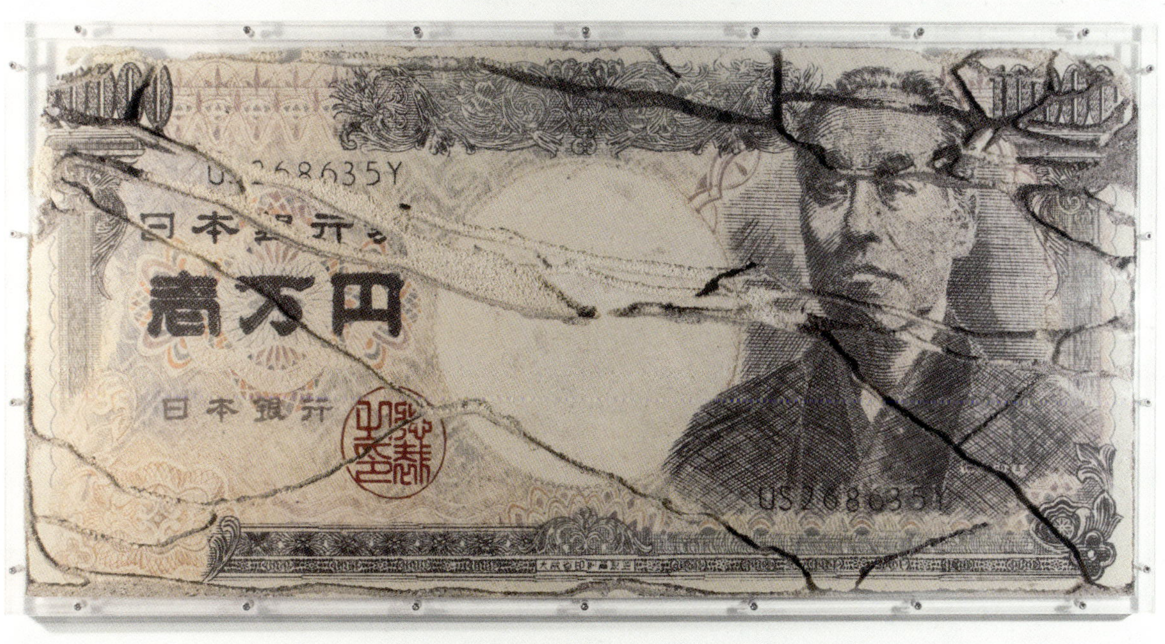

The 'heads', or obverse, side of a coin has depicted the image of a monarch or leader for thousands of years. The tradition originated in ancient Persia (modern day Iran) in the fifth-century BCE and has survived into the modern era. During the 70 year reign of Queen Elizabeth II between 1952 and 2022 — the longest of any British ruler — five official royal coin portraits appeared on UK coinage, with each successive effigy reflecting her ageing appearance. This understated work by Gavin Turk (b.1967) comprises rubbings taken from a couple of two-pence coins, each bearing a different portrait of the Queen. The effigy on the left was introduced in 1985; designed by sculptor Raphael Maklouf (b.1937), it was the third definitive coin portrait of the Queen, who appears flatteringly youthful for a 59 year old. The rubbing on the right features the Queen's fourth portrait from 1998, designed by sculptor Ian Rank-Broadley (b.1952) and displaying a visibly older, more jowly Queen. The technique used by Turk is also known as frottage, which involves using a pencil or crayon to rub over an object placed underneath a sheet of paper to form images with a shadowy, almost spectral quality. Falling somewhere between drawing, printmaking and sculpture, it was a favourite practice of the Surrealists, whose methodologies have greatly inspired the British artist. Here, Turk uses everyday coins to offer a haunting meditation on the passing of time, the ageing process, and the impermanence of life.

     Gavin Turk

Before and After (detail), 2002
Pencil on paper
190 × 240 cm (74 3/4 × 94 1/2 in.)

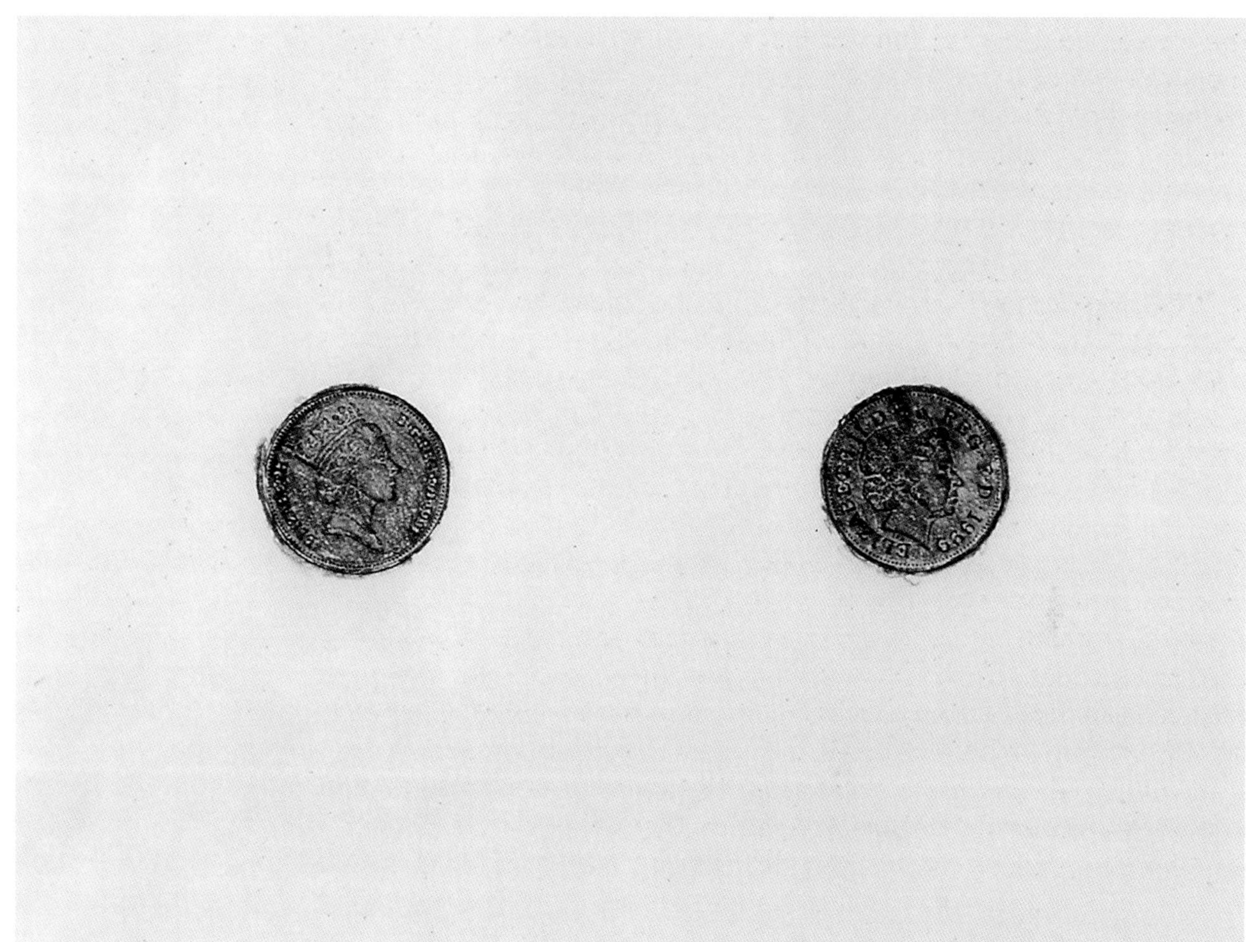

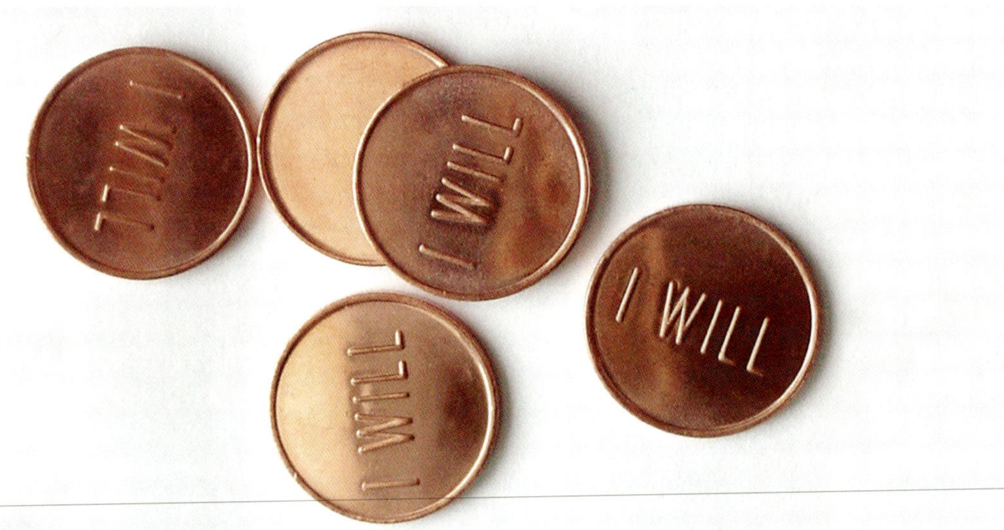

These small copper coins, each embossed with the phrase 'I Will,' require the bearer to make a pledge to another person, from something as small as fetching a neighbour's groceries to more significant promises, such as providing someone with a place to stay. Instead of legal tender being exchanged in return for an object or service, they are given as a symbol of a promise made and a means by which the beneficiary can hold the donor to account while in turn becoming a pledge maker themselves and paying it forward. Envisaged by the Malaysian-born Canadian artist Germaine Koh (b. 1967) as an alternative form of currency, *Pledge* is based on serial reciprocity, where individuals reciprocate for what they have received by providing something to a third party, regardless of whether a return is made to the original giver. The project is intended to operate outside of the traditional monetary system as a way of recognising and encouraging non-commercial transactions and interpersonal exchanges. The coins were freely distributed by hand, from one person to another, at exhibitions, events, and even the artist's wedding. Unlike conventional commerce, there is no economic reward associated with *Pledge*. Rather, by giving concrete form to promised intentions, the project sought to foster social bonds of trust, resulting in individually-defined social, psychological and cultural benefits. As with other works by Koh that incorporate everyday objects and actions, these coins rely on the active participation of people, though with no formal documentation, *Pledge* is only experienced by those with direct involvement.

Pledge, 2002
5,000 copper tokens for distribution
Each: 2.5 cm (1 in.) diam.

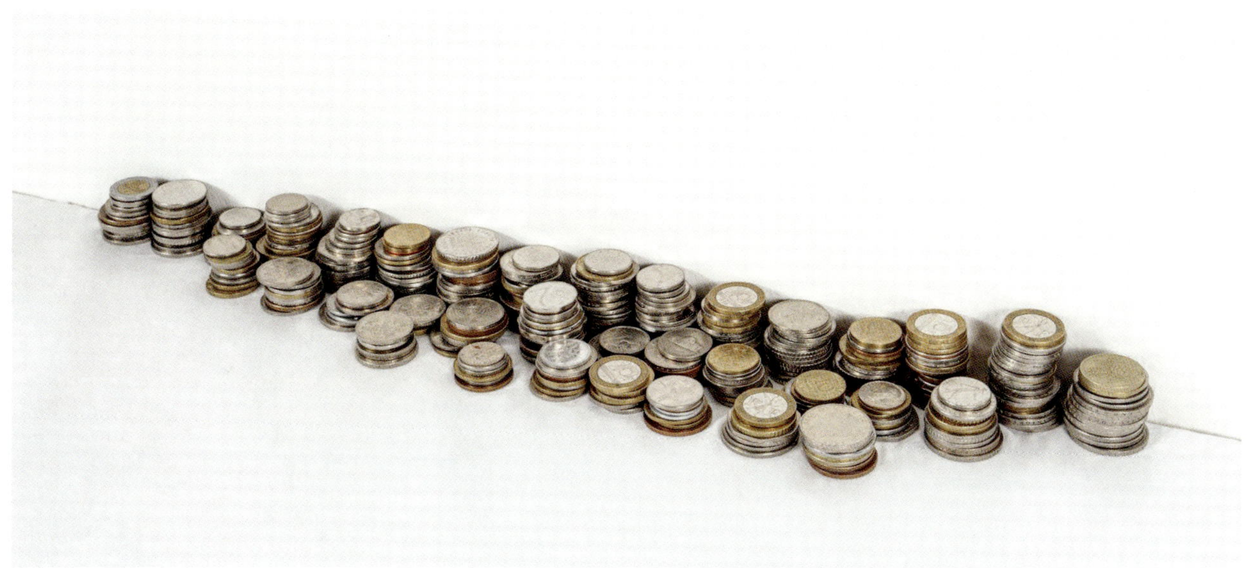

South Korean-born artist Koo Jeong A (b. 1967) describes her place of work as 'everywhere'. This transnational approach to life is echoed by this untitled installation, which on first glance resembles a collection of different currencies of the type typically accumulated by the seasoned global traveller. In piles of various heights, lined up on the floor against a wall, the arrangement of coins is both deliberate (each is neatly organised from large to small) and casual (the stacking of loose change being a common, even unwitting, action for many people). As with many of Jeong A's installations incorporating everyday materials, the very familiarity of its constituent parts might render it overlooked as an artwork, were it not for its presence within an art gallery. This context invites closer inspection, upon which emerges a wide range of currencies and denominations, along with the many differences of shape, colour, face designs and reeded or grooved edge patterns. Created the year after 12 European Union countries adopted the euro as their official currency, the presence here of the recently defunct French franc and German deutsche mark speaks poignantly to the impermanence of life's apparent certainties. Furthermore, their rapid demise from legal tender to obsolescence reinforces the fundamental materiality of coinage that underlies any ascribed, yet mutable, face value.

Untitled, 2003
Coins
Dimensions variable
Installation view, Yvon
Lambert Gallery, New York

Coins have been used in conjuring tricks for millennia and, on first sight, this video by Cuban artist Diana Fonseca (b.1978) might appear to be a demonstration of this form of close-up magic. The camera focuses our attention on the artist's open palms, each of which contain two pesos. Suddenly, the coins disappear, leaving behind only dirty, halo-like stains. Whether we are witnessing a cunning sleight of hand or basic video manipulation becomes less important than the fact that money is shown to be elusive — a reflection of the economic context in which this work was made. In 2005, Cubans were experiencing economic hardship; the US had imposed a trade embargo against the country, many products were scarce or prohibitively expensive, salaries were low and people struggled to cover their basic needs. For a large number of citizens, their pesos seemed to literally evaporate before their eyes. Fonseca's video is one of several works entitled *Pasatiempo* ('pastime'), in which she revisits small gestures that connect to simple childhood activities; in this case, the playful rubbing of coins until their grimy patina unwittingly transfers to the hands. For adults, such dirt arouses discomfort, an indicator of the unsanitary nature of physical money. Yet in reminding viewers of how naive and inattentive children can be, Fonseca wistfully points to a state of being where economic concerns similarly vanish into thin air.

Pasatiempo (dinero) ('*Pastime (money)*'), 2003
Video
52 mins, 8 secs

     Diana Fonseca

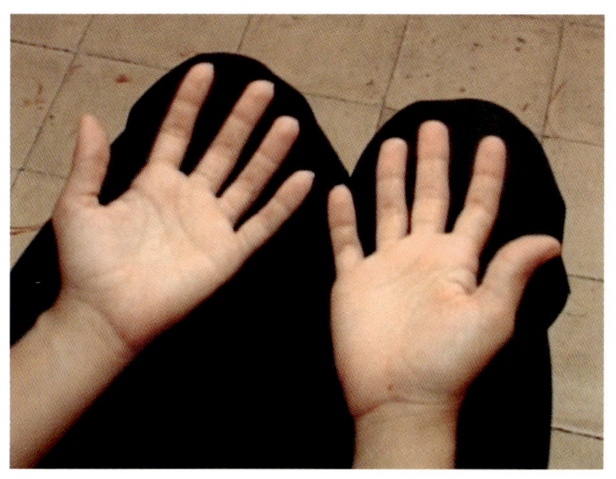
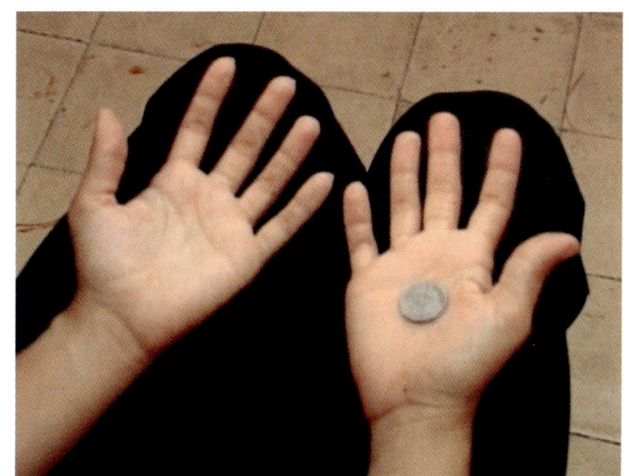
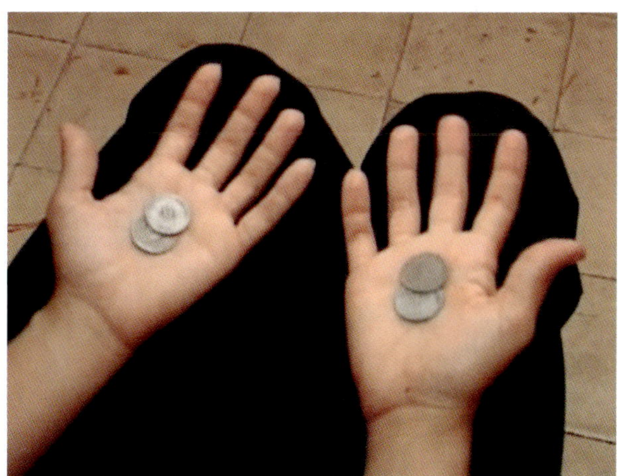
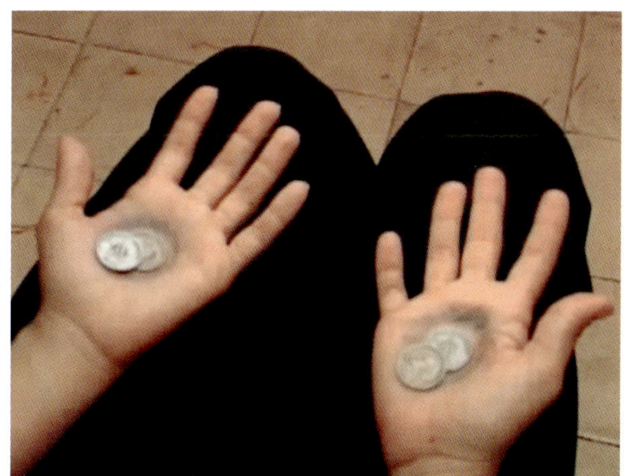
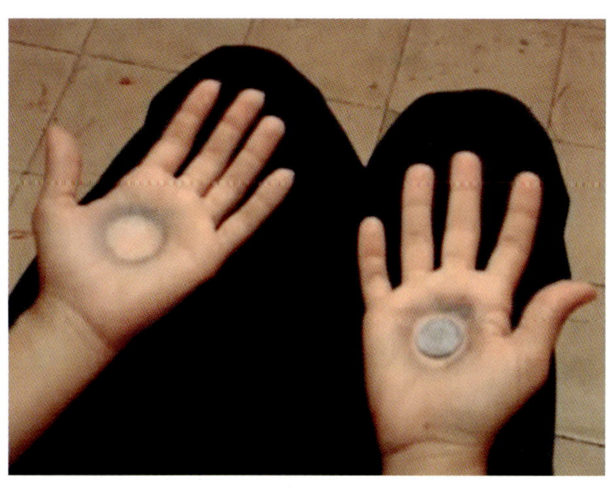
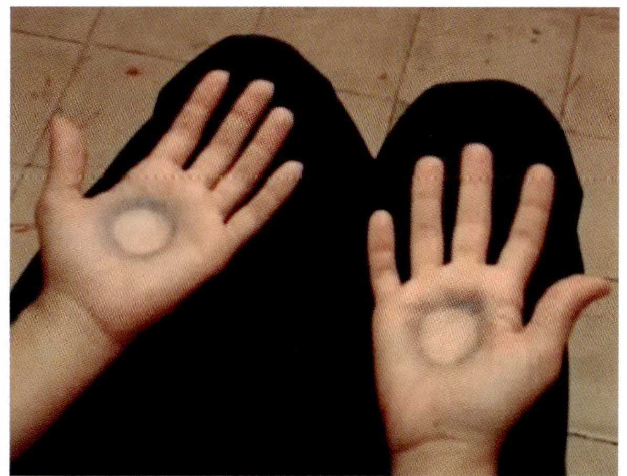

A rotund, cartoonish gentleman wearing a suit and top hat struggles to hold a collection of oversized one cent coins, which slip from his grasp as he gives, or perhaps takes, one from a tiny figure of a girl so small that she balances on another penny. The diminutive sculpture is one of more than 130 whimsical bronzes portraying people and animals in various situations by American artist Tom Otterness (b. 1952) that are permanently installed throughout the New York City subway station at 14th Street and 8th Avenue. Titled *Life Underground* and taking nearly a decade to complete, the project drew inspiration from the creation of the subway system in the late nineteenth century. Otterness studied period photographs of its construction, which informed several character designs, such as the many blue collar workers that scuttle around the station carrying oversize tools. Otterness also became fascinated in the work of the influential political cartoonist Thomas Nast (1840–1902), remembered for his depictions of New York's famously corrupt politician William M. 'Boss' Tweed (1823–78) with a bag of cash for a head. The motif is used liberally by Otterness to lampoon the greed of rich businessmen, including one sculpture in which an alligator emerging from a manhole cover devours a man with a moneybag head. Elsewhere, figures clutch bags of coins and busily sweep up piles of pennies. The contrast between overflowing riches and apparent poverty is a running theme which, in the context a public transport system where panhandlers in dire financial needs often look to the kindness of strangers, has a poignancy that contrasts starkly with the otherwise playful spirit of the installation.

Life Underground (detail), 2004
Bronze
This sculpture: *c.* 25.4 × 25.4 × 50.8 cm
(*c.* 10 × 10 × 20 in.)
Metropolitan Transit Authority and Arts for Transit,
14th Street and 8th Avenue, New York

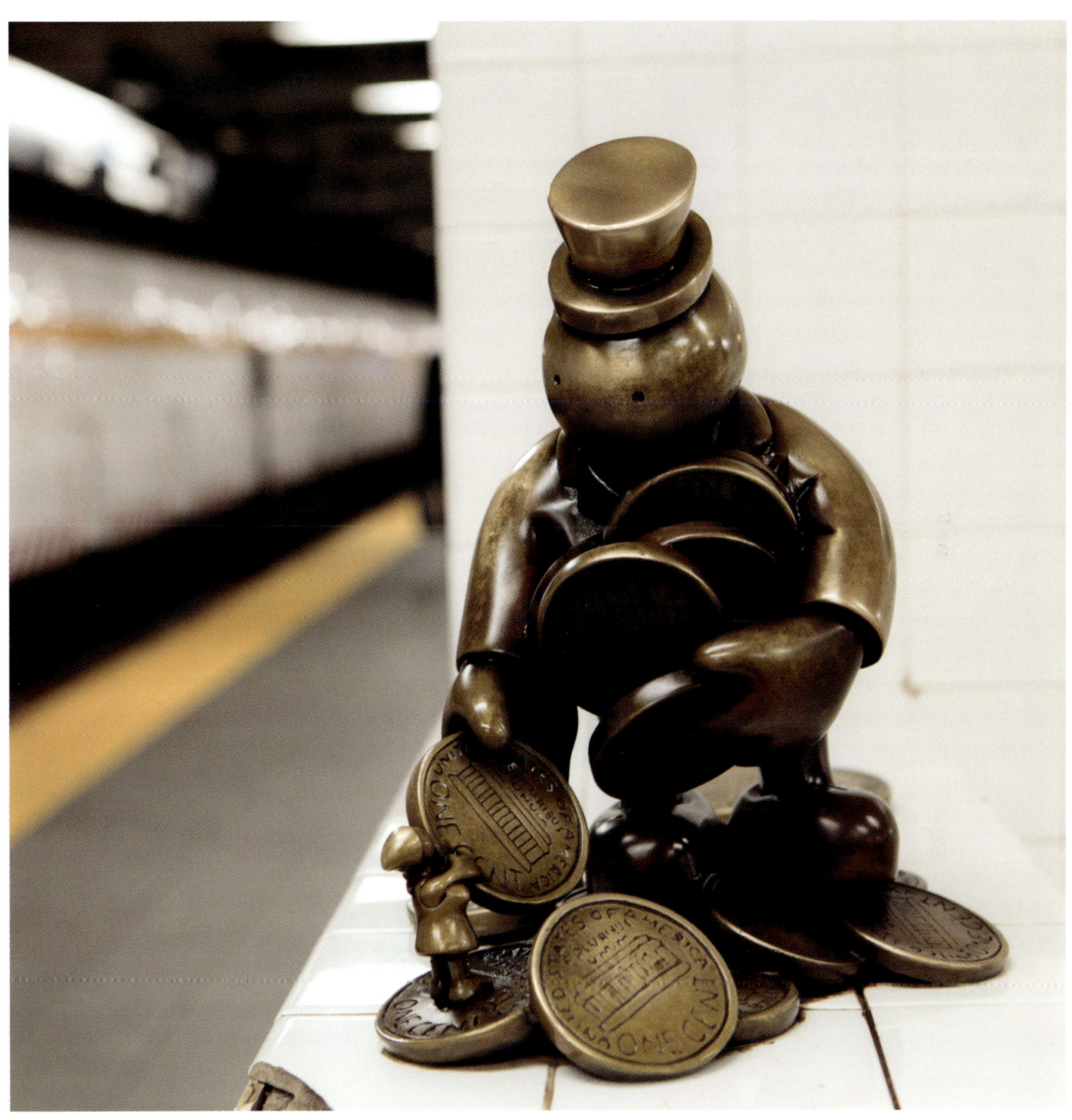

These concentric, mandala-like compositions are made from gradated black-and-white prints of various international banknotes. Reproduced at actual size, some display strong, dark tones, while others are desaturated and faint. The currencies were chosen for the personalities depicted on them, each of whom is connected to a war, conflict or, as in the titles of these works, a 'face-off'. For American artists Jud Fine (b.1944) and Barbara McCarren (b.1958), who have worked collaboratively as McCarren/Fine since 1996, these international conflicts inevitably have money and power as their motivating force. Among the figures included in *Face Off I* are Israeli prime minister David Ben-Gurion (50 Sheqalim), who led Israel during the 1948 Arab-Israeli war; Peruvian revolutionary leader Tupac Amaru II (50 soles de oro), who fought the Spanish conquistadors; and Vietnamese revolutionary Ho Chi Minh (10,000 dong), whose forces fought and defeated the Japanese, French and Americans. *Face Off II* repeats many of the notes but introduces others such as Iraqi president Saddam Hussein (25 dinars), who waged war on Iran and Kuwait and was later removed from power by a US-led coalition. Both works are bookended by US dollars and British pounds: nations that have instigated and fought countless wars. The use of black and white is deliberate and references the oversimplification of debates surrounding conflict and the binary terms political leaders use to justify violent aggressions, framing their rhetoric in terms of 'good versus bad, freedom versus subjugation' and so on. For McCarren/Fine, physical currency is as symbolic as a national flag, a kind of self-portrait reflecting how a state wishes to be seen in the world at a given time, but which is slowly fading as cashless payment methods become more prevalent.

          McCarren/Fine

Face Off I and *Face Off II*, 2004–5
LaserJet print on paper
238.8 cm (94 in.) diam.
Installation view, 'McCarren/Fine: Currency',
Ronald Feldman Fine Arts, New York, 2005

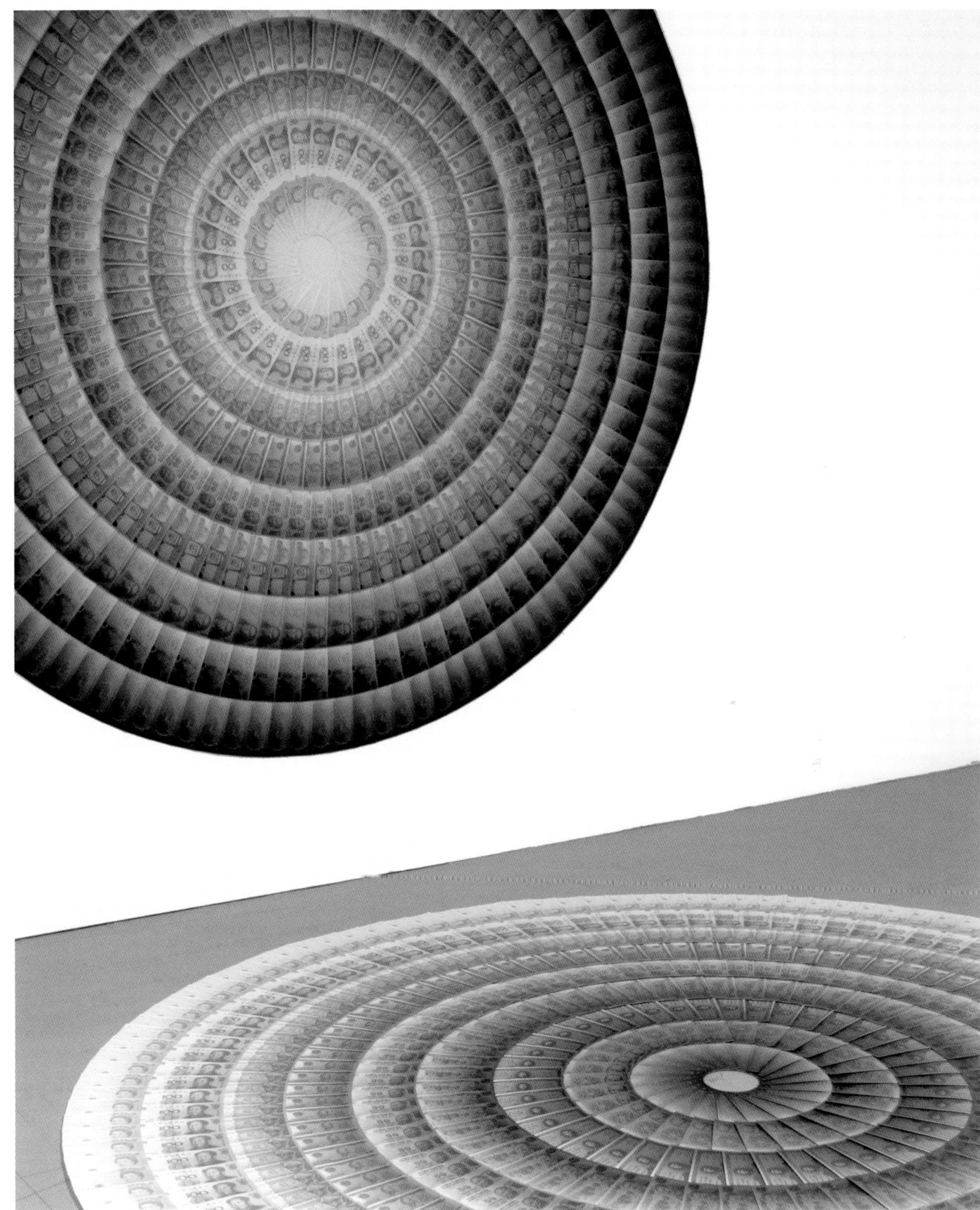

Characterised by colourful language as well as colourful brushwork this painting by American artist Mel Bochner (b. 1940) illustrates the rich vocabulary used to describe money in the English language and in particular in his native country. Each slang word or informal term has been painted in a different hue, their breadth reflecting the pervasive influence of currency in US society. Some are fairly recent additions to the lexicon: 'chump change' emerged from Black slang in the 1960s, while 'moolah', a word with unknown origins, has been used to refer to money since the 1930s. Others are older: 'greenbacks' dates to the American Civil War (1861–65) when the US government introduced green ink to the reverse side of paper banknotes to combat counterfeiters. 'Shekels', in use since the 1820s, derives from the unit of currency used in ancient Israel. The list even includes a biblical reference to money as the 'root of all evil', from St Paul's first letter to Timothy warning against the love of riches. Bochner is an avid collector of synonyms, filling his notebooks with interesting words from which he makes his paintings. A pioneer of Conceptual art in the mid-1960s, he initially forsook the fabrication of traditional art objects in favour of using working drawings, notes, diagrams and lists to explore language, meaning and systems. From the early 1980s, he focused on paintings with words and phrases, creating images inspired by the conventions of everyday language. As here, each of his painted lists ends with a comma, suggesting that many more words could be added.

 Mel Bochner

Money, 2005
Oil and acrylic on canvas
152.4 × 203.2 cm (60 × 80 in.)

MONEY, MOOLA, MAZUMA, GELT, SCRATCH, SKINS, SIMOLEONS, SHEKELS, DINERO, WAMPUM, GREENBACKS, CHINK, BREAD, DOUGH, PEANUTS, CABBAGE, GRAVY, CHEDDAR, CHICKEN FEED, DO-RE-MI, JACK, LOOT, BOODLE, PENNY ANTE, SMALL POTATOES, DEAD PRESIDENTS, CHUMP CHANGE, BIG BUCKS, ALMIGHTY DOLLAR, ROOT OF ALL EVIL, HARD CASH, LIQUID ASSETS, FILTHY LUCRE, $, $, $,

Comprising a transparent Plexiglass cube atop a low wooden plinth, this work by American artist Jonathan Horowitz (b. 1966) calls to mind minimalist sculpture of the 1960s. Yet the presence of a narrow slit on its top side invites gallery visitors to insert coins and bills as a donation to the United Nations High Commissioner for Refugees (UNHCR), the logo of which is emblazoned across its front. *Contribution Cube (UNHCR)* confronts the viewer with a choice to financially support the plight of refugees or to pass on by (if indeed they recognise this sculpture as a functioning donations box at all). The volume of the hollow cube is contrasted by the small amount of money it contains, raising questions about the extent to which gallery visitors trust that the money collected by Horowitz will make its way to the stated cause, and the issue of public confidence in charitable giving more broadly. Horowitz has been making his 'Contribution Cubes' since 2004, usually dedicating them to causes that he personally endorses. In 2016, as the US presidential election loomed, he presented an installation of the sculptures at The Brant Foundation in Greenwich, Connecticut, that fund-raised for conservative organisations such as the National Rifle Association and Catholic Charities USA, as well as liberal groups including Black Lives Matter and Greenpeace. As the six-month exhibition progressed against a backdrop of political division and polarisation, the boxes accumulated varying levels of cash, reflecting the differing concerns and priorities of those who visited.

    Jonathan Horowitz

Contribution Cube (UNHCR), 2004/2016
Plexiglass vitrine, vinyl sticker and wood base
79 × 76 × 76 cm (31⅛ × 29⅞ × 29⅞ in.)

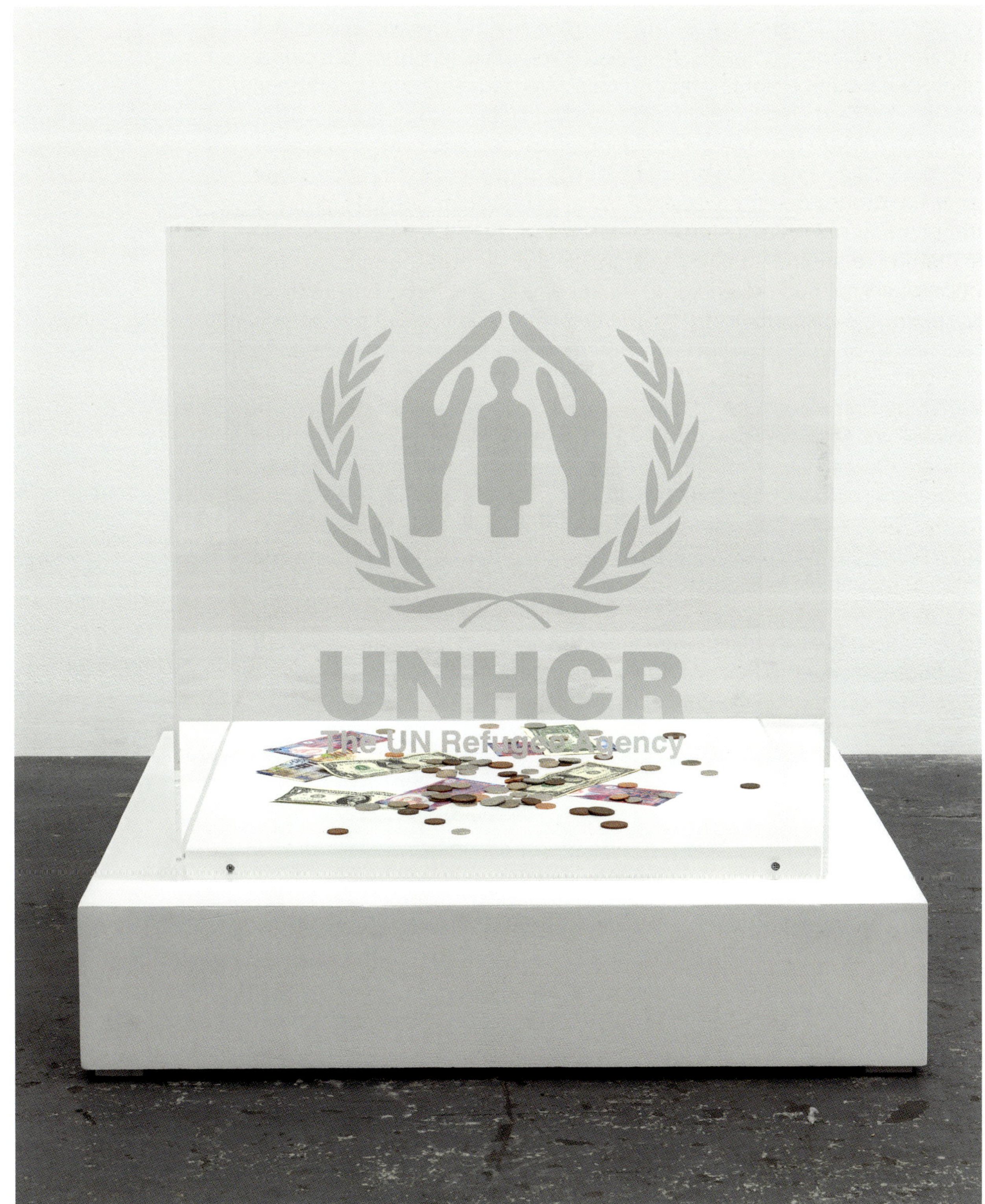

UNHCR
The UN Refugee Agency

A spectacular array of paper money from around the world features in these two digital collages, revealing a remarkable variety of colours and designs. Assembled geometrically, the banknotes that comprise *56.066.792.000* show world leaders and significant cultural figures, while *556.142.346.000* features the many important buildings and landscapes celebrated on notes. Each title indicates the aggregate numerical value of all the money depicted, regardless of actual worth, speaking to the nature of currency fluctuations, which means that relative worth of one in relation to another is constantly moving, or — more poetically — the impossibility of putting a number on happiness and fortune. The works were made with banknotes that Hong Hao (b.1965) bought at flea markets in Beijing or collected while traveling abroad. They relate to the Chinese artist's series 'My Things' (2001–13), a twelve-year project meditating on the nature of consumerism and the social construction of value, for which he used a flatbed scanner to record every single object that passed through his hands, and then organised them by colour and type to create elaborate digital collages. Hong emerged in the late 1980s as part of a new generation of Chinese avant-garde artists whose rise was enabled in part by the Chinese Communist Party's 'Opening and Reform' policies under Deng Xiaoping, which saw the country's socialist economy adapt to free-market principles and embed itself in the global capitalist system. Here, the scanned banknotes evoke the flow of international money into China's economy, now the world's second largest after the United States.

    Hong Hao

56.066.792.000 and
556.142.346.000, 2005
Chromogenic prints
Each: 165 × 270 cm (65 × 106¼ in.)

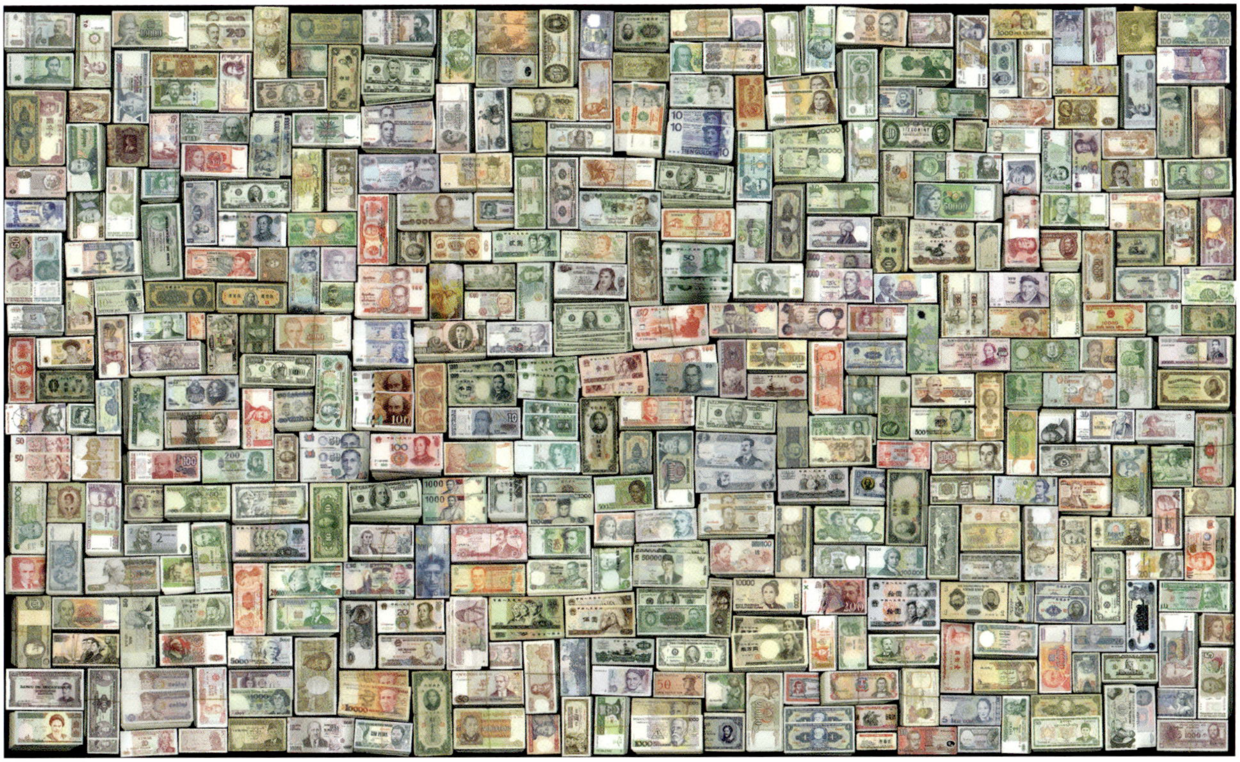

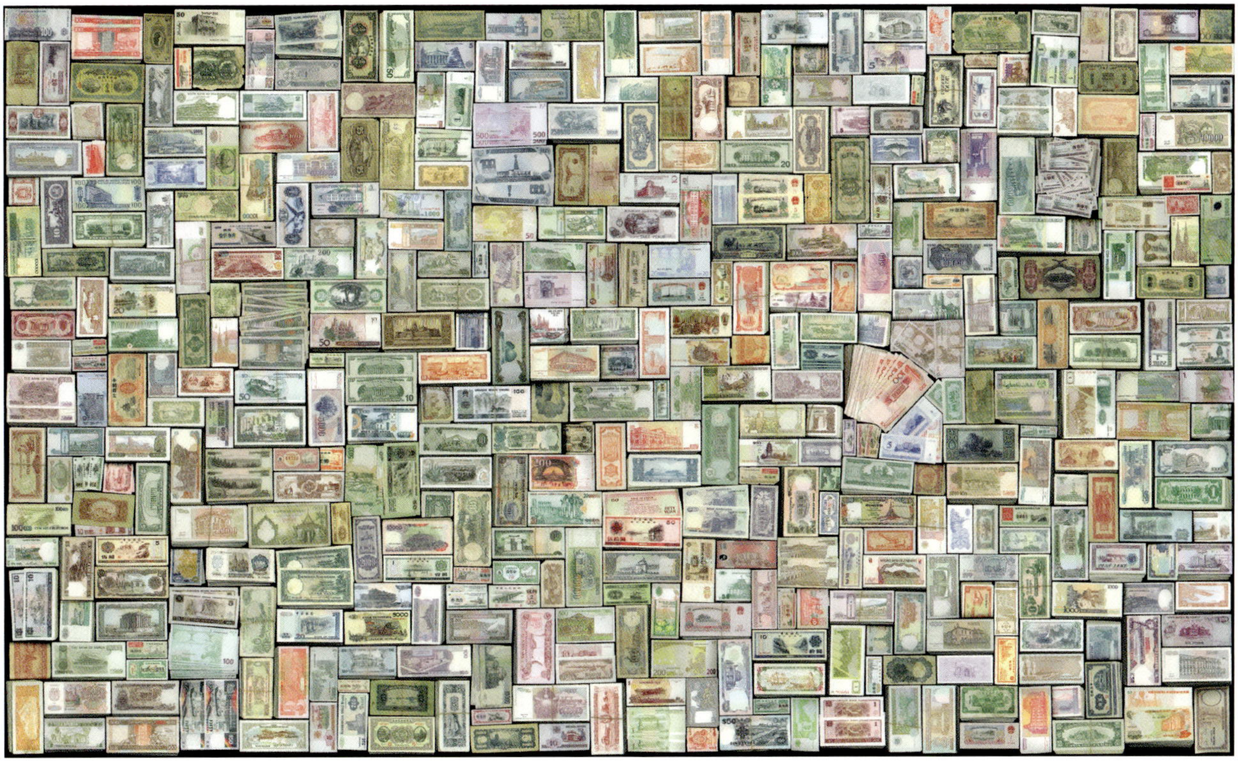

As with any tool, money can be used for good or to cause harm. It has the potential to make the world a better place but can corrupt those who place too much weight on its accumulation. Rarely though has physical money been considered a dangerous object, especially something as innocuous as the US quarter. However, in this work by the provocative conceptual artist Claire Fontaine (founded in Paris in 2004 by Fulvia Carnevale and James Thornhill, an Italian-British artist duo who declare themselves her 'assistants') small change is transformed into a weapon by outfitting the coins with retractable boxcutter blades. In the minds of many, and especially US citizens, concealed boxcutter knives will be associated with the horrific terrorist attacks of 9/11 in 2001, when smuggled blades of this kind were used in the hijacking of four commercial airliners. By metaphorically drawing a connection between capital and notions of terror, *Change* invites a consideration of the hidden violence embedded within the capitalist system, from colonial injustices of the past to the contemporary arms trade and government funding of overseas wars. While the work's title refers to coins of a low denomination, it also evokes ideas relating to social change, or even violent revolution. If the status quo of capitalism is to be challenged, the work suggests, then meagre resources will need to grow into significant weapons of change.

Change, 2006
Twelve 25-cent coins, steel box-cutter blades, solder and rivets
Dimensions variable
Private collection

     Claire Fontaine

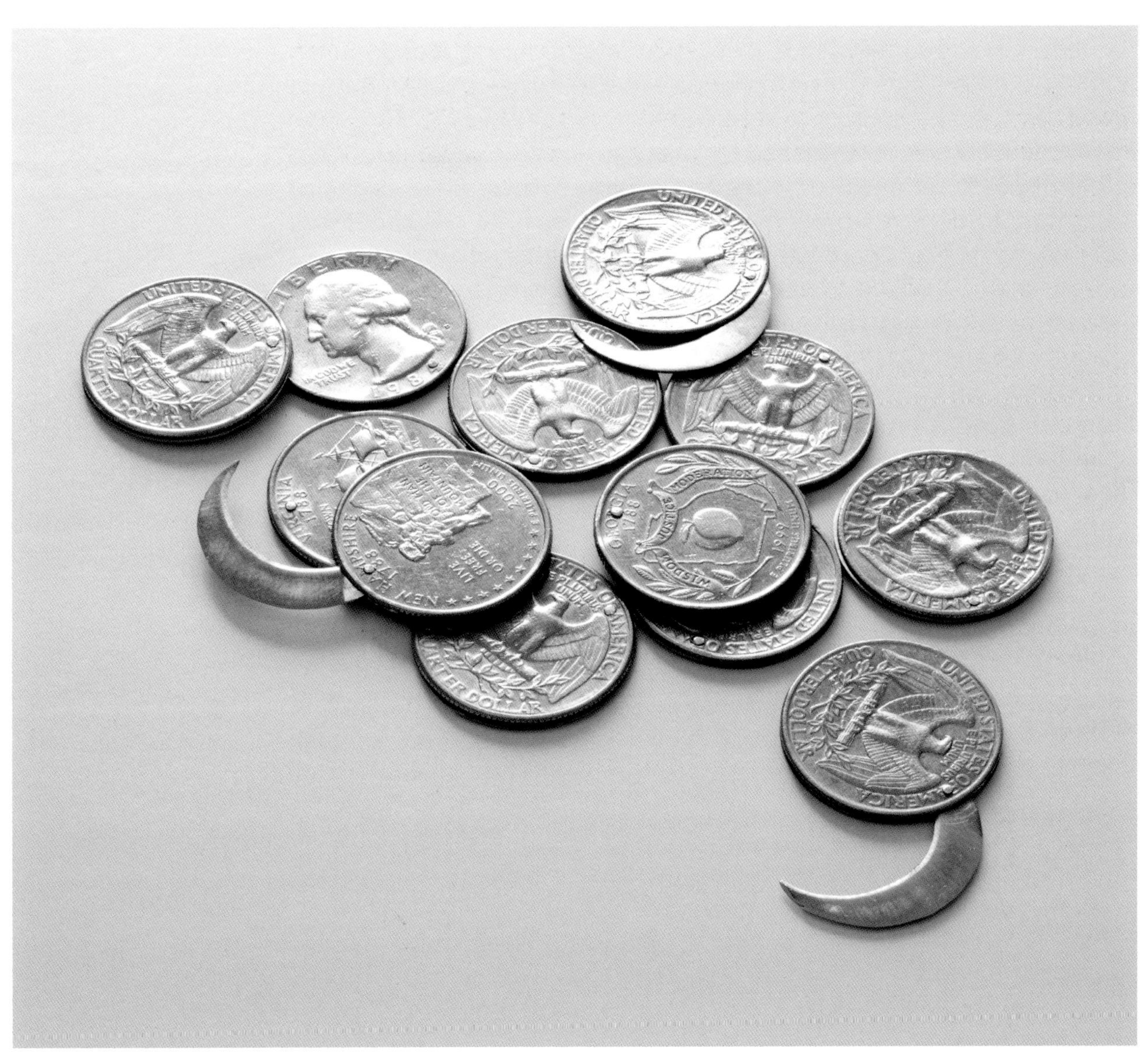

For American artist C. K. Wilde (b. 1972), money is a tool of oppression and exploitation that the powerful use to foment inequality through low wages, job insecurity and debt. By cutting up banknotes for his currency collages, he symbolically disrupts these power structures, undermining the power that money holds and critiquing the capitalist system that prioritises profit over people (the irony of commodifying his dissent through participation in the art market is, however, not lost on Wilde). *E Pluribus Unum* is a self-portrait made entirely from the faces of national heroes, political leaders, presidents and monarchs that have been cut from a vast array of international currencies. While some are more recognisable due to their global fame — Queen Elizabeth II, Mahatma Gandhi, Mao Zedong — others are less well known, such as Rafael Yglesias Castro, the 16th president of Costa Rica, and Kenneth Kaunda, the first president of Zambia. Many of these portraits have been rendered unrecognisable where Wilde has combined one or more faces, mixing up mouths, noses and eyes to create surreal visages. The work's Latin title, meaning 'out of many, one', is the traditional motto of the United States; printed on every dollar bill, it refers to how a single nation emerged from the original thirteen colonies. By using multiple currencies to create an image of his own face, Wilde hints at the influence that competing economies can have on individual lifestyles in an increasingly globalised and interconnected world.

E Pluribus Unum ('*Out of Many, One*'), 2006
Currency collage
22 × 16 × 1 cm (8⅝ × 6¼ × ⅜ in.)
Private collection

     C. K. Wilde

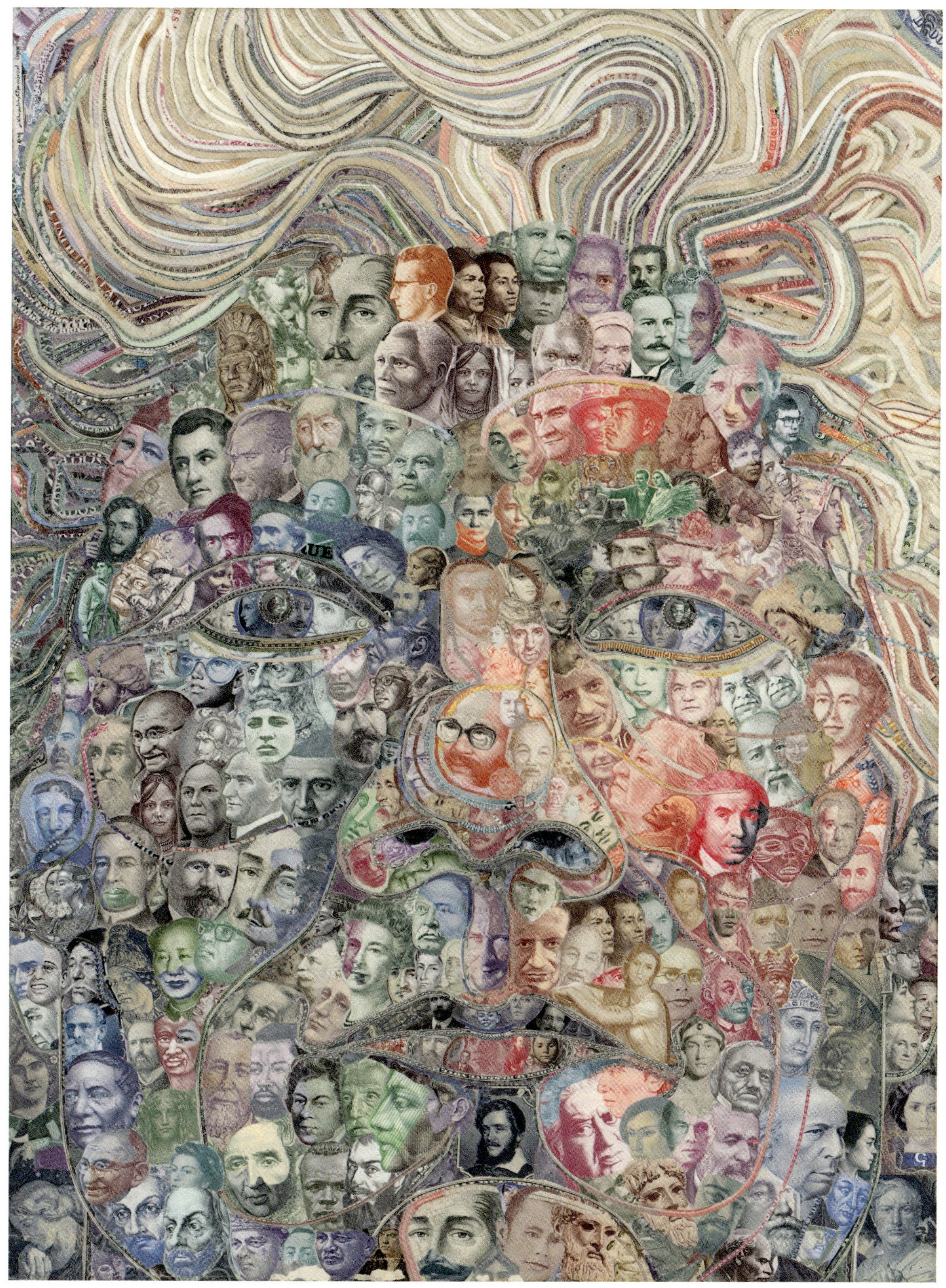

For many children, their first encounter with physical currency is in the form of 'pocket money' provided by a parent or guardian. In this piece, Roman Ondak (b. 1966) has strewn nine euro coins — the pocket money of his nine-year-old son — over a small, laminated chipboard shelf made from a table. At the time, the Slovak conceptual artist was living between Bratislava and Berlin, and the work, which was produced in an edition of ten over several weeks, used the currency of whichever country he and his family happened to be in, whether euros or koruna (the currency of Slovakia between 1993 and 2009, after which it adopted the European single currency). The allowance was willingly sacrificed by Ondak's son, who had numerous conversations with his father on the topics of value in art, whether he would miss the money, and how he might potentially benefit from 'investing' in the creation of an artwork about parent-child attitudes toward finances. Detached from the monetary system, these coins, once valuable to the artist's son, have gained new value as part of the art market's system of economic exchange. Many of Ondak's projects are born from his observations of post-communist society in his home country. Regularly using 'found objects' in his works, he disrupts the boundaries between art and everyday life, the private and the public, the personal and the institutional.

　　Roman Ondak

Pocket Money of My Son, 2007
Coins, shelf made from a section of a table
2.5 × 30 × 21.5 cm (1 × 11¾ × 8½ in.)
Edition 2 of 10
Collection Thomas Waldschmidt, Cologne

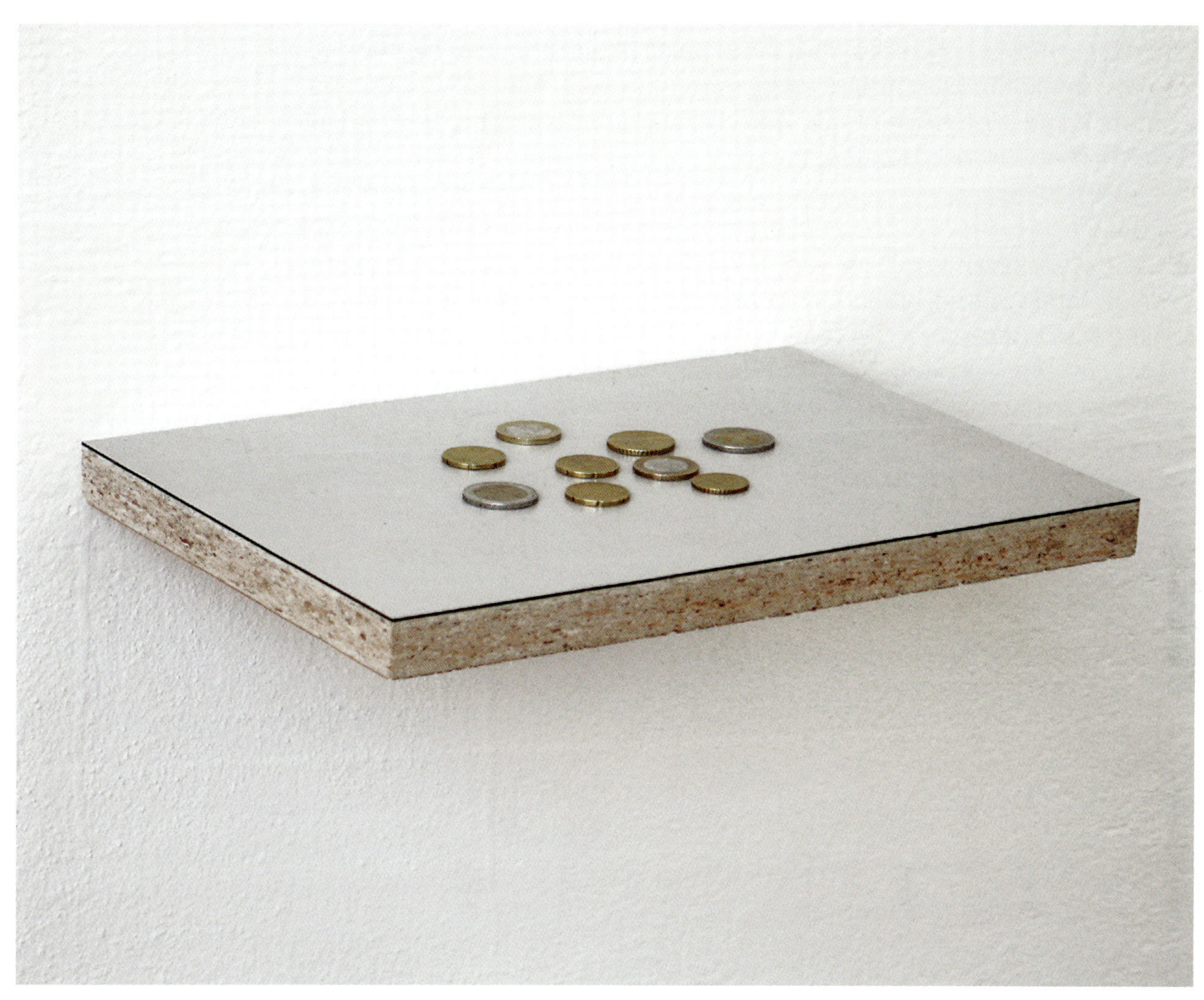

 Kim Rugg

Whereas many countries around the world have introduced harder-wearing polymer banknotes into circulation, the US still uses bills composed of linen and cotton. The average life expectancy of a one dollar note is around six and a half years bfore it needs to be replaced due to wear and tear. At first glance, the crumpled and creased dollar bills in these three images by Canadian artist Kim Rugg (b.1963) appear to be reaching the end of their life; having ostensibly passed through hundreds of thousands of hands, they have become worn and damaged. But on closer inspection it becomes clear that this money has undergone a very different type of transformation. With razor-sharp scalpels and a steady hand, the artist has arduously dissected each banknote into tiny pieces and reassembled them so that they appear distorted and fragmented. In addition to money, Rugg has performed similar procedures on newspapers, postage stamps, comic books, cereal boxes and maps. In each work, matter is neither created or destroyed but profoundly altered. The treatment of these dollar bills, for instance, amplifies the character of the source material, drawing our attention to every stain and blemish. Existing somewhere between collage and sculpture, each one remains recognisable though it is doubtful whether any could pass as legal tender. What is certain, however, is that, as an artwork, each is now worth far more than its apparent face value.

Folded Dollar, *Bent Dollar* and *Creased Dollar*, 2007
US dollar bills
Each: 15.6 × 6.6 cm (6⅛ × 2⅝ in.)

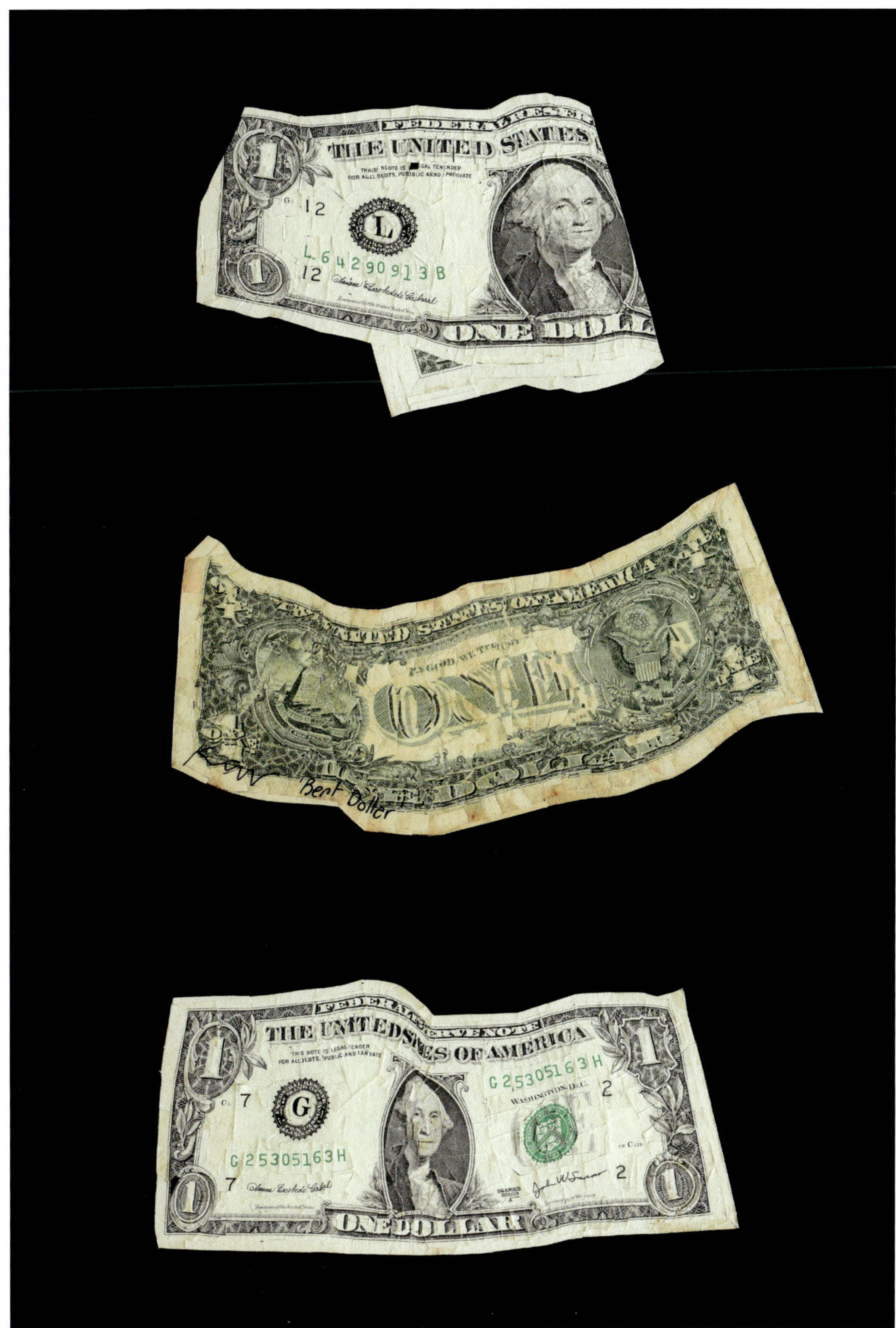

Each country in this map of Europe is represented by a banknote of its respective currency prior to the introduction of the euro on 1 January 2002, which was initially adopted by twelve of the European Union (EU) member states. British artist Justine Smith (b. 1971) has been incorporating money into her collages since 1998, fascinated by the power and authority invested into what are essentially pieces of paper. Her first currency map, *Money Map of the World* (2005), featured every country that used paper money, including the smallest island state and protectorate. This led to others, including *Money Map of Africa* (2007) and *The British Isles* (2010), all of which are laboriously cut from real banknotes. The French francs, Greek drachmas, Spanish pesetas, Finnish markkas and other obsolete currencies seen here feature imagery reflecting each country's values and sense of national identity. Smith sees money as a form of propaganda that reveals how states wish to portray themselves internally and to the rest of the world. Though titled *Old Europe*, this map captures a continent in flux (a pre-1989 version, for example, would look very different). Money is always changing too, regularly replaced with new designs and sometimes new currencies. Many European nations now use the euro and Smith's related map, *Euro Europe* (2007) depicts the same region but using EU banknotes to represent the thirteen countries that had by then joined the single currency. By 1 January 2023, with Croatia's adoption of the euro, that number had grown to twenty.

	Justine Smith

Old Europe, 2007
International banknotes on paper
89.6 × 83.1 cm (35 ¼ × 32 ¾ in.)

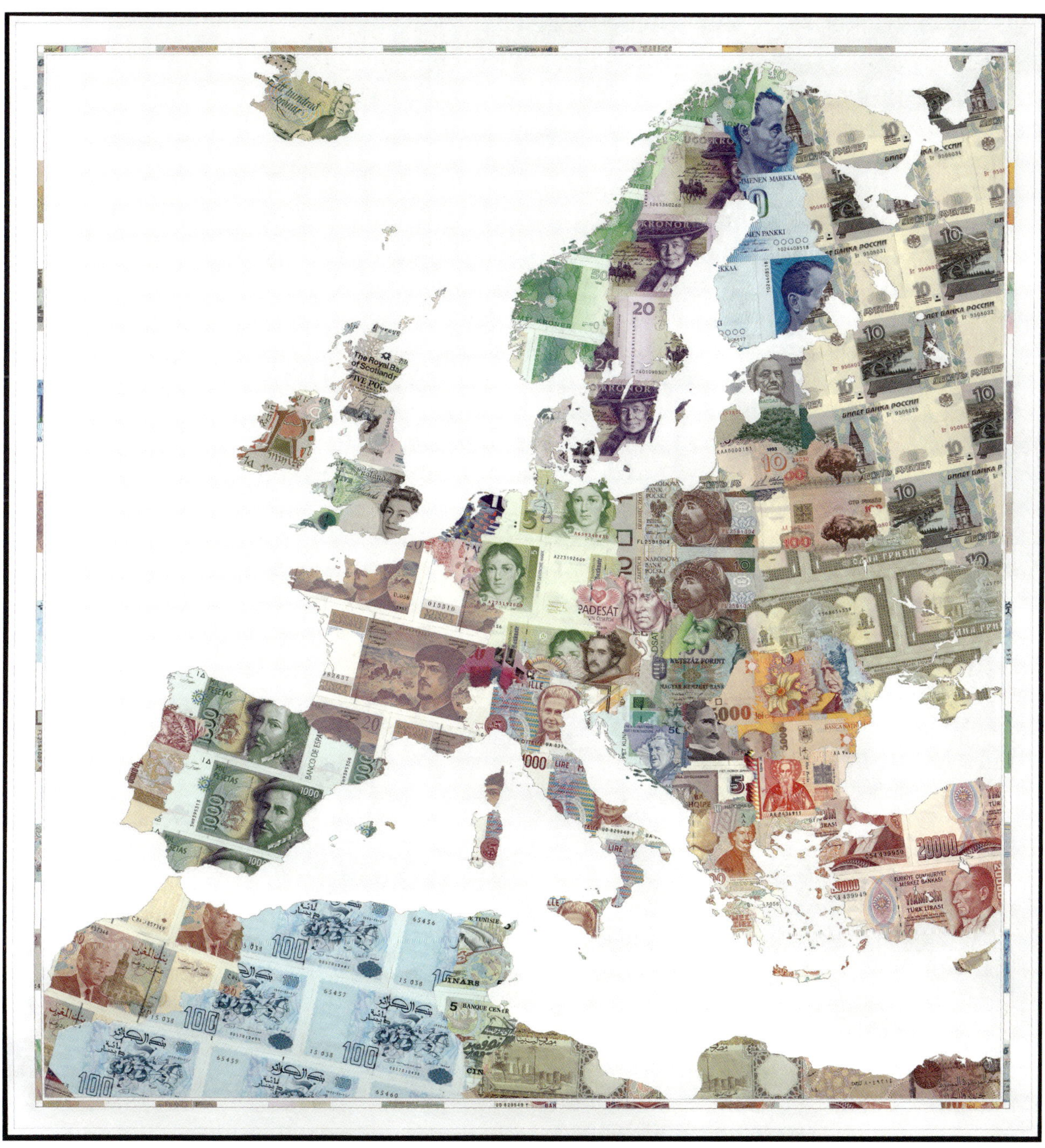

A noose fashioned from US dollar bills hangs ominously from a gallery ceiling, one of six in this installation by French-Peruvian artist Jota Castro (b.1965). When he created this unsettling work, the enormity of the 2007–8 global financial crisis — the worst since the Great Depression — was still unfolding. As banks collapsed, homes foreclosed and lifetime investments dissolved, the US's faltering economy was causing much pain and suffering. This work is at once an allusion to the suicide of financial institutions prompted by poor business decisions, and of individuals pushed to despair by economic turmoil. Its title, *Mortgage*, specifically points to the subprime mortgage crisis in the United States, a rapid decline in the stability of the country's housing market and associated financial bonds — both previously thought to be low risk, high yield investments — which disrupted the stock market and triggered a global economic downturn. The word 'mortgage' derives from the Old French words 'mort' (meaning death) and 'gage' (meaning pledge), referring to the agreement made by a borrower to repay their debt over a specified amount of time until their obligation was either fulfilled or the security (in the form of property) taken back through foreclosure — in either event, the deal would be considered 'dead'. Castro's provocative sculptures, installations and performances draw on his background in political science and diplomacy and law, offering cutting commentaries on complex social and political issues.

Mortgage (detail), 2009
American one dollar notes and rope
Dimensions variable

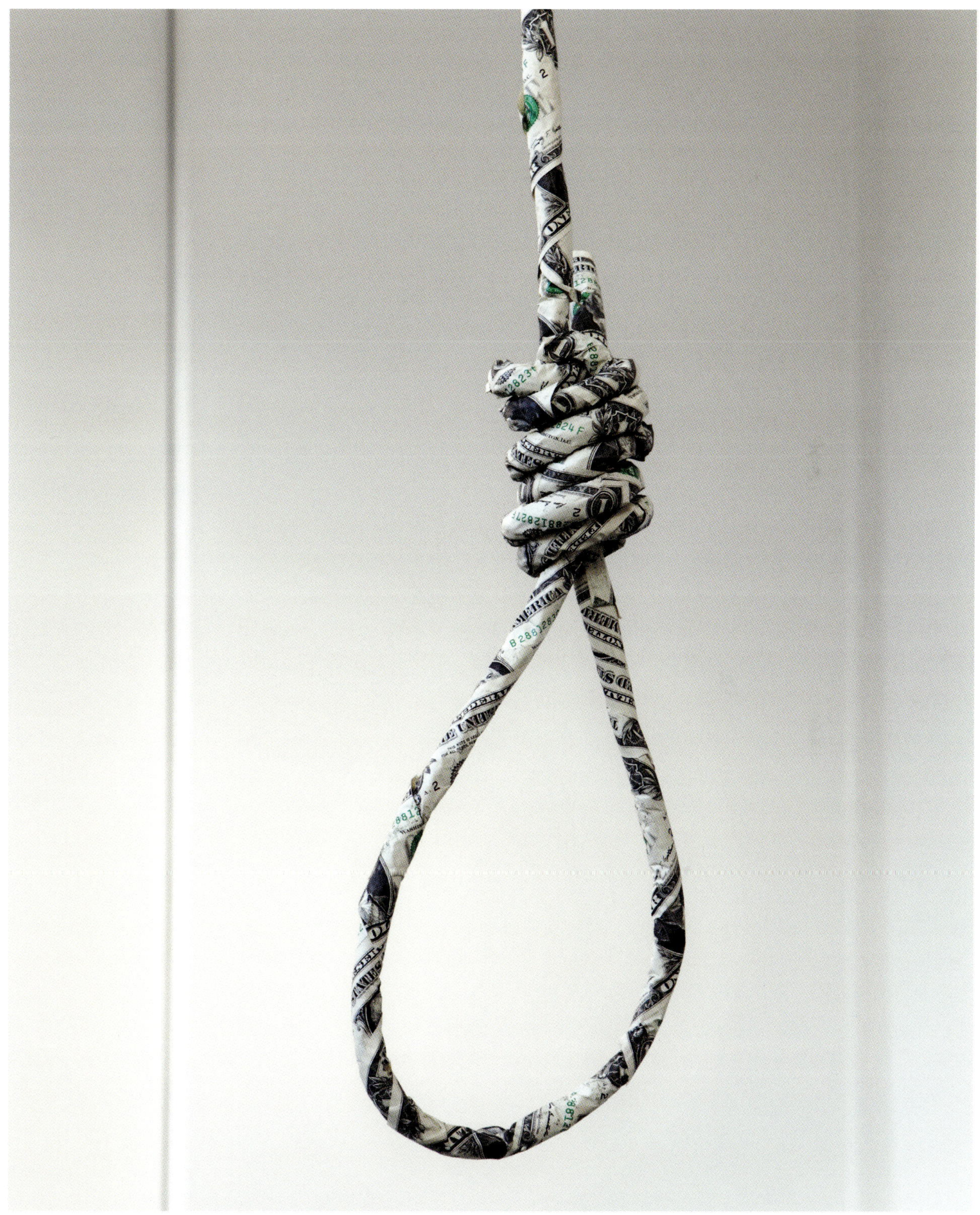

Paper money is rarely the object of contemplation. It is typically stored out of sight, in wallets and purses, being removed only when it is needed to complete a transaction, which is usually over in seconds before the note vanishes from sight again. This installation by the Italian artist Gianni Motti (b.1958) encourages viewers to consider money from a different perspective. The work consists of 20,000 crisp US one-dollar bills (a sum representing the project's budget), suspended on wires from a gallery ceiling. Like festive bunting, the bills flutter in the slightest breeze, creating a shimmering cloud of green and black above viewers' heads. His use of the US dollar reflects its dominance on the world stage and the widely-held acknowledgement of it as the most important reserve currency. Motti conceived of *Moneybox* in the aftermath of the global financial crisis of 2007–8, which had its roots in the US housing market, a reflection on the dire state of the world economy and specifically the implications for the cultural sector. Moreover, the work is a celebration of physical cash over electronic forms of money. Motti uses debit and credit cards as little as possible, noting in a video interview for Perrotin gallery that he enjoys 'pockets full of notes' and is concerned about the growing trend for cashless payments. By placing the dollar bills high up and out of reach, he points to the waning presence of paper currency in daily life.

     Gianni Motti

Moneybox, 2009
Dollar bills, paper clips and steel wire
Dimensions variable
Installation view, Migrosmuseum für
Gegenwartskunst Zürich

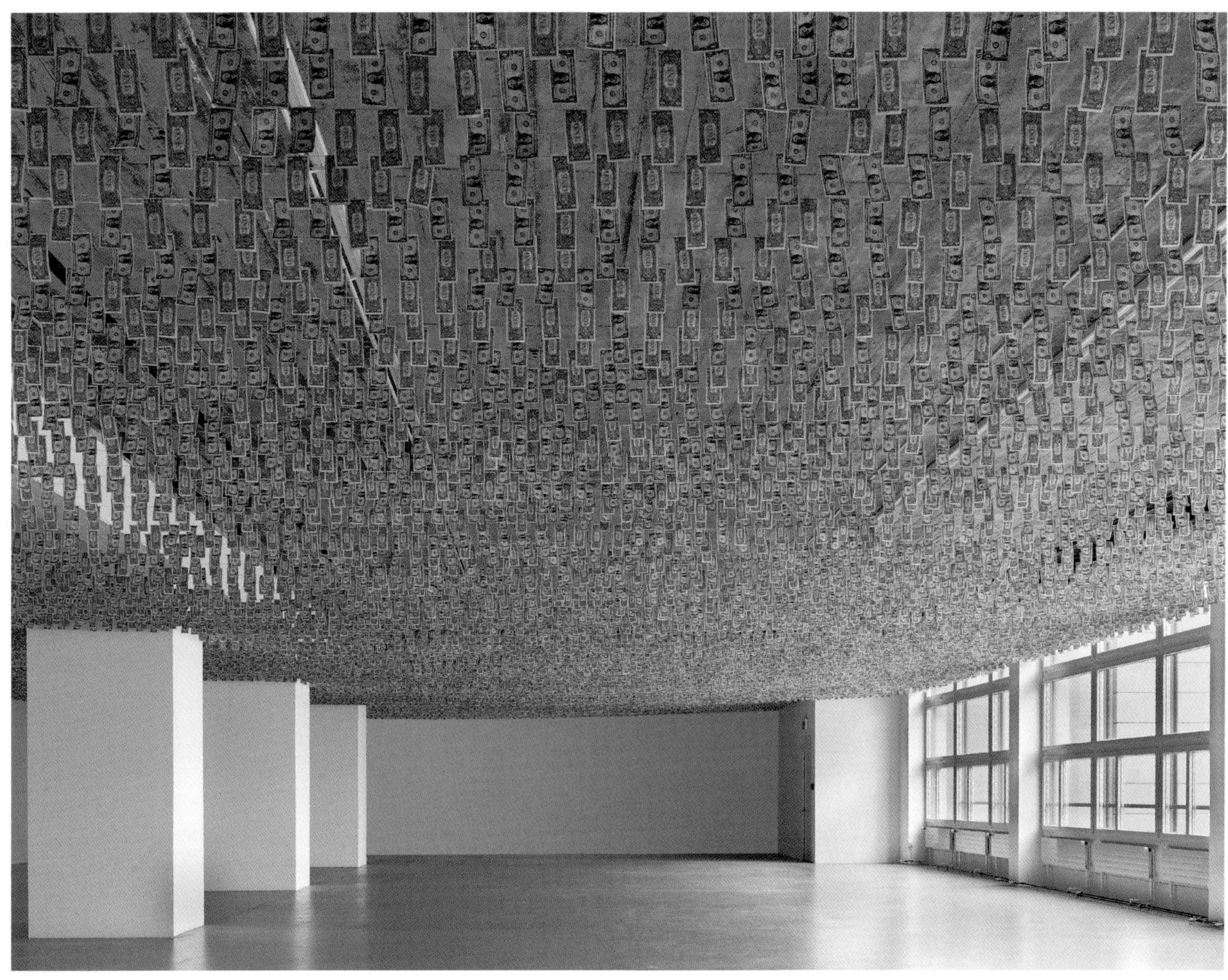

In 2010, when Louis Vuitton's flagship store opened in New Bond Street, London, its shop floor was occupied by a towering kinetic sculpture by Michael Landy (b.1963) made from rusty saws, scissors, levers, stuffed toys and an ominous looking wood chipper. When activated, the eccentric contraption whirred into life, mechanically creating an abstract drawing hand-signed by the artist for any customer willing to have their credit card shredded. The irony of obliterating payment cards in a luxury retail space is typical of the British artist's subversive practice, which is preoccupied with systems of value. This *Credit Card Destroying Machine* was also shown at the Frieze Art Fair in 2011, where it despatched around 400 cards. The apparatus is modelled after another destructive machine by Jean Tinguely (1925–91) titled *Homage to New York* (1960). This enormous device of over 6 metres (19 feet), composed of bicycle wheels, motors, metal drums, a go-cart, a bathtub and other found objects, spectacularly imploded before an audience at the city's Museum of Modern Art, as an anarchic expression of the Swiss artist's disillusionment with the overabundance of modern life. In Landy's case, destruction is offered as a form of liberation from the excesses of consumerism, a theme he memorably explored in *Breakdown* (2001), which saw him publicly destroy all his material possessions over a two-week period — leaving him with nothing intact but the boilersuit he was wearing.

     Michael Landy

Credit Card Destroying Machine, 2010
Mixed media
600 × 300 × 300 cm (236¼ × 118⅛ × 118⅛ in.)
Installation view, 'Dream On', Hellenic Parliament +
NEON, Athens, 8 June – 17 November 2022

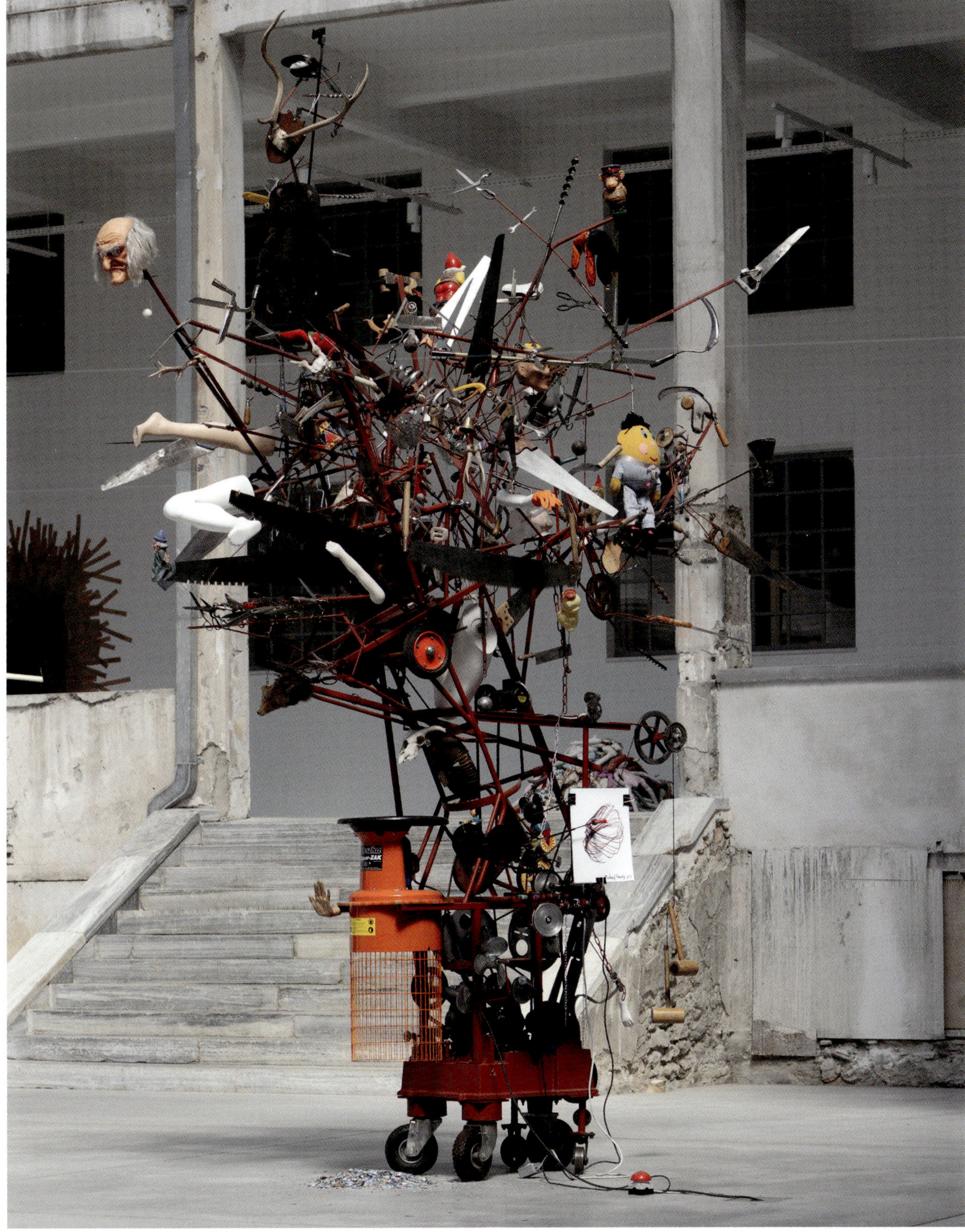

As winner of the 2010 Hugo Boss Prize (a biennial award recognising significant achievement in contemporary art), German artist Hans-Peter Feldmann (1941–2023) was presented with an honorarium of $100,000 and an invitation to exhibit at the Guggenheim Museum in New York. Deciding to create an installation, he cashed his cheque and pinned the entire amount to the museum's walls in a neat grid of overlapping one-dollar US bills. It took Feldmann and his assistants nearly two weeks to arrange the 100,000 uniquely numbered banknotes, each of which displayed signs of its life in circulation with creases, wrinkles, tears and scribbled jottings. Having potentially passed through thousands, if not millions of hands, the pungent smell of the used money permeated the space. By eschewing crisp new notes, the artist drew attention to the subtle differences between the bills, which were at once mass produced and unique. Once the exhibition closed, Feldmann removed the banknotes and slowly put them back into circulation via day-to-day spending and cash deposits in his bank account. As a result, the work could never be precisely recreated, nor could it be bought or sold. This typified the attitude of Feldmann, who regularly resisted the art world's commercial structures by issuing unsigned, unlimited editions and even giving up art making altogether for nearly a decade in the 1980s. Raising questions about notions of value in art, The Hugo Boss Prize continued Feldmann's long term interest in seriality and repetition, which characterise his signature archives of photographs and found objects.

     Hans-Peter Feldmann

The Hugo Boss Prize, 2010
100,000 US one-dollar bills and pins
Installation view, Solomon R. Guggenheim Museum,
New York, 20 May – 2 November 2011

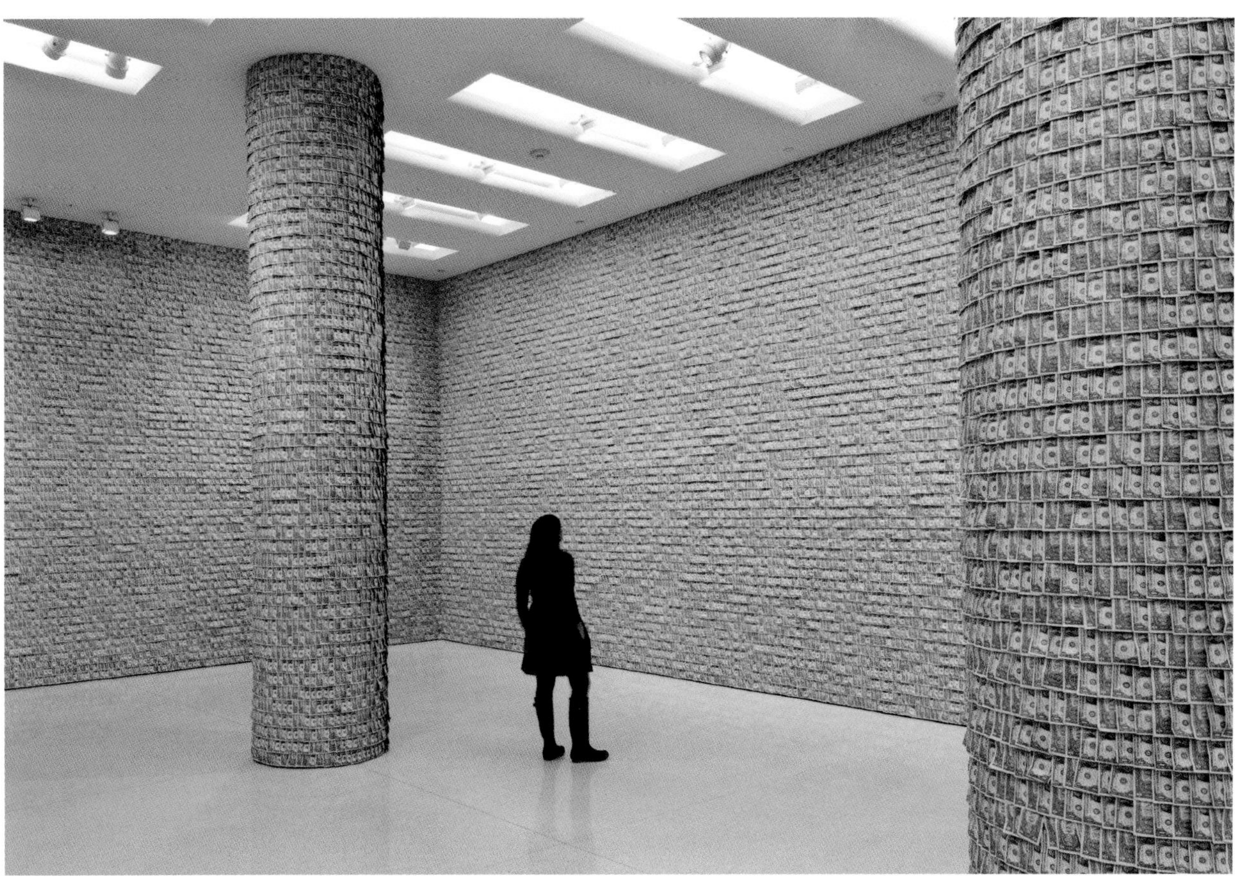

Glueing a coin to the floor is a classic practical joke but, in this instance, victims of the prank are encouraged to consider the prospective value of currency in the eurozone, the union of twenty member states of the European Union (EU) that have adopted the euro. As anyone bending down and attempting to pick up what seems to be a one-euro coin will see, it purports to have been minted in the year 2036 and its face value is in fact 25 euros, an amount reflecting an average inflation rate of 13.8 percent per year over twenty-six years. Made by Ryan Gander (b. 1976) six years before the UK voted to leave the European Union (EU) in 2016 (although like other EU members including Denmark and Sweden, Britain had never joined the single currency), the coin also features an expanded map of Europe and an updated number of stars (twenty-four instead of twelve). It is one of several similar works that the British artist has made using different world currencies, including UK pounds and US dollars, which appear to have impossibly fallen from the future. By ruminating on what different economic landscapes could look like in years to come, these works use humour to strikingly visualise the fact that the value of money, far from staying static, is subject to continual fluctuation and its purchasing power diminishes as inflation rises over time.

          Ryan Gander

We never had a lot of € around here, 2010
Single metal coin
2.5 cm (1 in.) diam.

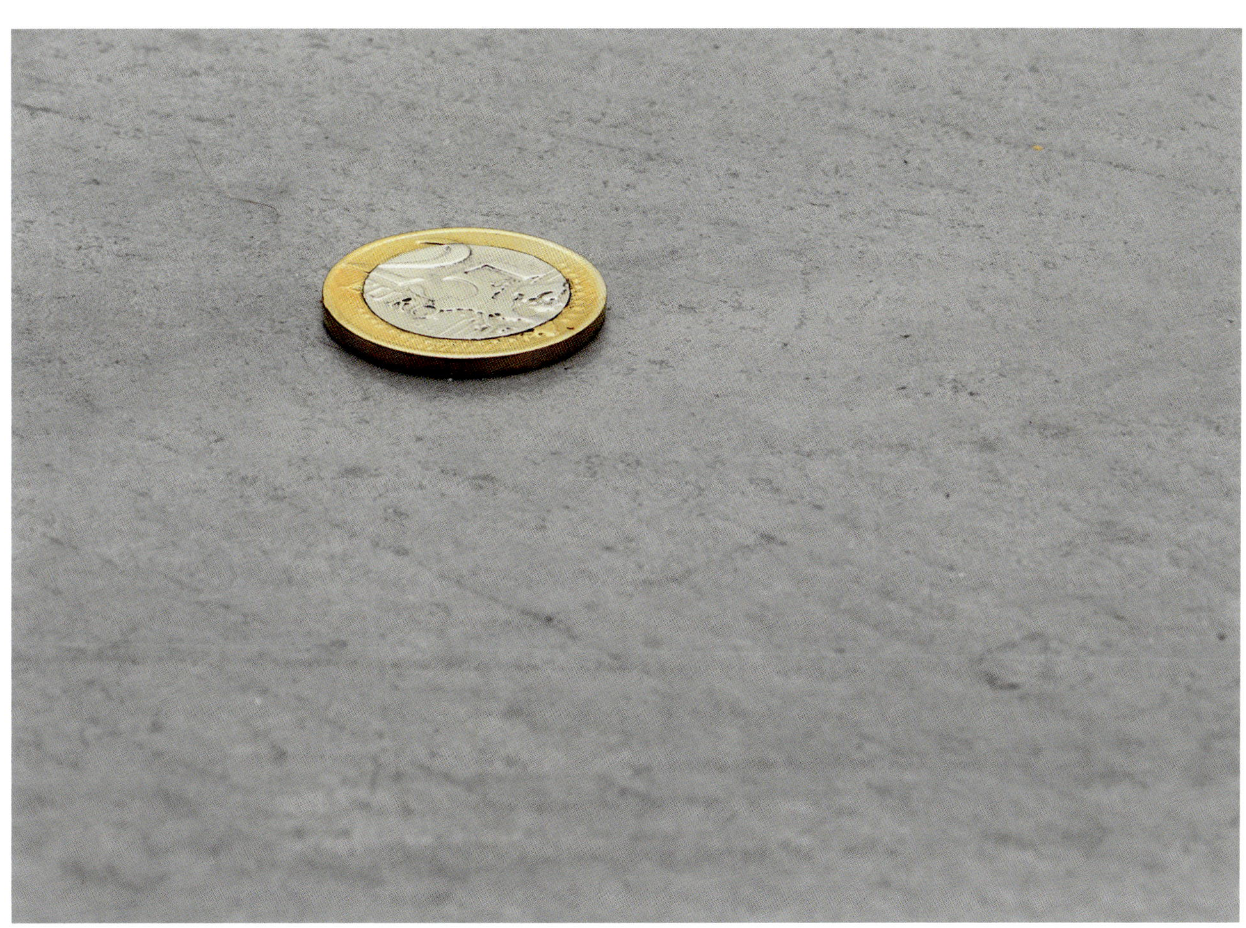

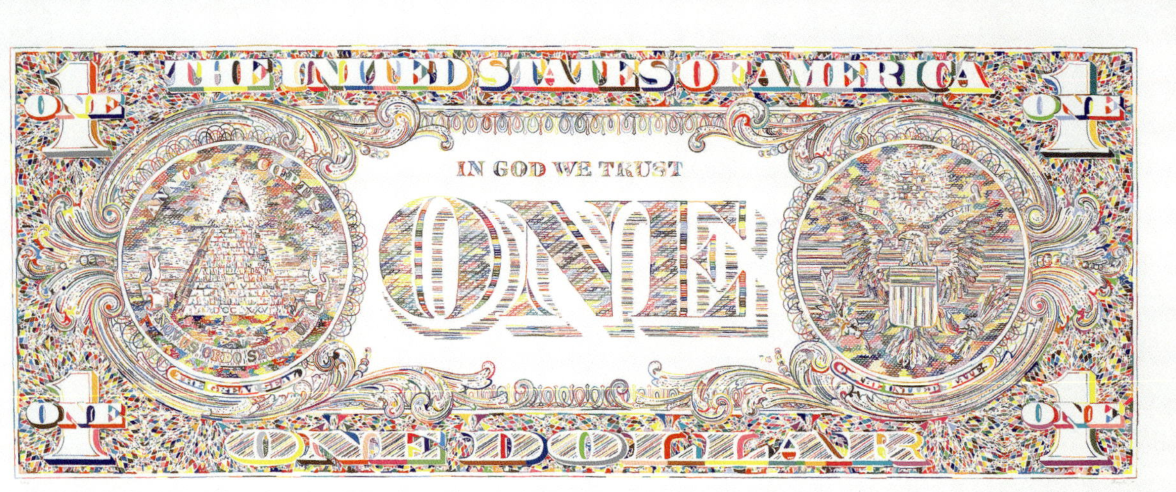

Featuring George Washington on one side and a wealth of arcane late-eighteenth-century symbolism on the other, the US one-dollar bill has carried the same design since 1957. Its distinctive green and black colourway dates back to the American Civil War, introduced as a way of thwarting counterfeiters; because photographic technology of the day was unable to reproduce colour, the federal government decided that the back of the bills should be printed in green, a colour associated with stability and which earned them the nickname 'greenbacks.' In this oversized, variegated rendering, American artist Tom Friedman (b.1965) has diligently reproduced every element of the reverse of the note, but made its familiar design seem strange and exotic through a multi-coloured palette. The vibrant and technically demanding screenprint is based on an original coloured-pencil drawing and is typical of his whimsical yet exacting work, in which simple everyday materials and imagery are manipulated and distorted, to confound and surprise. This is the second time that Friedman has made work based on US currency. *Untitled (Dollar Bill)* (2000) is a gigantic representation of the front of the banknote but composed in a way that appears blurred and distorted, as if seen through patterned glass. In fact, the bill is a collage of squares cut from 36 real dollar notes and arranged so that, though abstracted, the image remains discernible — a testament to the iconic bill's enduring design.

 Tom Friedman

Untitled (Dollar Bill, Back), 2011
Colour silkscreen on
Lanaquarelle paper
63.5 × 142.2 cm
(25 × 56 in.)
Edition of 100 + 10 APs

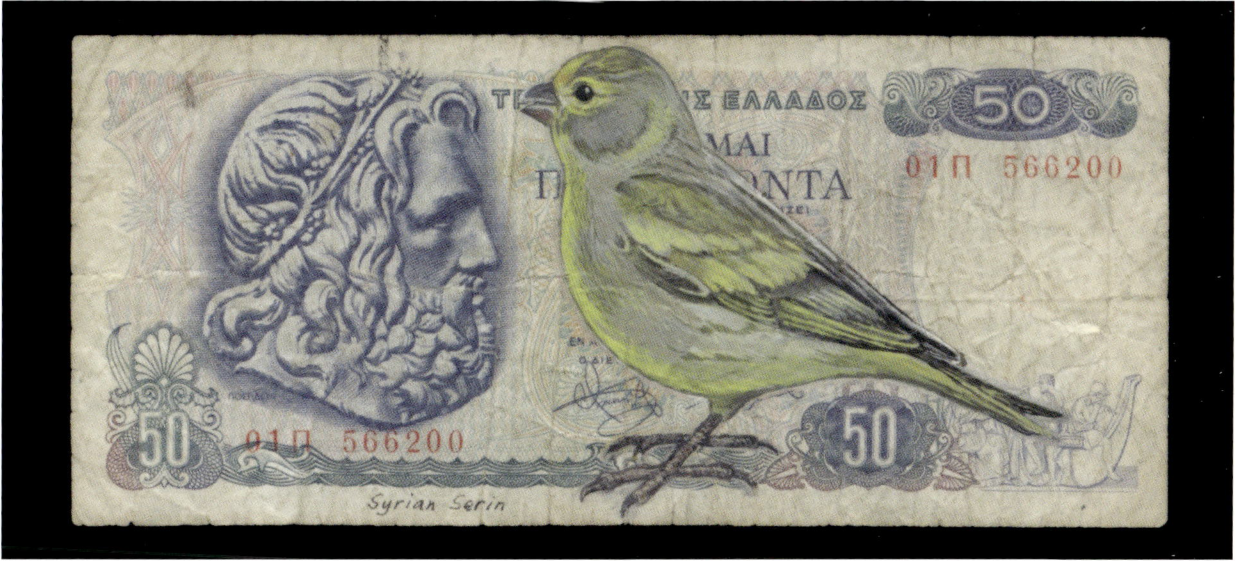

Born in Germany, Hanna von Goeler (b. 1964) moved to the United States as an infant and her dual identity and bilingual upbringing have influenced her outlook and artistic practice. Fascinated by the prevailing influence of money in society, she began painting on banknotes in the early 1990s, the gesture a reclaiming of agency; each work demonstrating how money can be controlled for the common good as opposed to a negative influence defining people's lives. In this piece, a Syrian serin occupies a Greek 50-drachmai note, a denomination that was in circulation from 1978 to 1986. The small bird of the finch family, which is more elongated than the European serin, faces Poseidon, the god of the sea in Classical mythology. The work is from von Goeler's series 'Migration', which feature intricate paintings of migratory birds and was prompted by the Syrian Refugee Crisis that began in 2011 after escalating anti-government protests plunged the country into a civil war. Greece, which abandoned the drachma when it joined the euro on 1 January 2002, is one of a number of countries that struggled to cope with the influx of refugees escaping the Syrian conflict, especially in the context of its own debt crisis. While this piece alludes to the economic and cultural upheaval in relation to Syrian refugees, the wider series points to the role that global economic forces play in human migration — whether forced or voluntary — and also climate change, which is having an adverse impact on the habitats of both people and migratory birds.

Syrian Serin, 2011, from the series 'Migration'
Watercolour and gouache on Greek 50-drachmai banknote
14.4 × 6.4 cm
(5 ⅝ × 2 ½ in.)

The tantalising prospect of printing reams of your own money is proffered by this artwork: a plate for printing US 100,000-dollar bills. Created by Argentinian-born Thai artist Rirkrit Tiravanija (b. 1961), the design derives from a 1934 Great Depression-era gold certificate that was never put into circulation. Instead, the $100,000 banknotes featuring the 28th president Woodrow Wilson, were used to transfer funds between Federal Reserve banks. Possession of them aside from federal government was, and remains, illegal. Of course, printing any unauthorised money is outlawed, and with good reason — an economy depends on a carefully managed supply of physical money to avoid hyperinflation. Too much cash can lead to a currency's rapid devaluing. The work's subtitle, *Print Mo' Money*, recalls the 1997 hit song 'Mo Money Mo Problems' by American rapper The Notorious B.I.G., which discusses the troubles that come with affluence and was released posthumously just months after the musician's murder at the age of 24, in relation to hip hop rivalries that inflamed as the success and riches of those involved grew. Tiravanija's ironic gesture also explores notions of art's value given that — as an artist of international acclaim — inking up and taking printed impressions from the piece could potentially decrease its market value. In a further twist, a decade later, Tiravanija produced a variation as an NFT, *untitled 2021 (rich bastards beware)*, which hinted at the artist's scepticism of the then overheated market for NFTs, while at the same time exploiting it.

Untitled 2011 (Print Mo' Money), 2011
Copper etching plate
13.3 × 15.5 cm (5¼ × 6⅛ in.)
Edition of 100

     Rirkrit Tiravanija

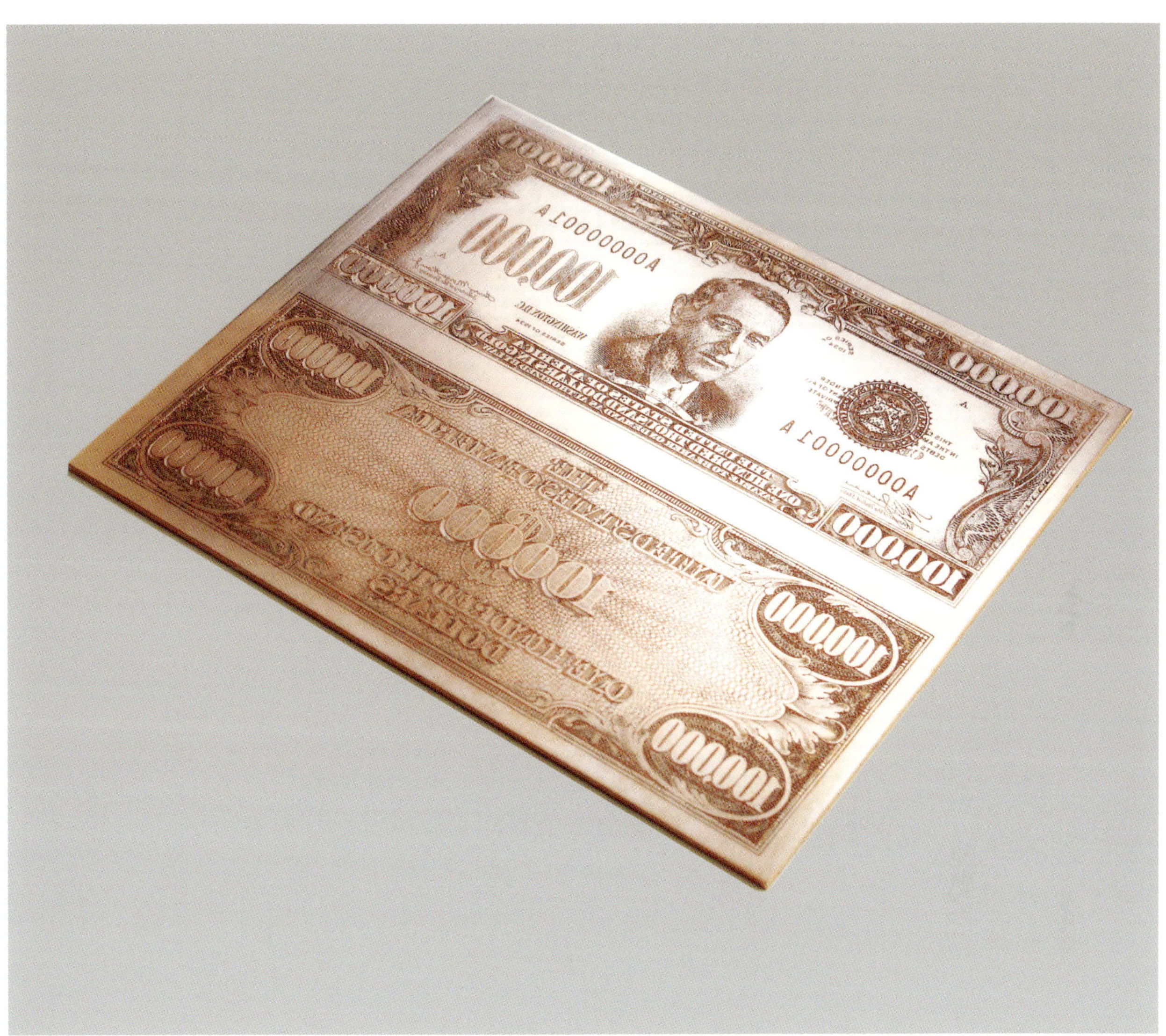

Each of the African traders that British artist Lubaina Himid (b.1954, Zanzibar) has painted onto these English five-pound notes are characters from an invented narrative revolving around money, memory, trade and history. The paintings are part of a project in which the artist was invited to respond to an object held in the Baring Archive, one of the most comprehensive archives of a financial institution anywhere in the world. Founded in 1762, Barings Bank was one of England's oldest merchant banks, which in 1995 collapsed as a result of colossal losses incurred by the fraudulent and unauthorised investments of rogue trader Nick Leeson. Himid was initially drawn to an engraving after Sutton Nicholls (1680–1740) of the opulent Devonshire Square in the City of London, where Barings had offices from 1793 until 1806. She reimagined the square as a site filled with African slave servants and street sellers — such as might be found in the satirical engravings of William Hogarth (1697–1764) — trading fresh fruit, singing birds and writing ink, or offering services such as knife sharpening and furniture repairs. From the seventeenth to the nineteenth centuries, the transatlantic slave trade was integral to London's banking, insurance, manufacturing, shipping and commodity trading with Europe. Himid's characters, painted directly onto symbols of wealth (albeit small ones — a reflection of the artist's own financial situation at the time), quietly acknowledge the contribution made by people of the Black diaspora to the immense wealth of the English capital.

   Lubaina Himid

Trading Places, 2011
Acrylic on banknotes
Each: 7 × 13.5 cm (2¾ × 5¼ in.)

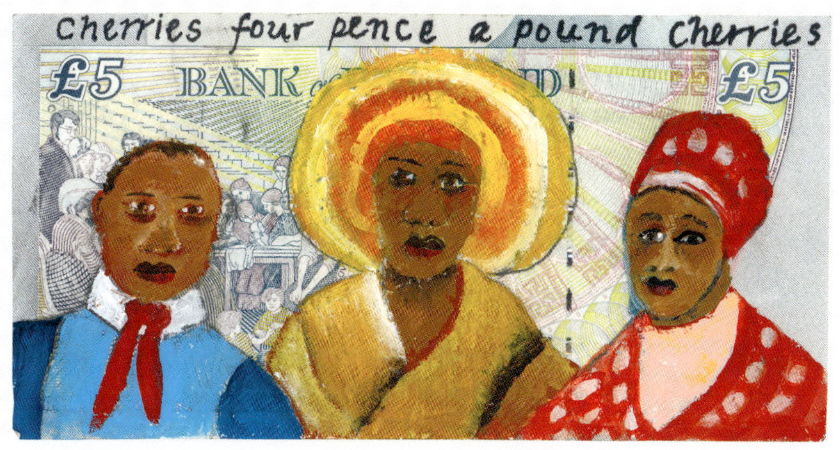
cherries four pence a pound cherries
£5
BANK OF ENGLAND
£5

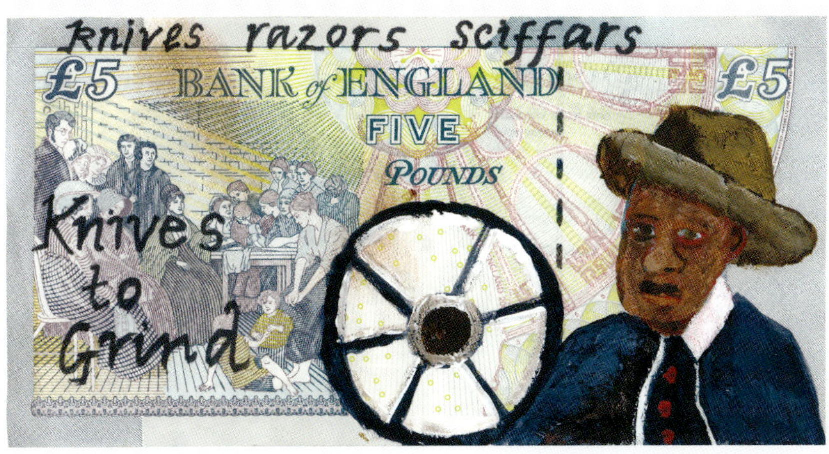
knives razors sciffars
£5
BANK of ENGLAND
£5
FIVE
POUNDS
Knives
to
Grind

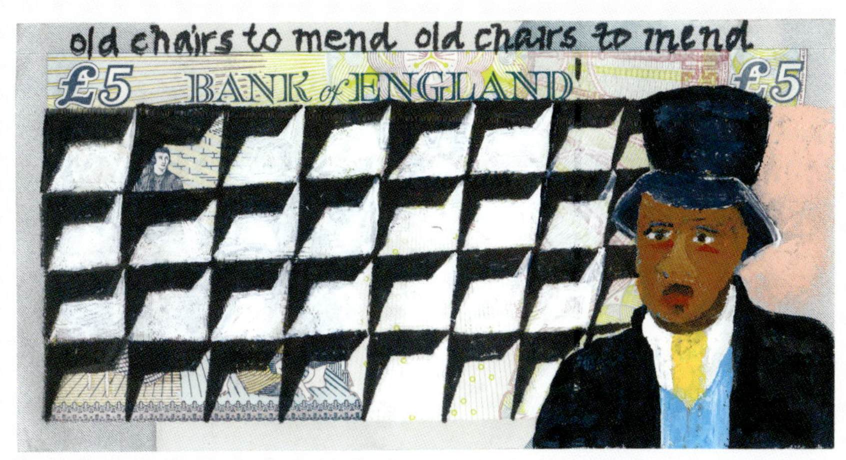
old chairs to mend old chairs to mend
£5
BANK of ENGLAND
£5

Most artists working with physical currency modify their medium in some way, whether by cutting it up and reassembling it as a collage, using it as a sculptural material, or re-presenting it in an unexpected way. For his 2011 project *Currency*, Australian conceptual artist Denis Beaubois (b. 1970) simply presented two bundles of unused, un-altered Australian 100-dollar banknotes with a total value of twenty thousand dollars. The sum was a grant from the Australia Council for the Arts and, as an experiment to pit the economic value of the money against the cultural value of the readymade sculpture, it was put up for sale at Deutscher and Hackett, a fine art auctioneer in Melbourne. While physical money is in principle generic and inter-changeable, the artist recorded the serial numbers of each bill to reinforce their specificity within the context of a unique artwork. The winning bidder committed to purchase the work for 21,350 Australian dollars: 1,350 dollars more than its face value. However, the ham-mer price was actually 17,500 dollars to which a 22 percent buyer's premium was added (including a value added tax of two percent). Beaubois thus received 15,960 dollars from the sale, effectively losing 4,040 dollars. The only party to make any money on the sale was the auction house. Inspired by the ambivalent relationship between art and financial exchange, *Currency* highlights how the distinction between artistic and commercial interests is often eroded by the structures and practices of art market institutions.

Currency, 2011
Two sections of uncirculated $100 Australian banknotes, 100 banknotes in each section
Each: 1.2 × 6.5 × 15.8 cm (½ × 2½ × 6¼ in.)
Art Nomad collection

   Denis Beaubois

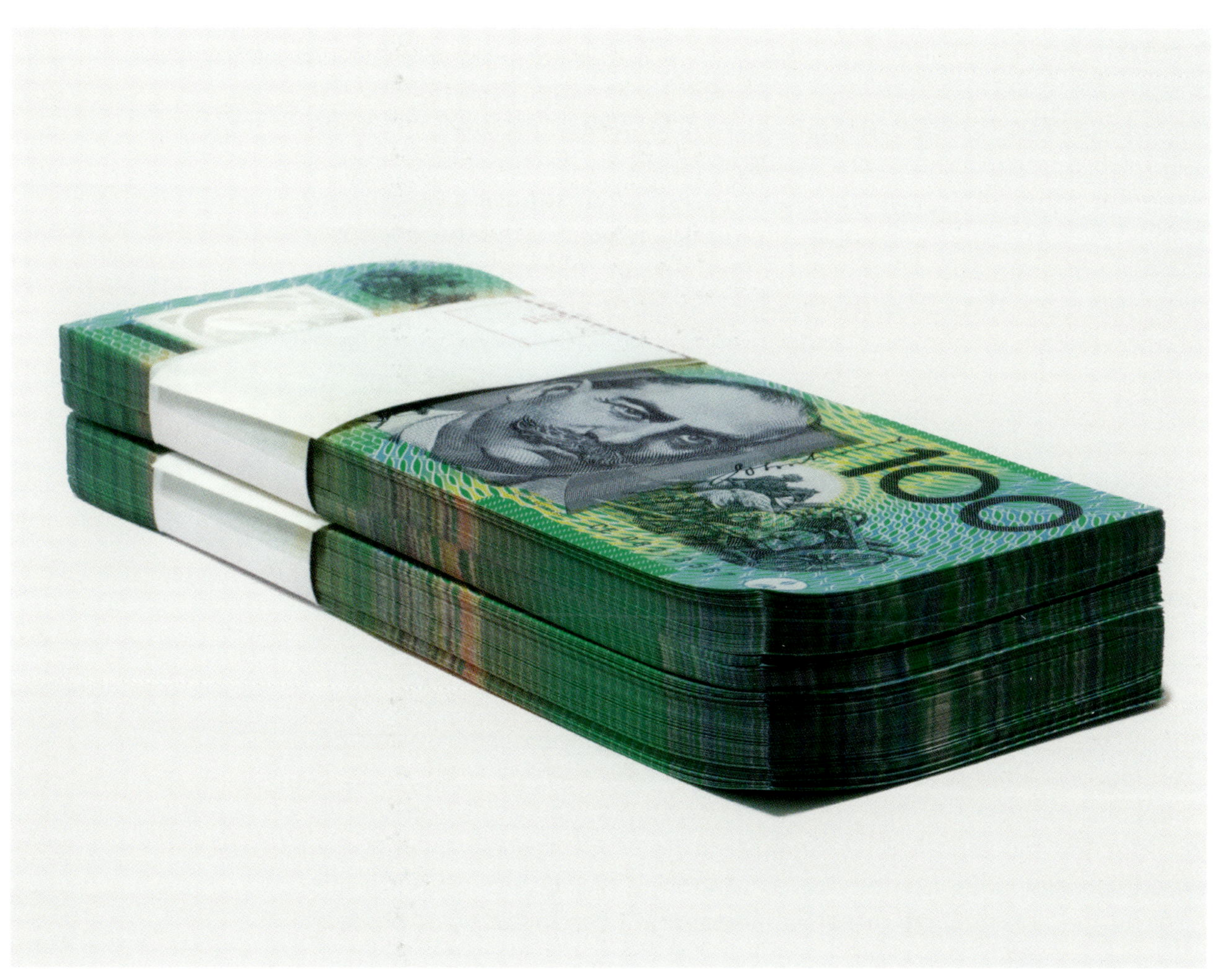

This unusual looking spacesuit has been laboriously constructed from decommissioned Zimbabwean banknotes and other materials by the Zimbabwean-born, South African-based artist Gerald Machona (b. 1986). It is both a sculpture and a prop, appearing in the short film *People From Far Away* (2012), which explores the rise of xenophobic attacks against African expatriates and immigrants living in South Africa, many of whom migrated there following the political and economic collapse of Zimbabwe in the late nineties, which led to a period of severe hyper-inflation culminating in the discontinuation of the Zimbabwean dollar in 2015. Wearing Machona's spacesuits, the film's 'Afronaut' protagonists venture as economic migrants into Makhanda (formerly Grahamstown), in the Eastern Cape province of South Africa. They appear like aliens, finding recognition only when meeting with other Afronauts — a metaphor for the artist's experience as an immigrant in South Africa. Machona often employs money in his works to explore the politics of African identity and cultural representation within post-colonial contexts. The banknotes used here serve as a reminder that paper currency was introduced to Africa by European colonial powers in the nineteenth century, replacing traditional exchange systems such as cowrie shells, beads, feathers, Kola nuts, teeth, and even livestock. After the decol-onisation of African countries in the mid-twentieth century, many of newly independent states continued with Western-style currencies in order to hold together national territories that had been artificially created under colonialism. But, as Machona highlights, violence, dis-crimination and political instability are among the legacies of colonial rule that persist to this day.

  Gerald Machona

Ndiri Afronaut ('*I am an Afronaut*'), 2012
Decommissioned Zimbabwean dollars, foam padding, fabric, wood, Perspex, rubber, plastic tubing, nylon thread and gold leaf
c. 190 × 60 × 50 cm (74 ¾ × 23 ⅝ × 19 ⅝ in.)

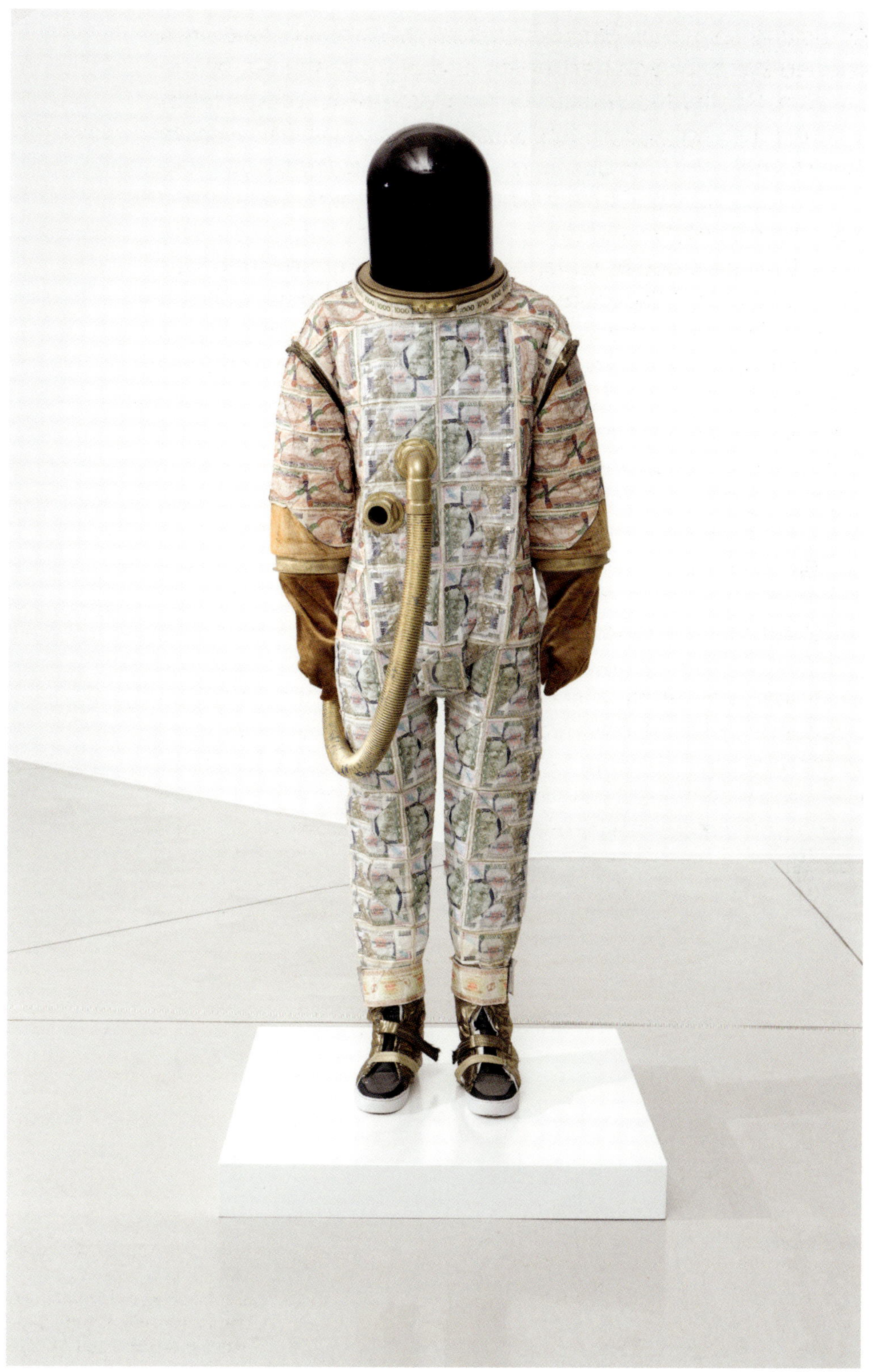

Ten enormous coins lie on a gallery floor, as if scattered by a giant hand. Weighing more than 100 kg (220 lbs) each, these glistening, brass-coated facsimiles of United States currency are instantly recognisable, reproducing every detail of real coinage except for its colour. The installation by American artist Kerry James Marshall (b. 1955) includes four pennies, three quarters, two nickels and a dime, which adds up to just 99 cents, a sum redolent of bargain bins, discount stores and budget shopping. Its title, however, indicates the enormous difference between the production cost of the work and the monetary value it depicts, revealing that the price of fabrication was $136,000, a figure reflecting the complex technical processes involved in sculpting, resin casting and finishing each coin with brass overlay. This echoes the economics of minting legal tender where, due to the high price of raw materials such as copper and zinc, the cost of manufacturing a US penny exceeds the coin's face value. As with Andy Warhol's silkscreened images of money and dollar signs (p. 30–1), Marshall's work points to the way that culture and currency are intertwined; a reminder that artworks belong as much to the market economy as grocery items bought for pocket change.

   Kerry James Marshall

99 cent piece (one thirty six thousand dollars in change), 2012
Cast resin with brass overlay: three quarters, two nickels, one dime and four pennies
Dimensions variable
Installation view, 'We Buy Gold: SEVEN', Jack Shainman Gallery, New York, 2023

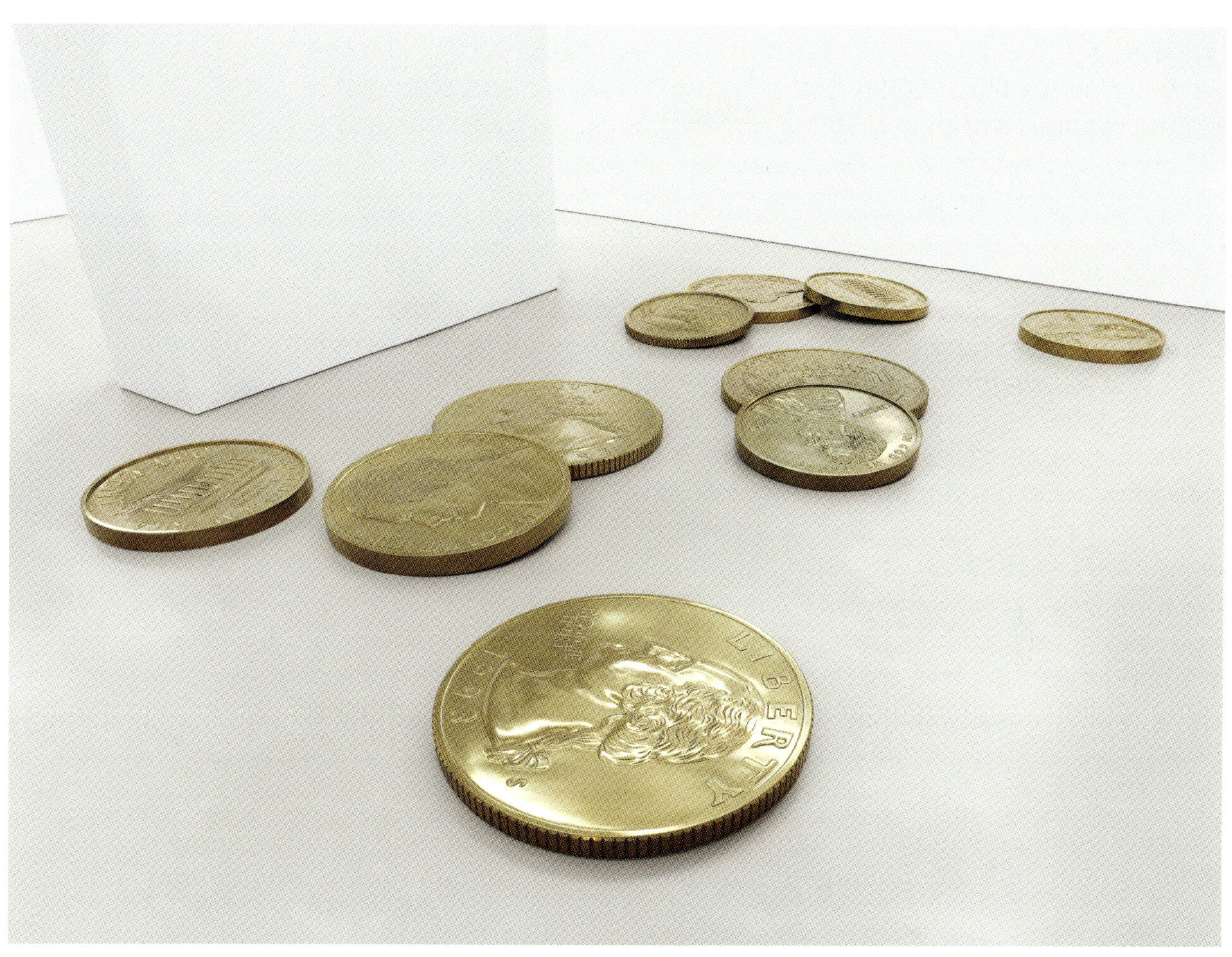

The multiple scaffold-like structures that constitute the *Tally Sticks* project by Colombian artist Santiago Montoya (b. 1974) appear strong and stable, yet are only held together by folded banknotes tied into knots. Standing several metres high, each monumental tower is carefully constructed from sustainable wood sourced from an area of the Cerro de Armas, in the Santander region of the Colombian rainforest, which has for generations belonged to Montoya's family, who are heavily invested in its protection and preservation. The work's title refers to an early form of accounting system: originating in the middle ages, a tally stick was a piece of wood scored with notches that was used to keep track of debts and payments. The word tally also relates to the notion of keeping score, a way of measuring one's successes or equally, one's failures. Implicit in Montoya's structures, then, is the idea of tallying the environmental burden of materialistic, consumer driven societies, where the latest and most desirable products are demanded at any cost. Teasing out connections between the global exploitation of natural resources and the economic drivers that foster such ecological disruption, *Tally Sticks* reflects Montoya's concerns about the environment of his native Colombia and the fragility of the world's financial structures, on which humankind relies.

 Santiago Montoya

Tally Sticks (detail), 2013–17
Bamboo wood and paper money
Dimensions variable
Collection Hugo Quinto and Juan Pablo Lojo

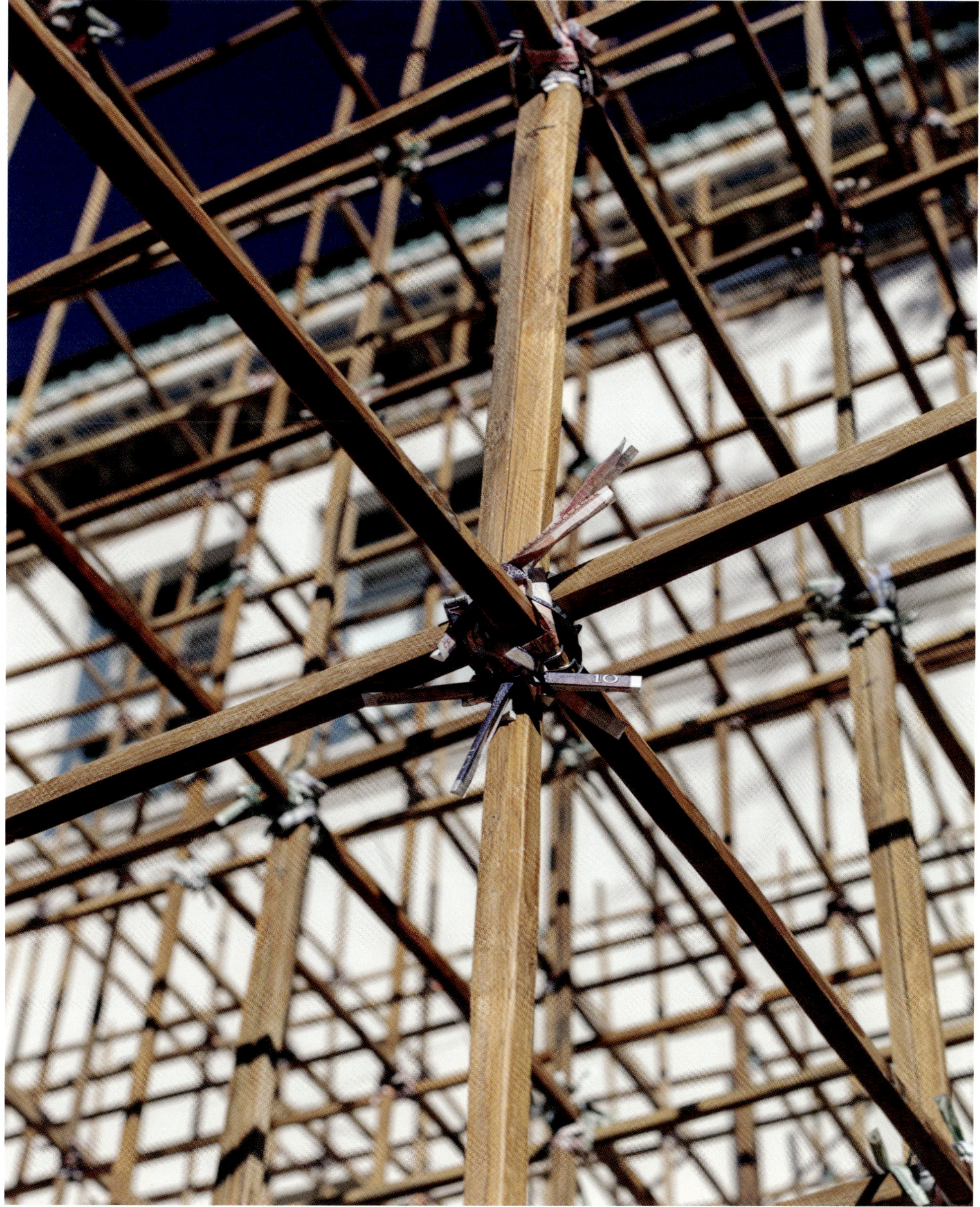

Employing the traditional weaving techniques of Native American Cherokee people, this paper basket features verdant forest imagery, reproductions of the Indian Removal Act of 1830 and, most prominently, hand painted US 20-dollar bills featuring the portrait of president Andrew Jackson that encircle the form and remain recognisable despite being fractured diagonally. The work was made by Shan Goshorn (1957–2018), an Eastern Band Cherokee artist who gained recognition for craft-based, politically-driven artworks that combine archival documents, photographs and other culturally-resonant materials to comment on Native American issues. Here, the basket's imagery addresses a specific act of terror committed against the Cherokee people in the nineteenth century by Jackson. His tyrannical approach to removing Indigenous people from their ancestral forest homelands in the Southeast region of the US displaced most of the tribes to lands west of the Mississippi leaving settlers (and Jackson himself) to claim their land. The applied gold foil splints, which hold the fragile structure together, refer to how the discovery of gold accelerated the process of Cherokee removal in the 1830s. The Cherokee people felt especially betrayed by Jackson who, despite having had his life saved by one of their warriors at the Battle of Horseshoe Bend in 1814, refused as president to even view the documents compiled by indigenous peoples disputing the legal authority of his actions. For Goshorn, it was galling that his portrait should remain on the 20-dollar bill and she considered it a bitter irony that the US currency was a similar colour to the lush mountain forests of her people's rightful homeland.

     Shan Goshorn

Color of Conflicting Values, 2013
Woven basket: archival inks, acrylic
paint on paper and gold foil
35.6 × 35.6 × 33 cm (14 × 14 × 13 in.)
Collection Edward J. Guarino

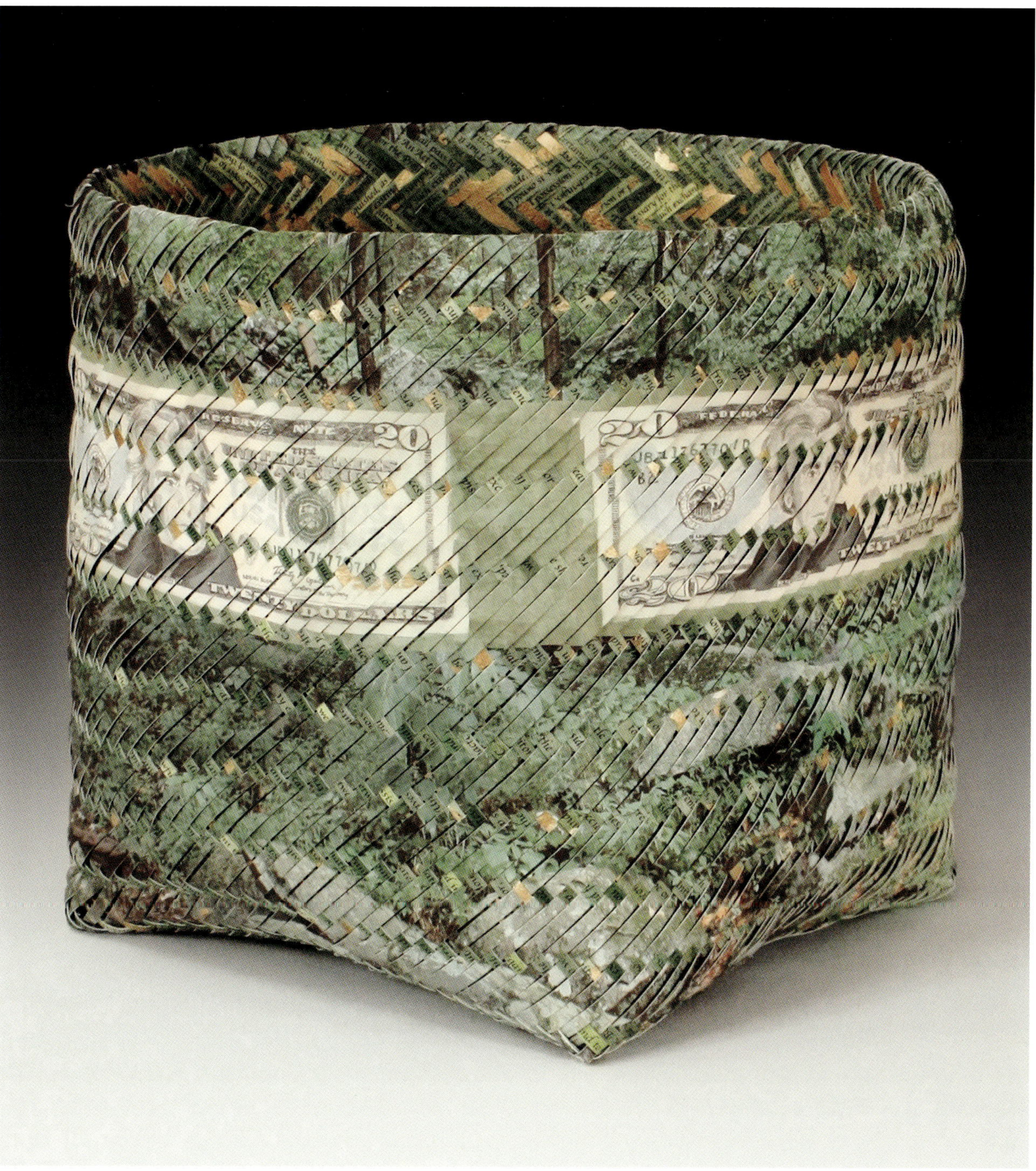

Appearing like the components of a dismantled clock mechanism, these eight German euro coins have been transformed into cogwheels, with each denomination from one cent to two euro given a meticulous, serrated edge. They are displayed in a row on individual marble shelves, though not strictly in order of face value. The coins are a witty visual allusion to the financial mechanisms that govern all our lives and keep the world in motion — as per the work's title. The installation is closely related to *Treibwerk* (2013), works in which similar euro cogs are horizontally interlocked and mounted on paper. Both projects question the extent to which artistic practice is itself beholden to economic machinery for validation and recognition. Playfully distorting everyday objects and materials in an effort to question the systems and structures of our world, Alicja Kwade (b.1979) creates enigmatic artworks across sculpture, film, photography and installation that engage with concepts of time, science and philosophy. The Berlin-based Polish artist has made numerous works interrogating the way in which value is assigned to objects, such as *Palette* (2006–9), which takes the form of a humble shipping pallet carefully recreated in varnished mahogany; *Kohle (Union 666)* (2008), where she covered stacks of coal bricks with gold leaf, and *Bordsteinjuwelen (Die 100 Auserwählten)* (2008), in which she had jewellers cut stone pebbles into the form of faceted precious gems.

Motion, 2013
Modified euro coins, marble shelves
Dimensions variable
Installation view, 'Solid Stars and Other
Conditions', i8 Gallery, Reykjavík, 2013
Private collections

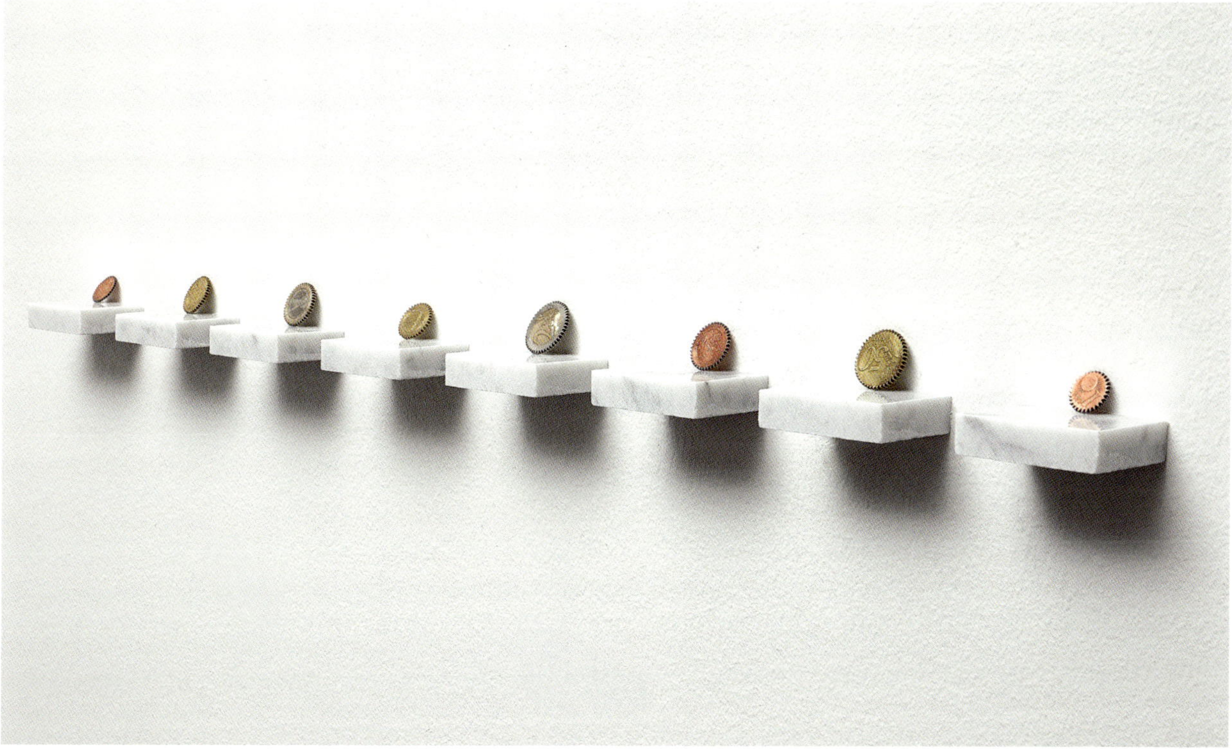

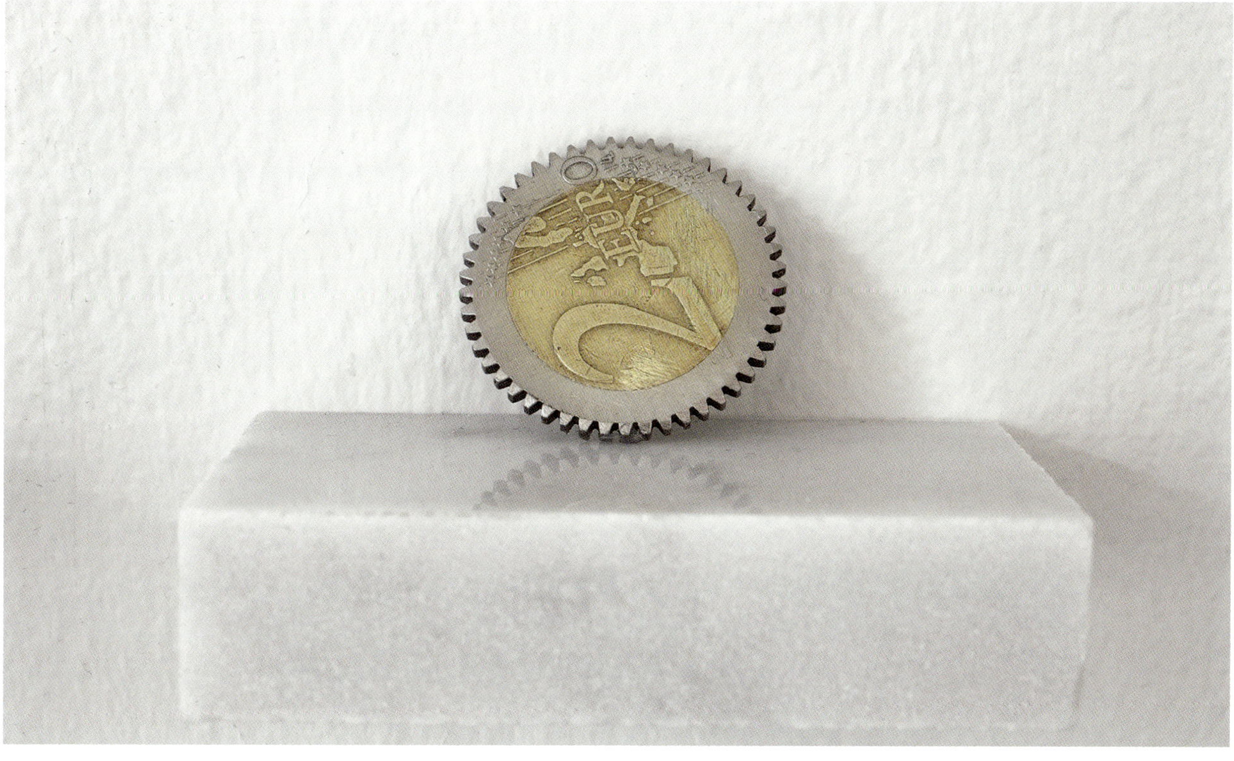

Launched in 2009 by the community-led action group Transition Town Brixton, the Brixton Pound (B£) is an innovative — if unofficial in the eyes of the Bank of England — form of local currency. It is used in parallel to pound sterling within an area of South London famed for its vibrant street markets and rich cultural history, especially in relation to the so-called 'Windrush Generation'. These were economic migrants who settled there in a wave of immigration from 1948 to 1962 that was facilitated by a UK government looking to bolster its post-war workforce with cheap labour from its former colonies, especially the Caribbean. The aim of the Brixton Pound was to strengthen the area's economy by encouraging spending within the community, particularly among locally-owned businesses. The first paper notes carried portraits of esteemed former residents, including Vincent van Gogh (1853–90) on the B£20 and the Trinidadian author C. L. R. James (1901–89) on the B£10. David Bowie (1947–2016) and basketball player p. (b. 1985) were added later on the B£10 and B£5 respectively. On the occasion of the currency's fifth anniversary, a special edition B£5 note was commissioned from Turner-Prize winning artist Jeremy Deller (b. 1966), whose eye-catching psychedelic design features an androgynous face surrounded by patterns of swirling curlicues on a rainbow background. On the reverse of the note is a provocative quote from the first volume of Karl Marx's *Das Kapital* (1867), an admonishment against fetishising money: 'Capital is money, capital is commodities… By virtue of it being value, it has acquired the occult ability to add value to itself. It brings forth living offspring, or, at the least, lays golden eggs.'

 Jeremy Deller with Fraser Muggeridge studio

Brixton Pound (obverse and reverse), 2015
7.2 × 14.1 cm (2 ⅞ × 5 ½ in.)
Commissioned by This Ain't Rock'n'Roll

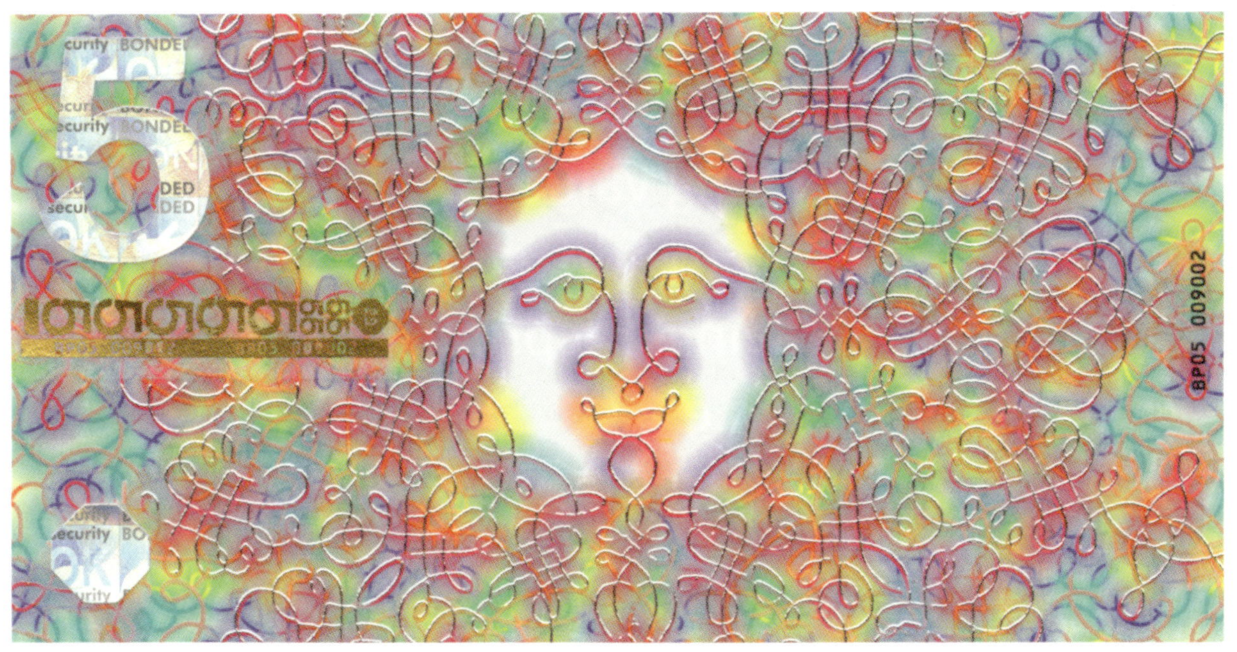

Capital is money, capital is commodities…
By virtue of it being value, it has acquired the occult ability to add value to itself.
It brings forth living offspring, or, at the least, lays golden eggs.

Karl Marx, *Capital*

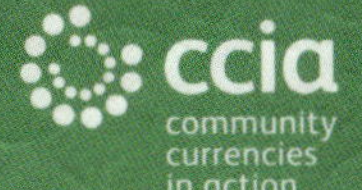

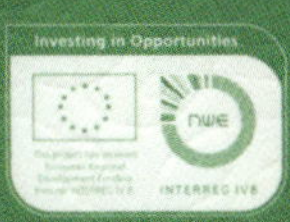

5

These colourful geometric canvases recall works by American abstract painters such as Frank Stella (1936–2024) and Kenneth Noland (1924–2010), though their designs in fact replicate details from patterns found on banknotes, old and new, from around the world. The work of Chinese artist Xu Qu (b. 1978), each one is painted with acrylic and spray paint on canvas and mounted back-to-back with another work from the series. Removed from their original context and enlarged many times, it is virtually impossible to identify which currencies Xu's paintings represent save for their titles, which reveal their country of origin and denomination. On the far left of this installation view, the green-hued *Dollar 2 old* (2015) derives from a withdrawn US two-dollar bill while, visible directly behind this, *RMB 5 yuan new* (2015) represents the Chinese yuan renminbi, the official currency of the People's Republic of China. Other currencies include English pounds and New Taiwan dollars. The title of the series, 'Currency Wars', refers to a phenomenon in international trade relations where nations seek to gain an advantage over others by manipulating the exchange rate of their currency to fall in relation to others. As a result, exports become cheaper and therefore more attractive to foreign buyers, though if too many countries adopt this strategy it can lead to a general decline in trade to the detriment of the global economy. For Xu, these paintings serve as visible symbols of this unseen conflict. Set on wheels, the abstract forms can be arranged in different configurations each time the installation is displayed, simulating the movement of world currencies as values rise and fall.

Currency Wars (various currencies), 2015
Acrylic on canvas and acrylic and spray paint
on canvas, each (without stand): 158 × 150 cm (62¼ × 59 in.)
Installation view, 'Currency Wars', Almine Rech, Paris

     Xu Qu

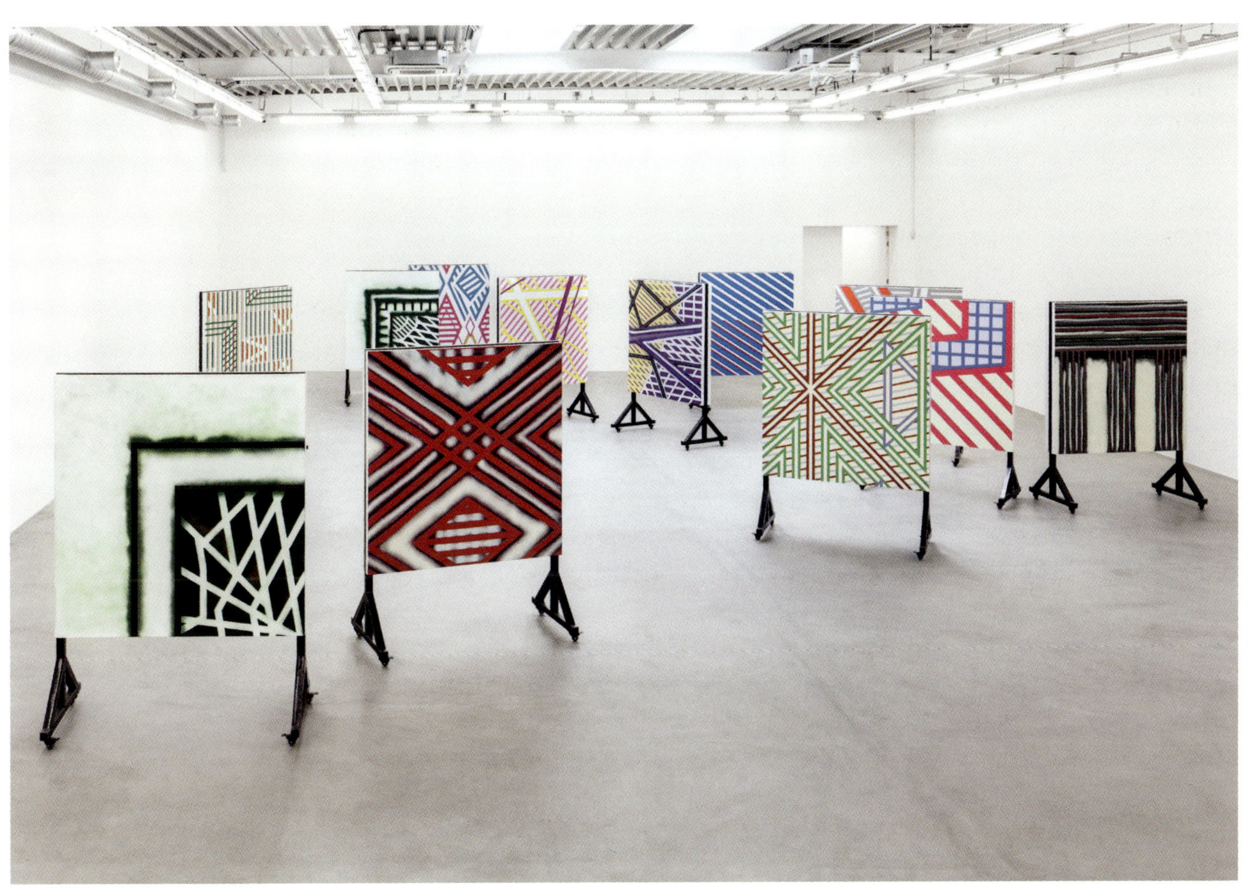

Notions of value, valuation and speculation lie at the heart of *Bitchcoin*, a digital asset developed by French-American artist Sarah Meyohas (b.1991), five months before the emergence of the trailblazing cryptocurrency platform Ethereum in 2015. Although similar to the revolutionary peer-to-peer electronic cash system Bitcoin, Meyohas's tokens can only be used to buy artworks she has made. When launched, *Bitchcoin* was backed by the artist's photographic series 'Speculations' (2015) — images of infinite reflections that are a metaphor for the limitless number of transactions possible with blockchain technology. Each coin, priced at one hundred US dollars, was worth 25 square-inches of a physical print, with twenty-five coins required to purchase a complete work. *Bitchcoin* has since migrated from Meyohas's own blockchain to Ethereum and 3,291 tokens are now linked to the same number of pressed rose petals from her 2017 performance, *Cloud of Petals*, for which each was plucked, photographed and analysed by artificial intelligence software that learned to generate its own digital versions. Whenever a physical petal is redeemed, its corresponding *Bitchcoin* is 'burnt' by being sent to an address on the blockchain that cannot be accessed. Addressing the ownership and utility of art in the virtual realm, Meyohas's project is an early example of an artist exploring the creative potential of cryptocurrency, using blockchain to track ownership of an artwork, and creating Non-Fungible Tokens (NFTs) long before the concept was embraced in the wider art world.

Bitchcoin, 2015–21
NFT

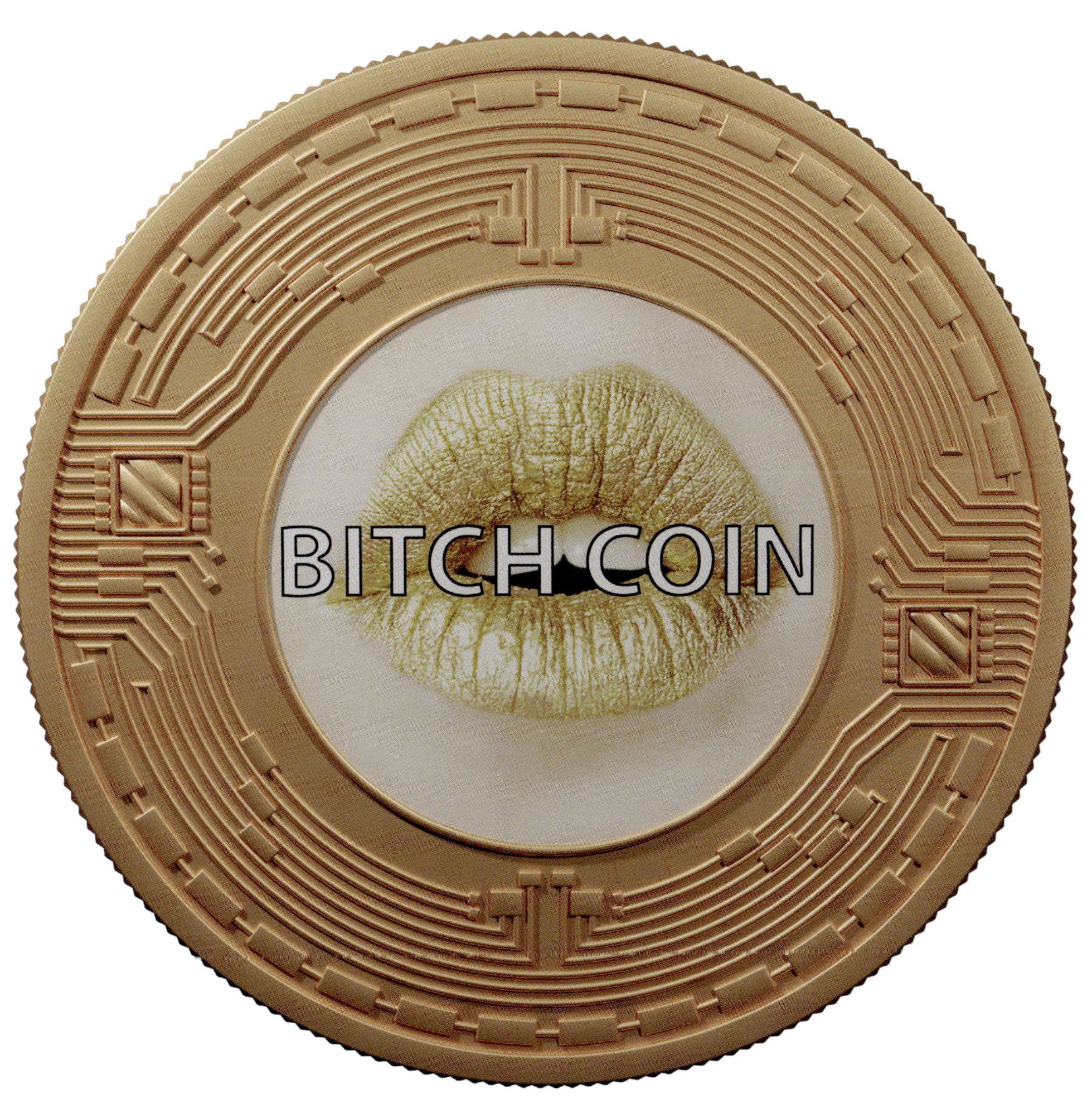
BITCH COIN

A country's banknotes are an important part of its national identity and much consideration goes into their graphic design. In addition to the portraits of current rulers and of political or historical figures, various aspects of a nation's culture are frequently included, from historic events and heritage landmarks to celebrated landscapes. A more overlooked element, often integrated into decorative backgrounds and borders, is the depiction of indigenous flora. These flowers and other plants may be representative of a region or have national symbolism. For his ongoing 'Herbarium' series, begun in 2015, German artist Philipp Valenta (b. 1987) has sourced international banknotes old and new, and painstakingly cut out an array of plant life. Each is framed individually, isolated against a plain background. Illustrated here are wild yellow roses prominently foregrounded on a 1991 Sri Lankan 10-rupee note, stylised irises from a 1987 Polish 10,000-złoty note, and cultivated roses from a 1993 Kenyan 20-shilling note. Others in the series include an Alpine carline thistle from Switzerland, an orchid representing Singapore's national flower and a hibiscus from Sierra Leone, which grows throughout the country. Although Valenta's specimens have been separated from their currencies, signs of their origins are still present: a partial serial number, a figure denoting a denomination, or the signature of a chief cashier. Flowers, of course, are no respecters of national borders and, while printed money is only legal tender within the territory of its issuing country, plants thrive wherever they can.

    Philipp Valenta

(clockwise from top)
10 Rupees, Sri Lanka, 2018
10,000 Złoty, Poland, 2023
20 Shillings, Kenya, 2023
from the series 'Herbarium', 2015–ongoing
Flowers cut from international banknotes
Each (framed): 18 × 24 cm (7⅛ × 9½ in.)

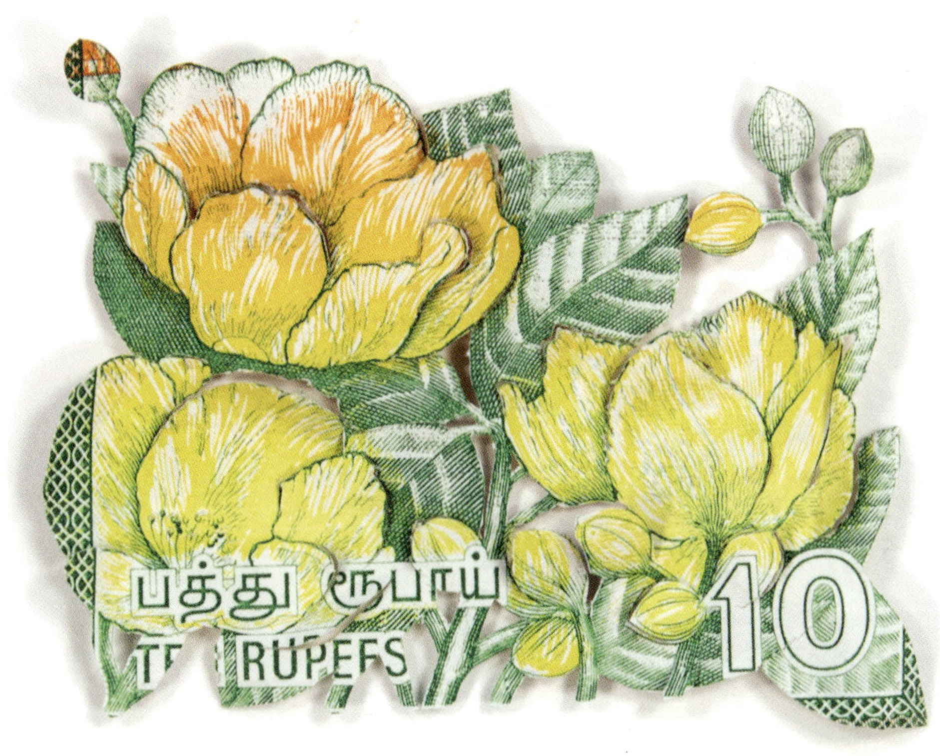

பத்து ரூபாய்
TEN RUPEES
10

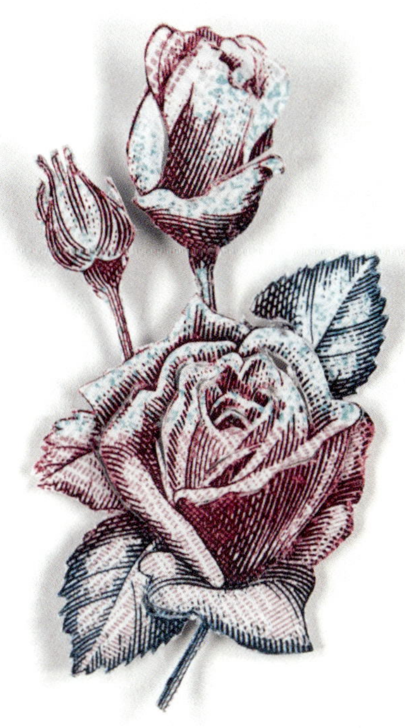

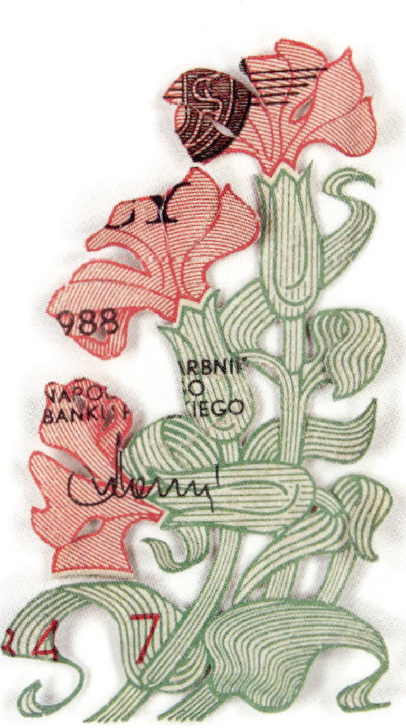

988
RBNIF
NARO
BANKI
IEGO
4 7

The intricately crafted collages of Mark Wagner (b.1976) are made exclusively from US dollar bills. Using just a knife and adhesive, the American artist assidously cuts up hundreds of the familiar green and black notes and reorganises the fragments into complex portraits, landscapes and fanciful allegories that reflect on issues of wealth, capitalism and American identity. In his work, former US presidents, including Abraham Lincoln and Barack Obama, appear alongside public and political figures such as Ben Bernanke, who oversaw the Federal Reserve's response to the 2007–8 global financial crisis. George Washington is naturally a recurring character and the Founding Father's portrait from the one dollar bill is used to depict him in a variety of playful scenarios, from mowing the lawn to rowing a boat. Sometimes, Wagner arranges the bay laurel leaves from the front of the notes to form topiary animals, dollar signs and, as here, words. The phrase 'hedge fund' refers to a type of high-risk investment scheme that uses a wide range of strategies to exploit the market and generate higher returns than normal. Run by professional managers, hedge funds have been known to generate huge gains for investors, even as more traditional investments have languished. Conversely, some have lost hundreds of millions of dollars. In neither condemning or celebrating such ethicaly questionable practices, Wagner's collage reflects the ambiguity that runs throughout his practice.

     Mark Wagner

Hedge Fund, 2016
Currency on panel
45.7 × 61 cm (18 × 24 in.)

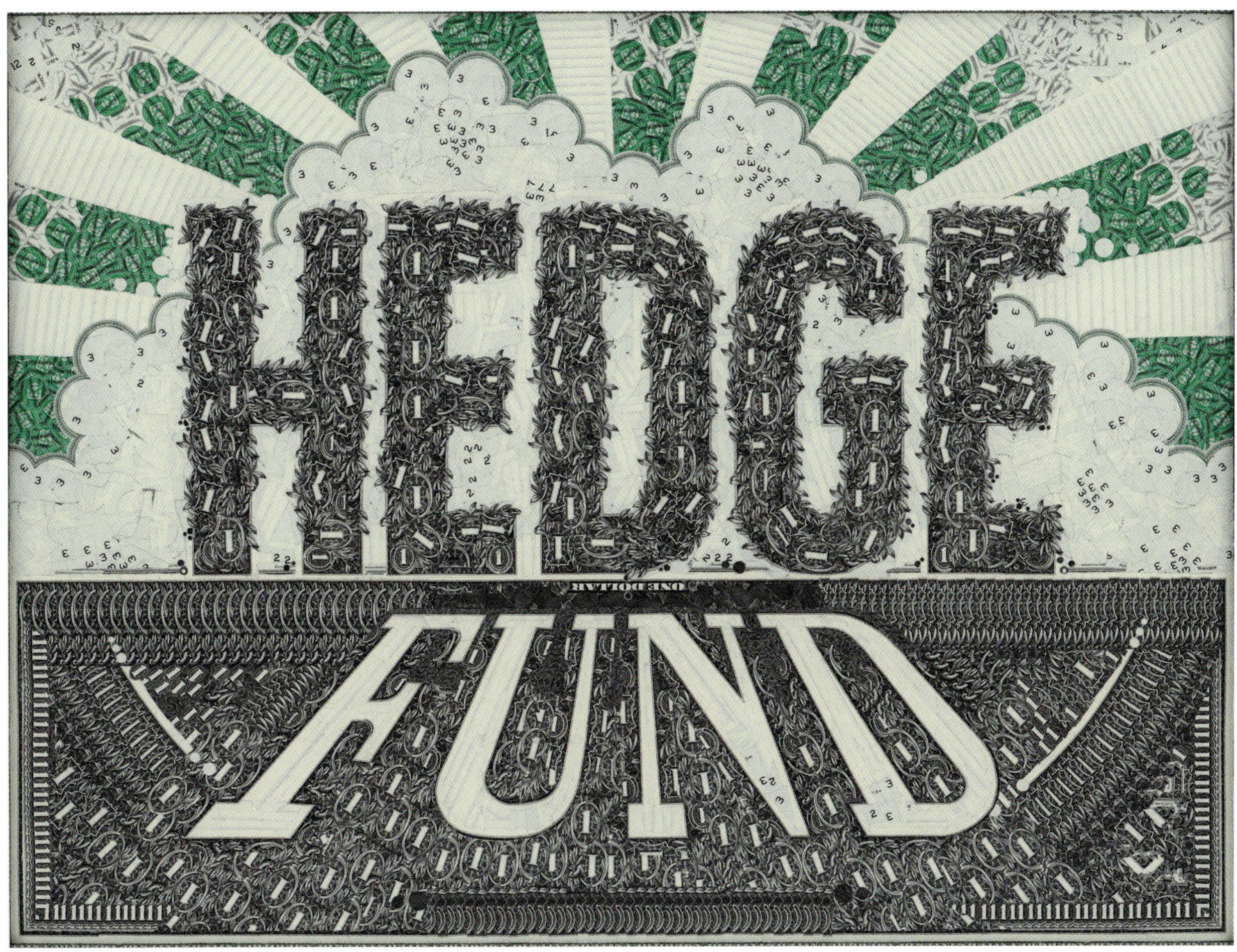

HEDGE
FUND
ONE DOLLAR

London's male-dominated financial world is the target of mockery in this glazed ceramic phallus by British artist Grayson Perry (b. 1960). Its erect form is covered with images of banknotes, designer goods, city bankers and George Osborne — the UK's Chancellor of the Exchequer from 2010 to 2016, in the aftermath of the global financial crisis that began in 2007–8 and for which several British banks were controversially bailed out by the UK goverment (at the taxpayer's expense), while austerity measures decimated public services to make up the shortfall. Perry produced this work while making a television programme on the theme of modern masculinity for British broadcaster Channel 4. Having explored the worlds of mixed martial arts and criminality, the artist turned his attention to high finance, visiting London's financial district — also known as The City — to speak with stockbrokers, traders and hedge fund managers. At the time of filming, 84 per cent of senior bankers were male and Perry suggested that exuberant, testosterone-driven decision making had contributed to the financial crash. While some bankers he spoke to claimed that this period had been an aberration and denied the existence of a rampant culture of toxic masculinity in the sector, one admitted to enjoying the chaos of the global crisis. Inspired by the attitudes he encountered, Perry created *Object in Foreground* as a deliberately derisive comment on the gender imbalance in The City. When the penile sculpture was unveiled to City workers, it was met with horror, anger and disgust.

    Grayson Perry

Object in Foreground, 2016
Glazed ceramic
95 × 38 cm (37 ⅜ × 15 in.)

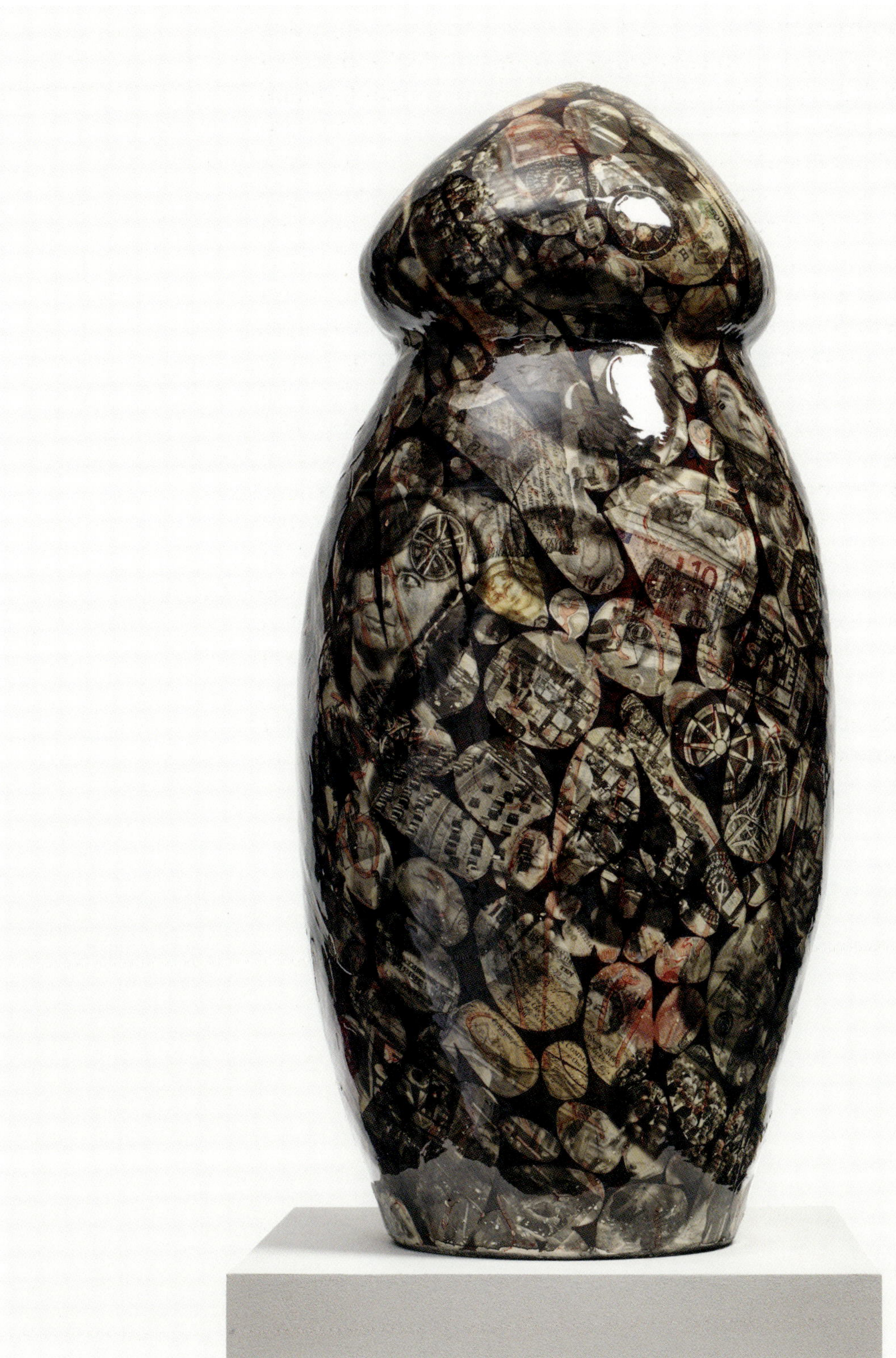

Piled up on a gallery floor is a total of 2,043,599 one penny sterling coins — a powerful visual representation of the £20,436 (minus one penny) that the UK government believed was the annual minimum that a British family of two adults and two children needed for basic survival in 2016. By removing a single coin from the sum, Michael Dean (b.1977) symbolically plunged the proverbial family below the poverty line, a strikingly political gesture alluding to the persistently high levels of poverty and inequality in the UK, particularly as experienced in the North East of England, where the London-based artist was born and raised. In the wider installation to which these coins belong, the family of four is represented by a ragged group of concrete structures, created by taking casts of corrugated fencing. Their proportions are based on those of Dean's own family and each one is punctured by a pair of holes that read as eyes, suggesting a certain poignancy between the figures — two parents, a young child and a teenager. Adjacent to these were detritus-like sculptures, concrete fists (cast from the hands of the artist, his children and their mother) and drug 'baggies' printed with Dean's own designs evoking the wider threats and challenges of the penurious urban environment. Together, these elements formed a monument to the many barriers (which are poetically referred to by Dean as 'shores') that keep people impoverished. Language and the struggle to communicate are central to Dean's sculptures and installations, which typically begin with his own writing and typographic designs that he translates into illegible, anthropomorphic forms using concrete, steel, soil, sand and other easily available materials. References to the body recur throughout his work; here, they suggest the detrimental effects of poverty on human experience.

  Michael Dean

United Kingdom poverty line for two adults and two children: twenty thousand four hundred and thirty-six pounds sterling as published on 1st September 2016, 2016
Installation view, 'Turner Prize 2016', Tate Britain, London

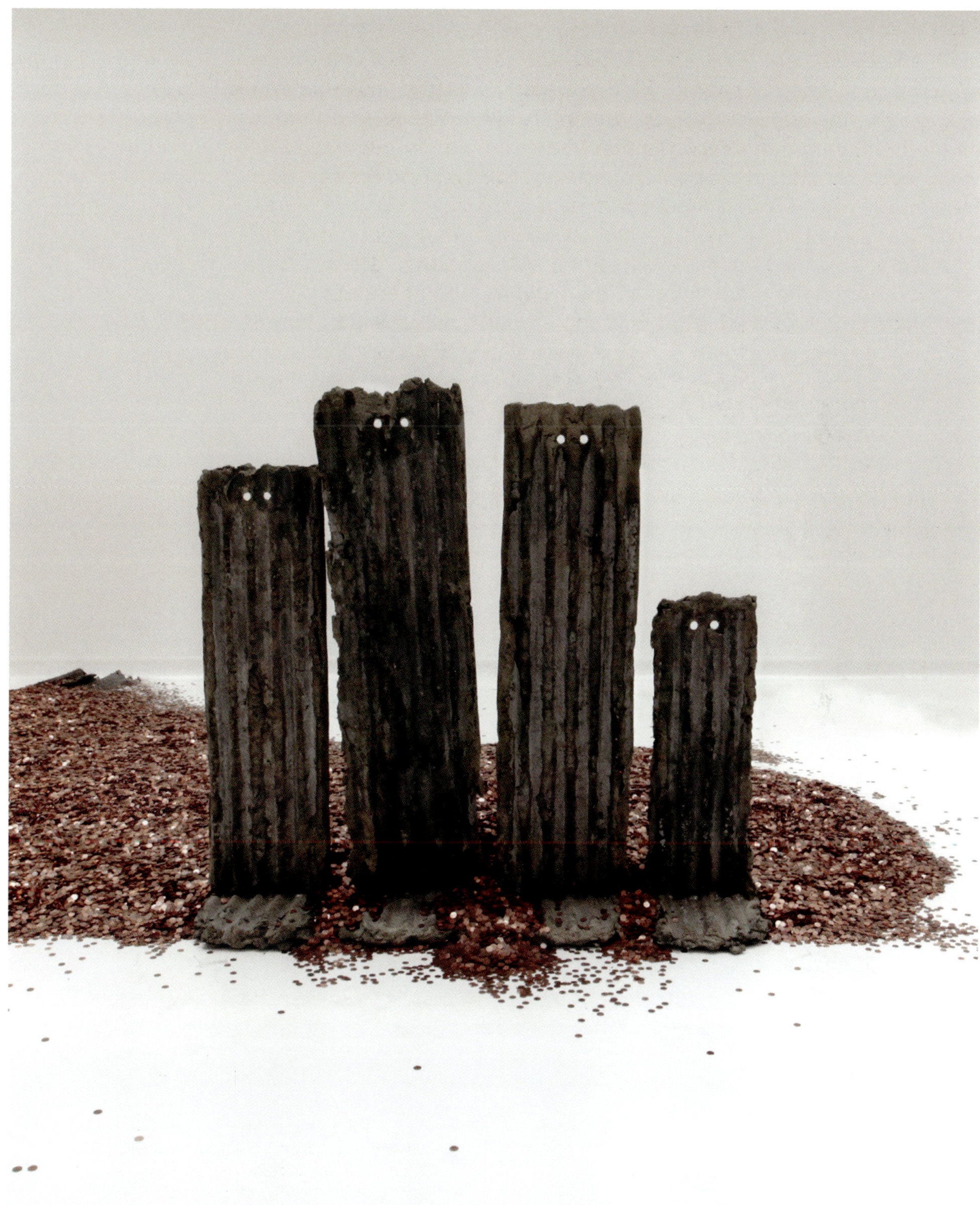

On a pine structure resembling a market stall, Beninese conceptual artist Meschac Gaba (b.1961) has laid out his wares, but the goods apparently offered for sale are Zimbabwean banknotes, tokens of exchange that became virtually worthless in 2015 when the currency ceased to be legal tender. The notes, variously pegged to wires and secured under stones, range from the one-dollar bill introduced after the country gained formal independence from British colonial rule and a new name in 1980, to the 100 trillion-dollar note, issued at the zenith of the country's hyperinflation, which hit a staggering 79 billion percent in 2008, in the latter years of Robert Mugabe's presidency. That year, the 100 billion banknote bought little more than a loaf of bread. Gaba has incorporated money into his work since the mid-1990s, when Benin, along with thirteen other West African countries, devalued their shared currency, the Communauté Financière Africaine (CFA) franc, by fifty percent — a bold decision made with the intention of encouraging sustainable growth by boosting exports and helping them become more competitive in the global market. His sculptures, installations and prints interrogate the systems that create and sustain value, whether social, cultural or economic. Many works respond to the economic challenges facing different African countries and the role played by market forces on Africa's position in the global art world.

    Meschac Gaba

Bank or Economy: Inflation, 2016
Wood, Zimbabwean banknotes, stones,
rope and pegs
200 × 200 × 120 cm (78¾ × 78¾ × 47¼ in.)
Installation view, 'Bank or Economy',
Stevenson, Cape Town

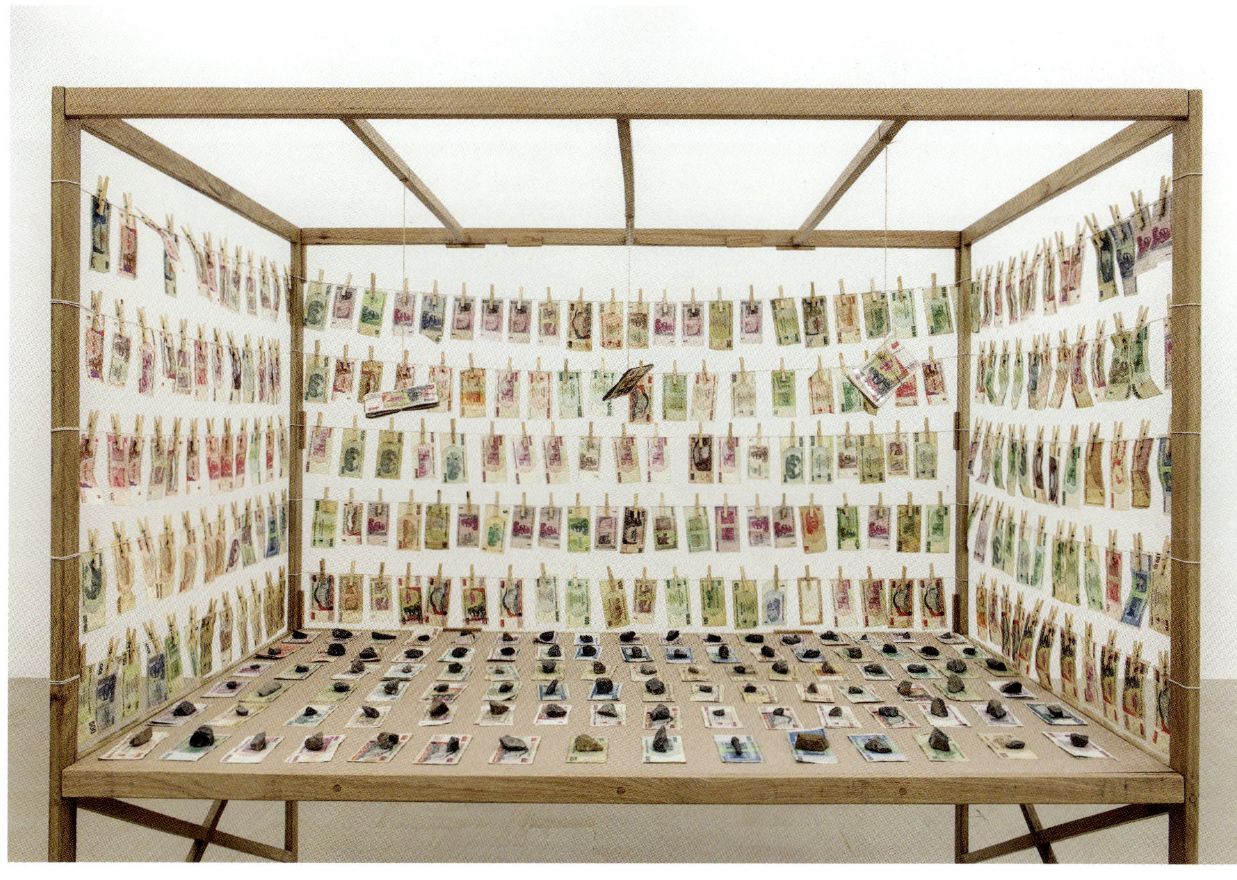

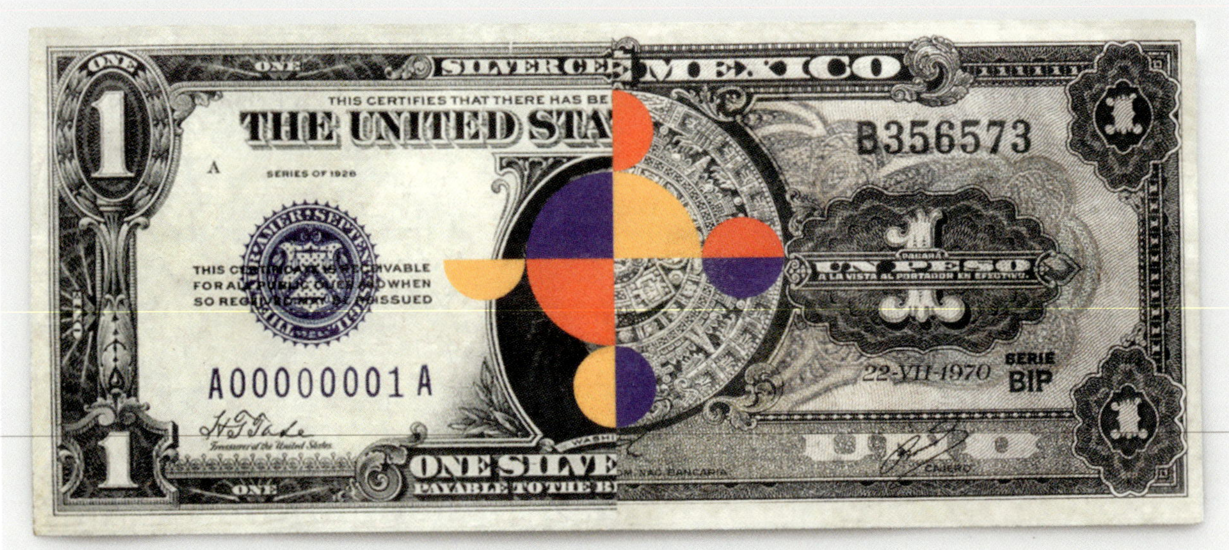

This hybrid banknote — half US dollar, half Mexican peso — is adorned with a logo-like design of circle segments. This is a recurring motif in the work of Mexican artist Gabriel Orozco (b. 1962) who created the currency to be used in his participatory installation, *OROXXO*, which ran for 30 days in February and March 2017. Transforming kurimanzutto gallery in Mexico City into a fully operational Oxxo (the largest chain of convenience stores in Latin America), Orozco filled its shelves with the snacks, drinks and other items one would expect to find. Visitors were given one of Orozco's bills, with which they could purchase any item, except for products carrying the artist's geometric logo, which were neither for sale nor authentic artworks but rather 'samples' of the 300 editions offered for sale in the second half of the installation. Alcohol, pharmaceuticals and tobacco products were also off-limits. Many 'customers' decided the better option was to keep hold of their banknote, reasoning that it would acquire more value over time than a bottle of soda. The second part was a more conventional gallery space displaying objects stickered with Orozco's gold, red and blue semicircles — cans of cola, bags of chips, shampoo bottles and breakfast cereal. Though identical in contents to the merchandise in his Oxxo store, each was priced at $30,000. *OROXXO* thus critiqued the fickleness of both the art market and consumer culture at large, demonstrating how even the most minor of gestures — the application of a logo — can transform items from quotidian to rarefied.

Oroxxo Dollar (detail of *OROXXO), 2017
Two-sided offset lithograph
c. 6 × 15.2 cm (c. 2⅜ × 6 in.)

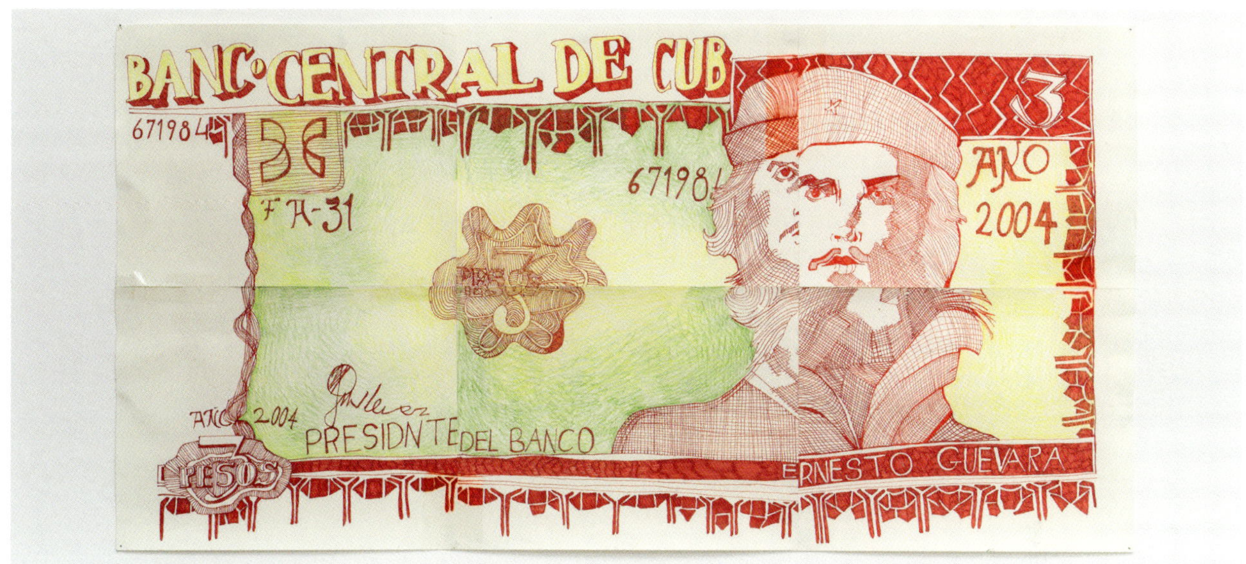

Rather than realism, Israeli artist Keren Cytter (b. 1977) seeks to capture the essence of the banknotes she draws: their vibrant colours, dynamic patterns and striking portraits. This highly stylised rendition of the Cuban three-peso bill featuring Marxist revolutionary Che Guevara demonstrates how she fragments and distorts the original design — using several smaller sheets of paper stuck together — while retaining its identifiable features. Her first such work was the new Israeli ten-shekel banknote: she was inspired by the beauty of its orange-yellow-tan colour-way and portrait of Golda Meir (Israel's only female Prime Minister and a prominent Zionist activist). She subsequently drew the Chinese one-renminbi banknote featuring Mao Zedong, another leader who, like Meir and Guevara, espoused socialist ideals and believed in controlled wealth distribution. Indeed, Guevara sought to correct what he perceived as grave injustices regarding resource allocation in Cuba, but in doing so presided over scores of firing-squad executions of political opponents. To these drawings Cytter added a US 20-dollar bill, which carries the portrait of president Jackson who, in the nineteenth century, vehemently opposed a federal bank, believing it was his duty to protect the masses from the rich and corrupt, yet he lacked such compassion for the Native American Cherokees (see p. 128). Cytter's drawings thus subtly highlight the way that adulatory portraits on currency can obscure problematic aspects of a nation's history.

Che Guevara (banknote),
2017
Coloured pen and
pencil on paper
43.2 × 83.8 cm
(17 × 33 in.)

To create his complex money-based text works, American artist Dan Tague (aka D-TAG; b.1974) folds and manipulates paper banknotes with precision so that only certain letters remain visible, which combine to form phrases such as 'Make Love Not War', 'The Price is Right' and 'Opiate of the Masses'. From common idioms to colloquial sayings, Tague's intricately arranged words use humour and irony to touch on social and political issues including civil rights, war, consumerism and the status of money itself. Each obsessively folded piece is photographed against a black background and printed larger than life to avoid accusations of counterfeiting. His earliest works were created using single US dollar bills whereas subsequent series have incorporated currencies from other countries, often combining multiple denominations into a single image to allow for a wider variety of words than the lettering of US dollars would allow. Several works feature the titles of popular songs such as *Come as You Are* (Nirvana); *Fight the Power* (Public Enemy); *Another One Bites the Dust* (Queen) and, as here, *Just Can't Get Enough* — the title of a 1981 top ten hit by British synth-pop group Depeche Mode. While Tague's reference to this catchy song may arouse an earworm for the viewer, the words can also be understood in relation to the subject of money and the theme of avarice — the rapacious desire to accumulate wealth well beyond one's reasonable needs.

     Dan Tague (D-TAG)

Just Can't Get Enough, 2017
Archival pigment print
100 × 100 cm (39⅜ × 39⅜ in.)

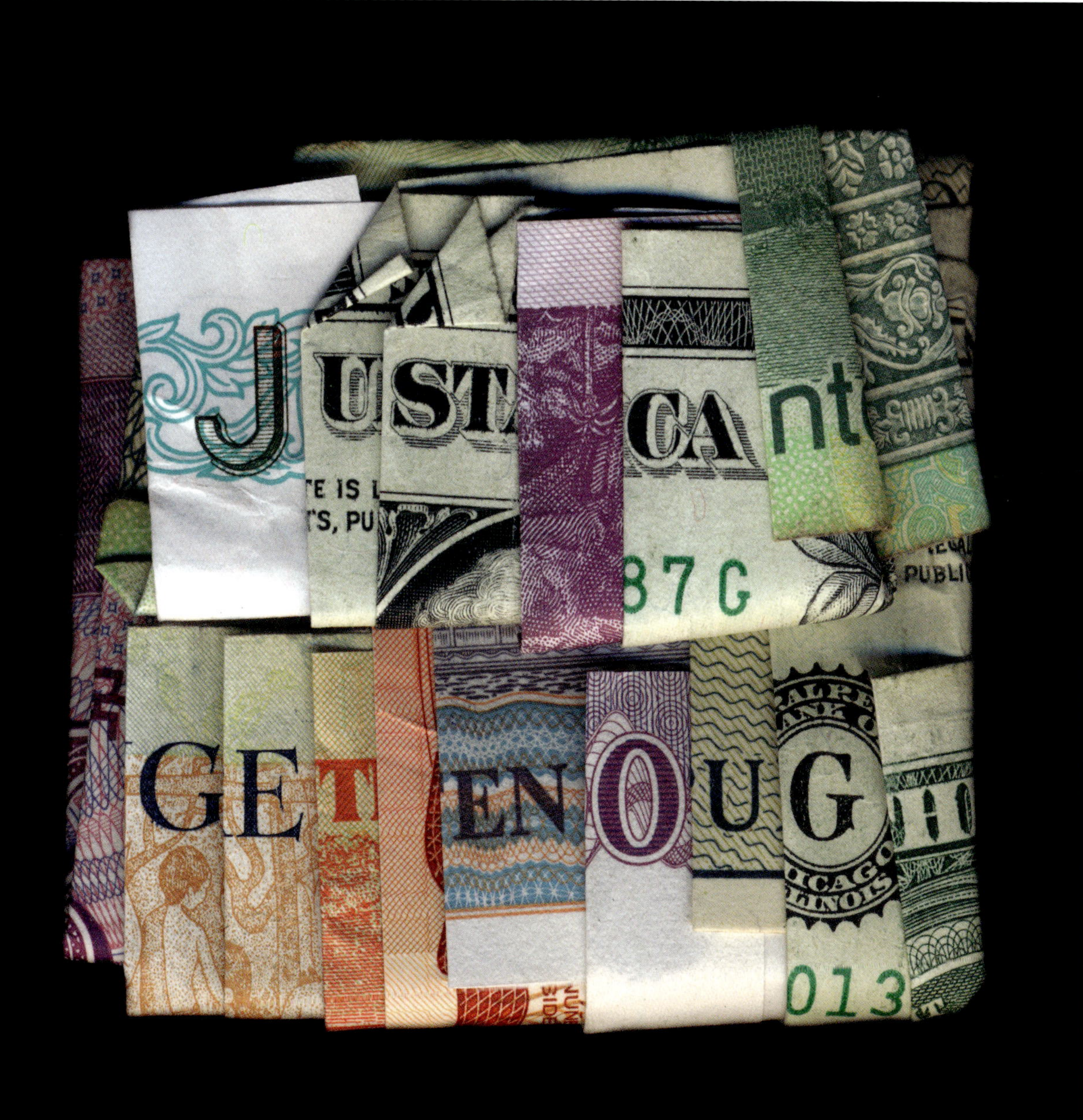

JUST CA nt
GET ENOUG H

This short video shows the hands of anonymous passersby as they open wallets and purses, revealing the personal cash and bankcards concealed within. Some are stuffed with Brazilian real (BRL) banknotes, others contain only small change or credit cards. Each brief close-up plays in slow motion and is accompanied by the evocative sounds of rustling bills or creaking leather. Jonathas de Andrade (b. 1982) filmed this work on the streets of the Brazilian cities of Recife and São Paulo against a backdrop of the biggest corruption scandal in the history of Brazil. A federal investigation dubbed 'Operation Car Wash' (2014–21) had uncovered a web of bribes and kickbacks worth billions of dollars involving the state-run oil company Petrobras, which resulted in dozens of high-profile Latin American business leaders and politicians being sent to jail, including several former presidents. De Andrade's moving-image works, photographs and installations reflect on social issues affecting Brazilian society, and while *Voyeuristico* invites the viewer to reflect on individual identity, socio-economic status, class, age and gender, it also alludes to the presence in society of hidden wealth associated with illicit financial activities. By emphasising the materiality of physical money and pocket wallets, the work additionally encourages reflection on the increasing shift towards cashless societies.

Voyeuristico, 2018
Video in full HD
4 min, 24 secs

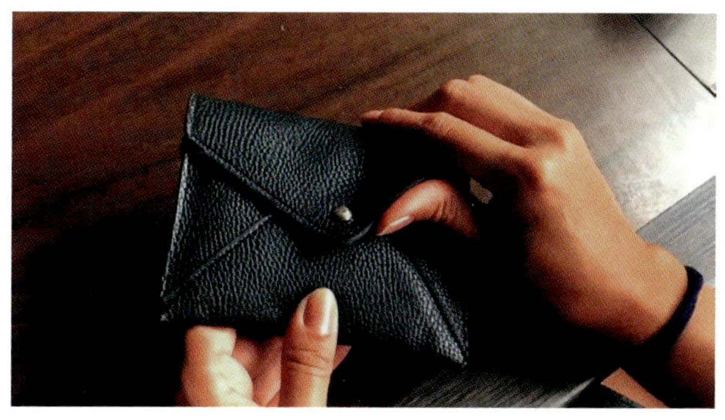
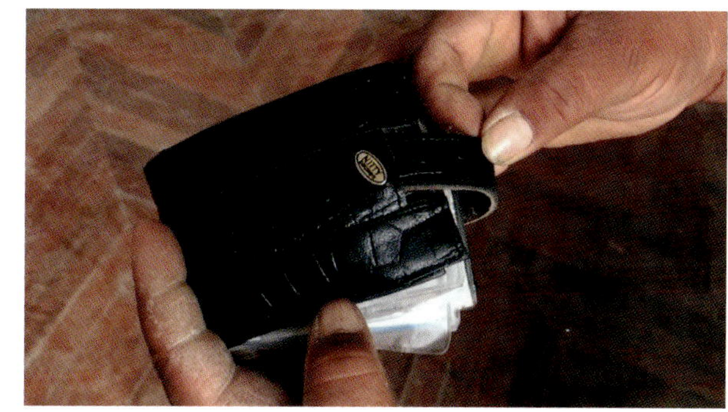
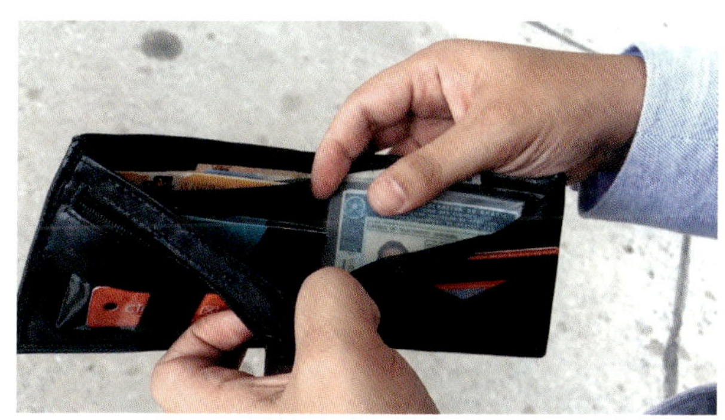
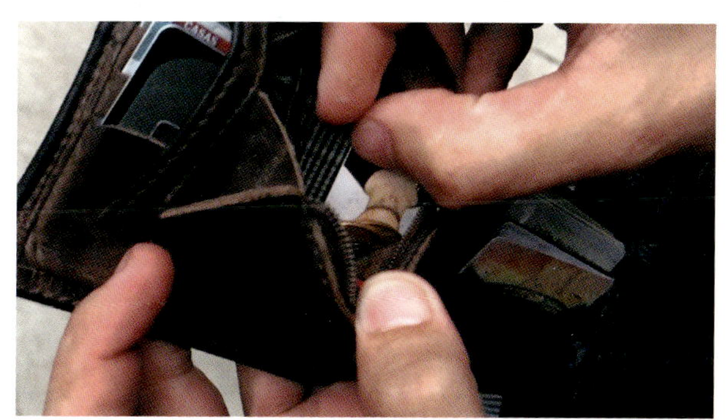
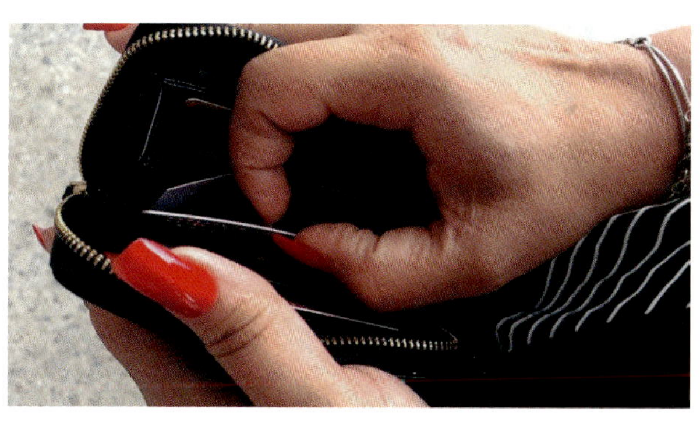
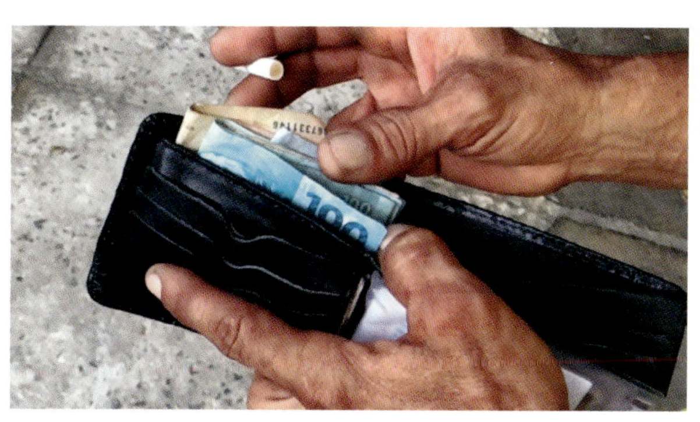
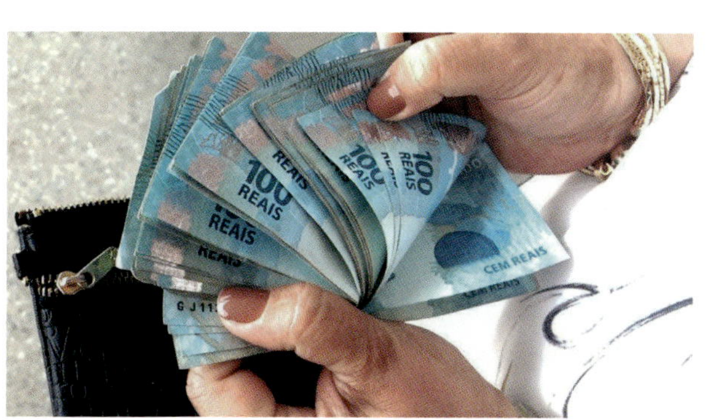
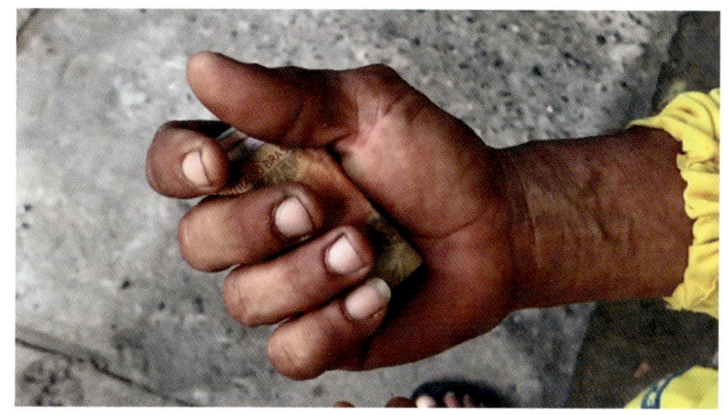

In this rudimentary collage, Swiss artist Thomas Hirschhorn (b.1957) overtly links the pursuit of wealth to the destruction of world heritage by picturing the late 2nd century BCE Temple of Baalshamin in Palmyra, Syria, disintegrating into a shower of coins. The theme of ruins is central to a broader series of collages that the artist began in 2016, after this ancient site was blown up and destroyed by militants of the Islamic State (also called Daesh) who, taking advantage of the upheaval caused by the ongoing Syrian civil war, gained control of large areas of Syria and Iraq from 2014 and 2017 in an attempt to form a global caliphate. The organisation's roots lie in the activities of jihadist groups who opposed the invasion and occupation of Iraq by a US-led coalition from 2003 to 2011. While positioned as an ideological fight against terrorism, the Iraq War has also been considered an 'oil war': Iraq has the second-largest petroleum reserve in the world. Hirschhorn uses simple means to address a complex subject matter, in this case emphasising how the desire to control the natural resources of foreign lands for financial gain can have ruinous consequences. His deliberately low-tech installations, sculptures and works on paper characteristically use inexpensive and commonplace materials such as cardboard, packing tape, tin foil, plywood and photocopies, yet are sophisticated critiques of contemporary geopolitics and the insatiable hunger for money and power that underpins the capitalist system.

  Thomas Hirschhorn

How Money Ruins, 2018
Cardboard, inkjet, coins, adhesive and metal
240 × 160 cm (94 ½ × 63 in.)

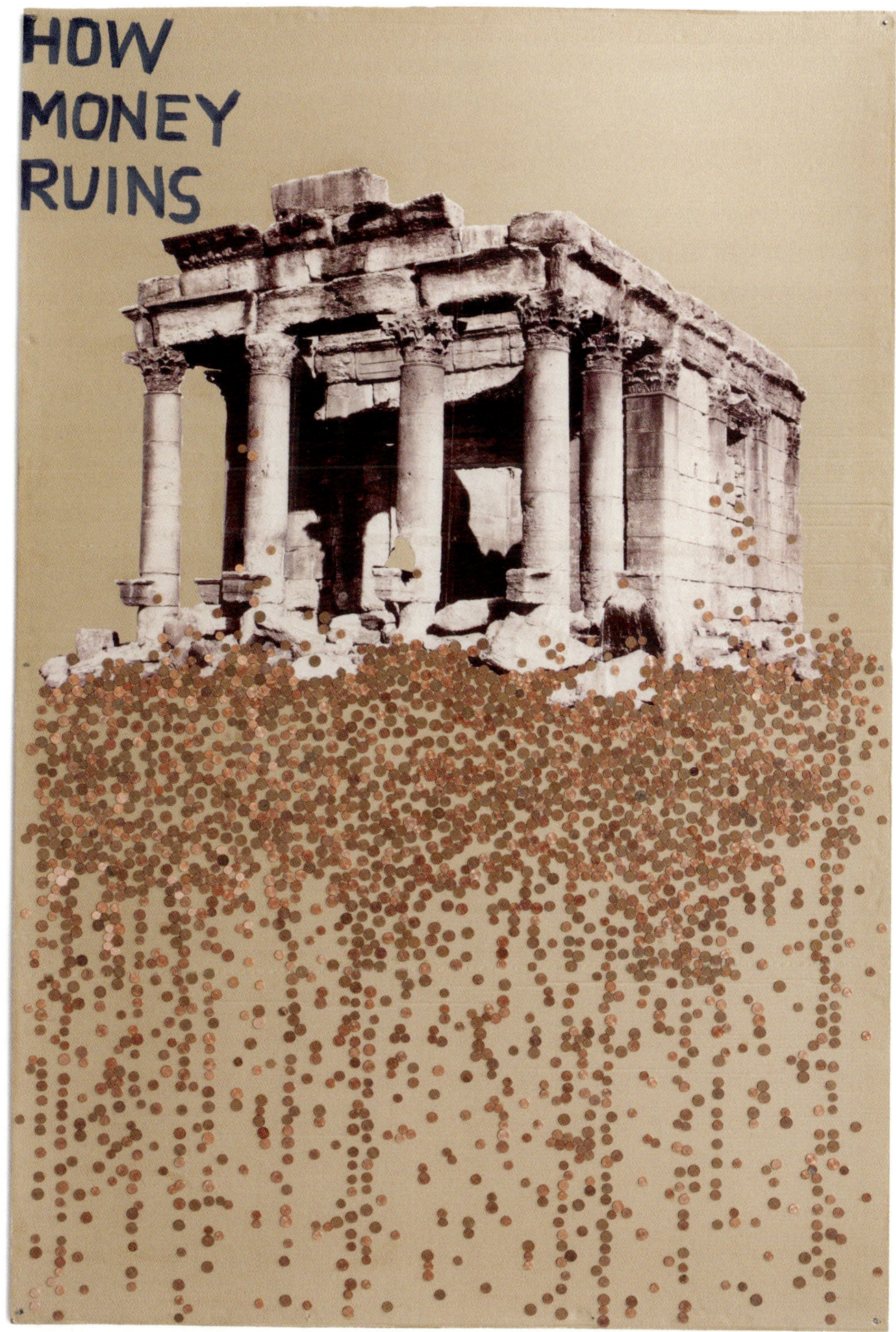
HOW
MONEY
RUINS

In a gloomy industrial building pierced by shafts of sunlight, multiple banks of networked computers are whirring away, bathed in a green electronic glow. What appears to be a traditional data centre is in fact a cryptocurrency farm, optimised for mining bitcoin. This image, taken by Greek-American photographer Christos J. Palios (b. 1979), belongs to his 'Absolute Powers / ex nihilo' series (2015–ongoing), in which an array of different objects — including gold dust, coinage, tulips and banknotes — are photographed to examine the slippery notion of value and the forms it has taken across time. The machines seen here, each of which is substantially more powerful than the average home computer, are stacked floor to ceiling in their thousands. They are running day and night to solve complex mathematical puzzles which, if successful, mints fresh bitcoins and adds a new block of transactions to the blockchain. The rewards of an operation like this can be high, but so too are the overheads because of the enormous amounts of electricity needed to run the specialist machinery (this particular company in Virginia Beach, US, filed for bankruptcy in 2019 after amassing more than $3 million in unpaid energy bills). Indeed, what isn't made visible by Palios's camera is the extreme heat alluded to in the work's title, a byproduct of the intense processing power. Analysts at Cambridge University have suggested that Bitcoin consumes more electricity annually than the whole of Argentina. This has attracted much criticism from those concerned with the negative environmental impacts of an otherwise intangible digital asset.

Hot Aisle, 2018, from the series
'Absolute Powers / ex nihilo', 2015–ongoing
Archival pigment limited-edition prints
Edition of 10: 53.3 × 76.2 (21 × 30 in.)
Edition of 8: 78.7 × 114.3 (31 × 45 in.)
Edition of 5: 101.6 × 147.3 (40 × 58 in.)
Edition of 4: 127 × 190.5 cm (50 × 75 in.)

     Christos J. Palios

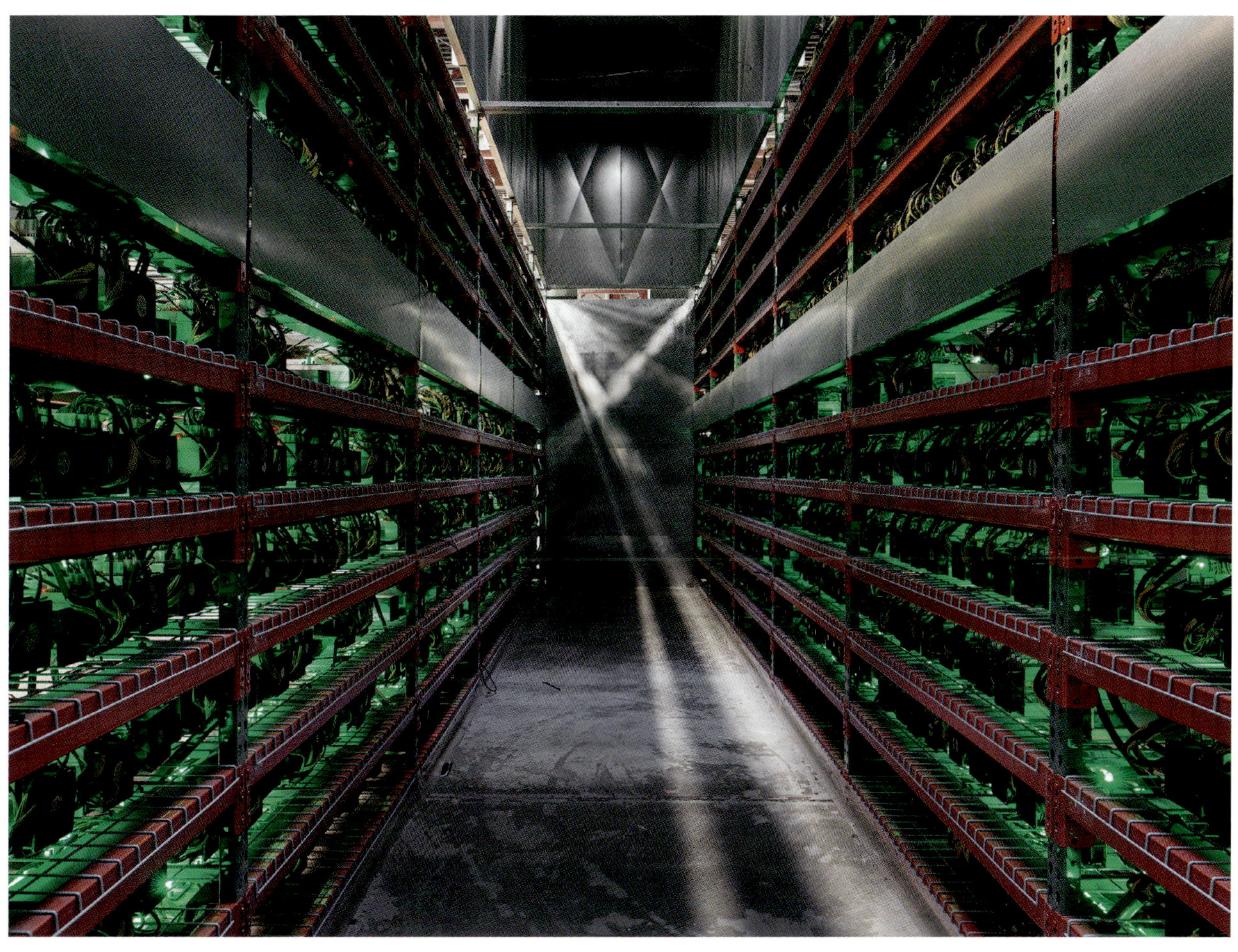

A band of spectral skeletons cavort around the passengers of a small but heavily-loaded rowing boat, alluding to the extreme risk involved in such journeys. British artist Hew Locke (b. 1959) painted the ghostly image onto a vintage loan certificate from 1924 relating to the 'Seven Per Cent Greek Government Refugee Loan', a total amount that exceeded £12 million, which was intended to help the semi-bankrupt Greek state support the settlement of hundreds of thousands of refugees, who arrived after the Greco-Turkish war (1919–22). The loan, backed by European and American banks, prevented Greece from descending into further economic chaos while allowing Britain and the United States to establish commercial interests in the region. Locke typically combines historic sources with contemporary political concerns across his multi-layered works, reflecting on how the past resonates in the present. When making this piece, Greece was recovering from a sovereign debt crisis sparked by the global financial crisis of 2007–8 and was again struggling to cope with an influx of refugees, with many travelling across the Mediterranean sea to escape conflicts in Syria and Afghanistan. Alluding to repeating cycles of conflict, debt and forced displacement, Locke's work is a poignant reminder that many continue to risk it all by piling into rickety boats in search of a better life.

     Hew Locke

Greek Government Refugee Loan 1924 II, 2019
Acrylic on antique paper share certificate
47 × 53.5 cm (18½ × 21 in.)

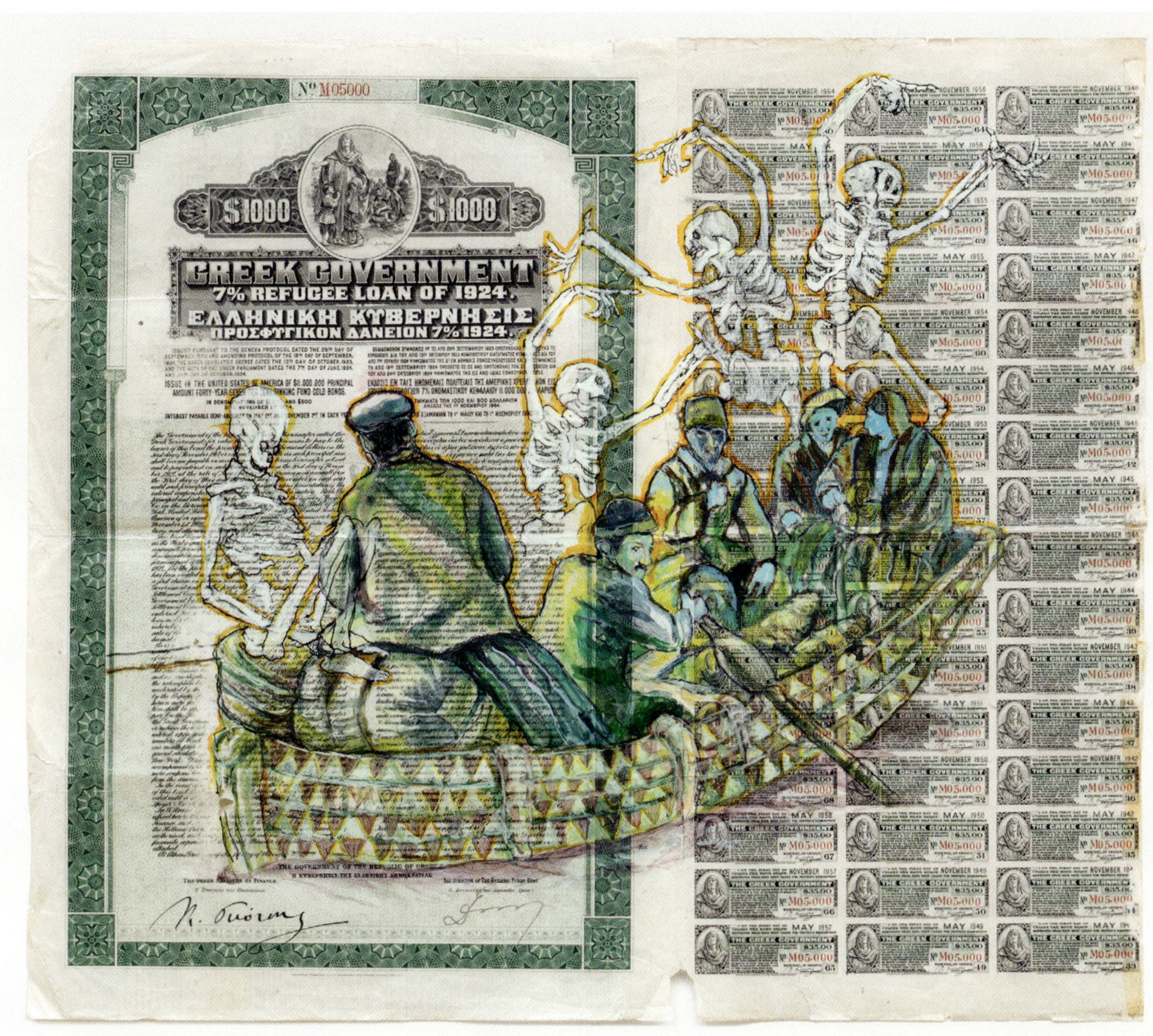

Nº M05000
$1000 $1000
GREEK GOVERNMENT
7% REFUGEE LOAN OF 1924.
ΕΛΛΗΝΙΚΗ ΚΥΒΕΡΝΗΣΙΣ
ΠΡΟΣΦΥΓΙΚΟΝ ΔΑΝΕΙΟΝ 7% 1924.

By subverting the iconic design of the American Express green card with imagery relating to the abolition of the transatlantic slave trade, Hank Willis Thomas (b. 1976) spotlights the role that slavery and racial exploitation played in the economic development of the United States between 1619 and 1808. In a wry allusion to the transportation of enslaved Africans across the Atlantic to the Americas, the card issuer's name has become 'Afro-American Express,' while the decorative border takes the form of shackled bodies from William Elford's infamous 1788 engraving of the slave ship Brooks, which epitomised the barbarity of transatlantic voyages. American Express's centurion logo is replaced by an 1860 image published in Harper's Weekly depicting the slave ship Wildfire crammed with illegal slaves (the 'Act Prohibiting the Importation of Slaves' took effect in the US in 1808), behind which is the iconic image of a kneeling black man in chains asking 'Am I Not a Man and a Brother?' popularised by Josiah Wedgwood's abolitionist medallion of 1787. Thomas describes the modern credit system as a form of indentured servitude that encourages the normalisation of debt and financial slavery. Indeed, when he made this and similar prints satirising the Discover and Chase brands, US credit card debt stood at $868 billion.

     Hank Willis Thomas

Amex, 2019
Digital c-print
73.7 × 111.8 cm (29 × 44 in.)

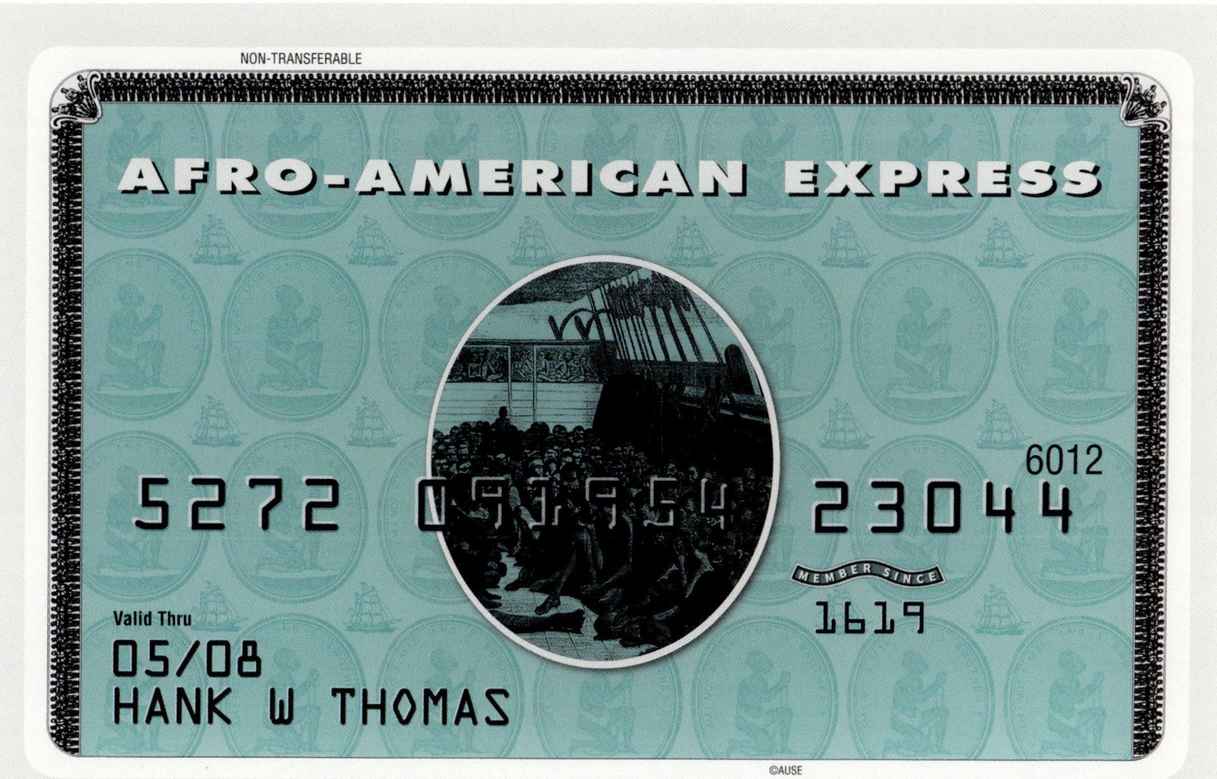
NON-TRANSFERABLE
AFRO-AMERICAN EXPRESS
5272 093954 23044
6012
MEMBER SINCE
1619
Valid Thru
05/08
HANK W THOMAS
©AUSE

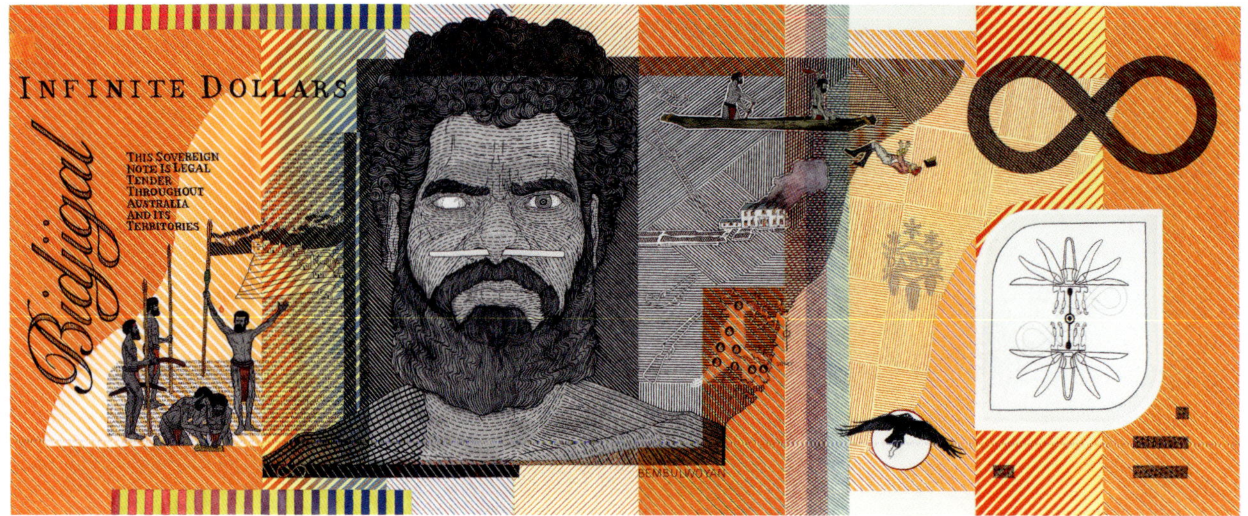

'Blood Money' is a series of watercolour paintings in which Australia's currency is reimagined with the country's Indigenous history at the fore. The expression refers to money obtained at the cost of another's life and in using it the Aboriginal artist Ryan Presley (b. 1987) highlights the violence and exploitation bchind Australia's great prosperity, which was built largely on the dispossession of the country's native inhabitants. Each of the paintings in his series depicts a different Aboriginal figure whose story offers an alternative to the myth that defiance to colonial encroachment was insignificant. This workfeatures the warrior Bembulwoyan (commonly known as Pemulwuy), a member of the Bidjigal clan who brought together Aboriginal people in a united twelve-year resistance campaign, vehemently defending their land and livelihoods from British colonists. Presley's bills contrast with the version of history represented on Australia's official currency, which primarily features white settler figures. In his designs, Presley replaces the word 'Australia' with the name of the Indigenous group represented and, as here, some replace the dollar sign with the infinity symbol to highlight the incalculable harm suffered by Aborigines at the hands of colonial settlers, the effects of which are still felt today.

Infinite Dollar Note – Bembulwoyan Commemorative, 2018, from the series 'Blood Money', 2018–ongoing
Watercolour on Arches paper
60.5 × 145.5 cm (23⅞ × 57¼ in.)
Museum of Contemporary Art, Australia

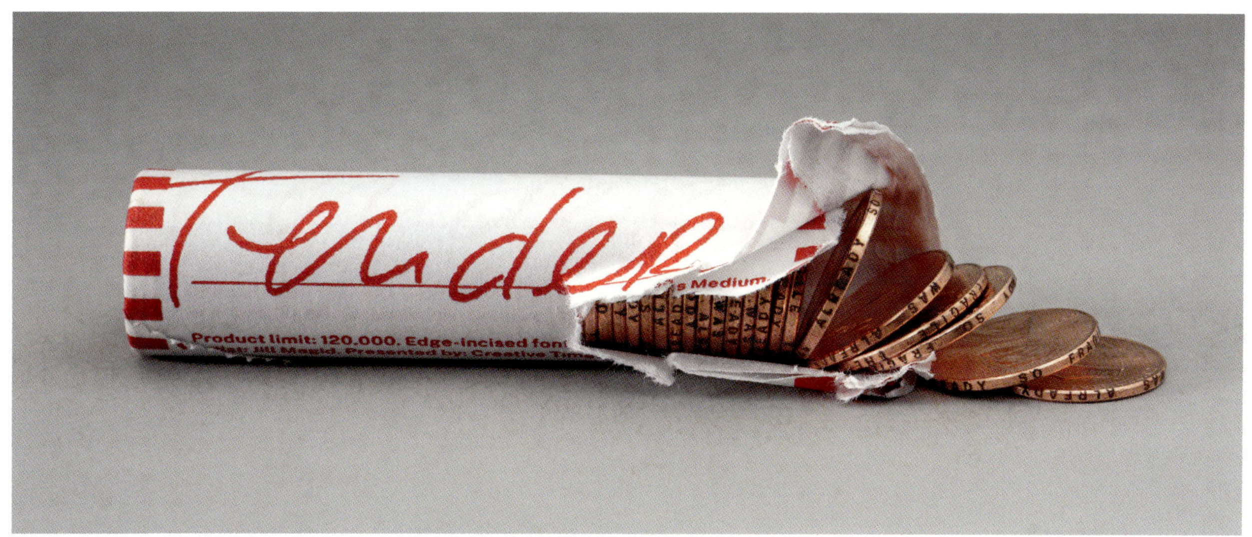

In March 2020, as COVID-19 was spreading globally, American artist Jill Magid (b. 1973) became troubled by US politicians' view of the crisis as a trade-off between saving lives and protecting economic interests. Her response was to infiltrate the economy with *Tender*, a substantial yet almost invisible public artwork comprising 120,000 newly-minted pennies with 'The Body Was Already So Fragile' engraved on their edges. The phrase speaks to medical and economic vulnerability, while drawing a parallel between the human body and the body politic. The value of the coins equated to the $1,200 stimulus payments issued to millions of citizens as part of the federal government's pandemic financial aid programme. While Magid sought the help of senior administrators at the US Mint to procure the coins, she did not disclose her intentions, ensuring that *Tender* remained an unofficial project, free from official oversight. Packaged in custom-designed wrappers with each roll of 50 bearing the name of the project in red, she introduced the coins into circulation via the small convenience stores (bodegas) found across New York's five boroughs, chosen for their ability to rapidly circulate coinage. Most were distributed by armoured cash-in-transit vehicles in autumn 2020, while some were used by Magid and others to make cash purchases at the stores. As the money was used and exchanged, passing from person to person, it echoed the virus' transmission. Magid, whose conceptual art interrogates structures of power and authority, describes *Tender* as a 'dispersed monument'. It is expected to stay circulating in the public realm for 40 years.

Tender, 2020
120,000 newly-minted,
edge-engraved pennies

In the 'Weaving Myths and Realities' series Pakistani artist Abdullah M. I. Syed (b.1974) splices and fuses together uncirculated banknotes from different countries to form hybrid currencies. Through an exacting process of cutting, collaging and weaving, he explores the interrelationship of capital, politics and nationhood, creating ambiguous narratives that mingle national mythologies and geopolitical realities. In the first of these two works, which uses a grid format to combine Pakistani and Indian 50-rupee notes, the majestic Karakoram Peak (K2) in the Himalayas intertwines with the Old Parliament House in New Delhi, a colonial-era building that served as the seat of India's government until 2023. Below, blending 500-rupee notes from the same countries, the iconic Mughal-era Badshahi Mosque in Lahore is interlaced with the Gyarah Murti, a monument in New Delhi commemorating the country's struggle for independence under the leadership of Mahatma Gandhi. Teasing out connections between politics and economics, these amalgamated notes allude to the fierce tensions between the two countries. Another in the series uses notes from China and the US, enmeshing the United States Capitol in Washington, D.C. and the Great Hall of People in Beijing. Syed additionally drew inspiration from the wormhole theory developed by physicists Albert Einstein and Nathan Rosen, which hypothesises that theoretical passages through the fabric of space-time could create shortcuts between distant regions of the universe. The artist's banknotes are thus speculative structures, linking not just opposing political values but disparate geographies and time zones. As an artist born in Pakistan and now living and working between Sydney, Karachi and New York, they also reflect on his own displacement and cross-cultural experience.

Weaving Myths and Realities: 500 Pakistani Rupee and 500 Indian Rupee (Structures, Verso) and *Weaving Myths and Realities: 50 Pakistani Rupee and 50 Indian Rupee (Structures, Verso)*, both 2020
Hand-cut and woven uncirculated 500 Pakistani Rupee and 500 Indian Rupee and archival tape
7.3 × 16.6 cm (2⅞ × 6½ in.) and 7.3 × 14.7 cm (2⅞ × 5¾ in.)

     Abdullah M. I. Syed

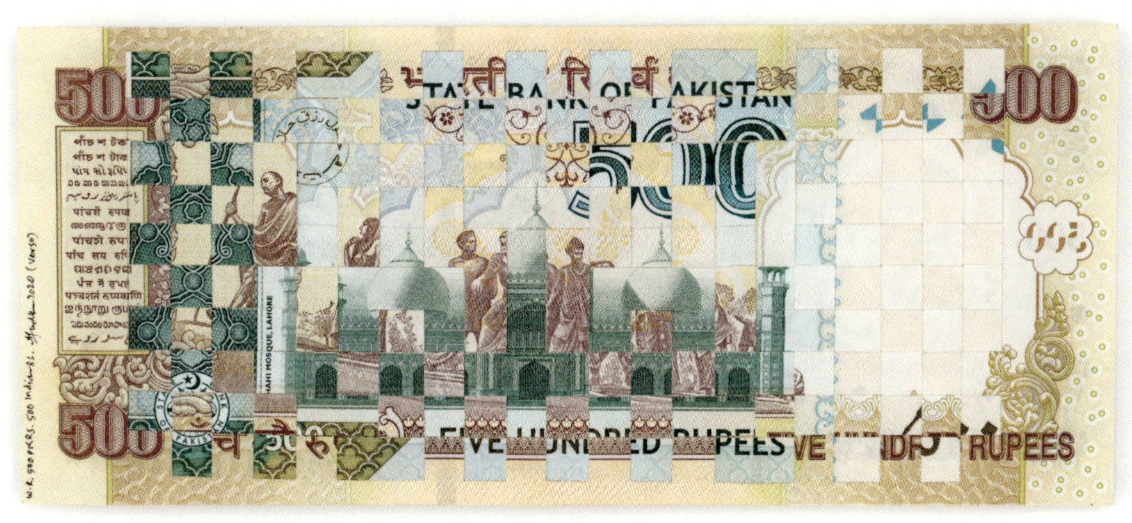

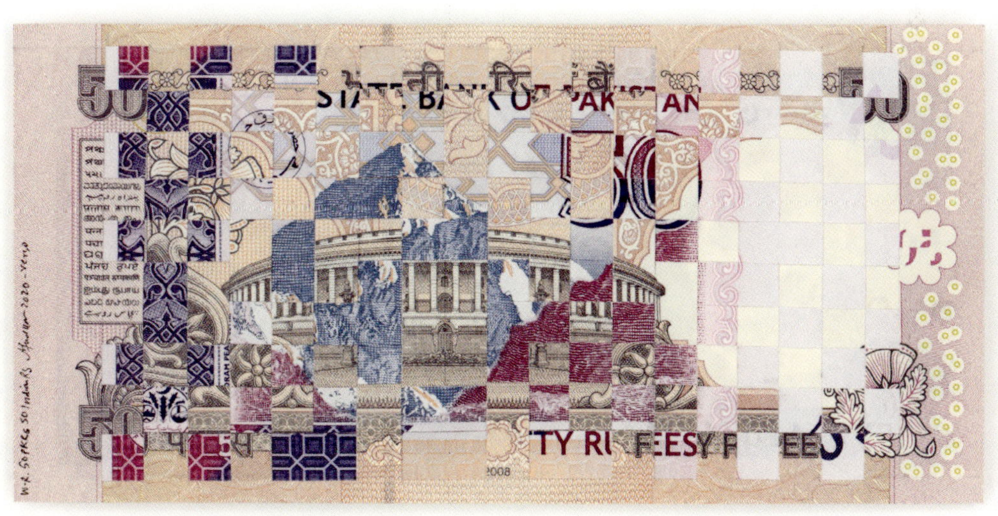

To the casual eye this dress appears to be constructed from multiple banknotes stitched together. In fact, American artist Liz Glynn (b. 1981) did not use real money but fabric printed with a pattern based on the reverse of a German 100-Papiermark note, a short-lived currency created by the central Reichsbank at the outbreak of the First World War in 1914. The Papiermark was demonetised after a period of rampant hyperinfla-tion in the Weimar Republic between 1921 and 1923, and replaced by the temporary Rentenmark before the Reichsmark came into use from 1924 until the fall of Nazi Germany in 1945. While Glynn's work references a specific moment in history when a particular currency was worth so little that it had greater value for its material properties than its financial power, it also recalls the practice of concealing money in clothing by sewing it into hems and other inconspicuous places during times of great social upheaval. Created in 2020, when the world was grappling to understand the COVID-19 pandemic (the most serious global crisis since the Second World War) *Panic Dress '23* resonates with the anxiety that people felt about the economic impact that the virus would have, which in many instances led to seemingly irrational behaviours such as panic buying and the stockpiling of food, toilet paper, pharmaceuticals and other goods in order to engender a sense of security.

Panic Dress '23, 2020
Silkscreen on muslin, Aqua Resin, acrylic,
fibreglass and steel
147.3 × 62.2 × 52 cm (58 × 24½ × 20½ in.)

    Liz Glynn

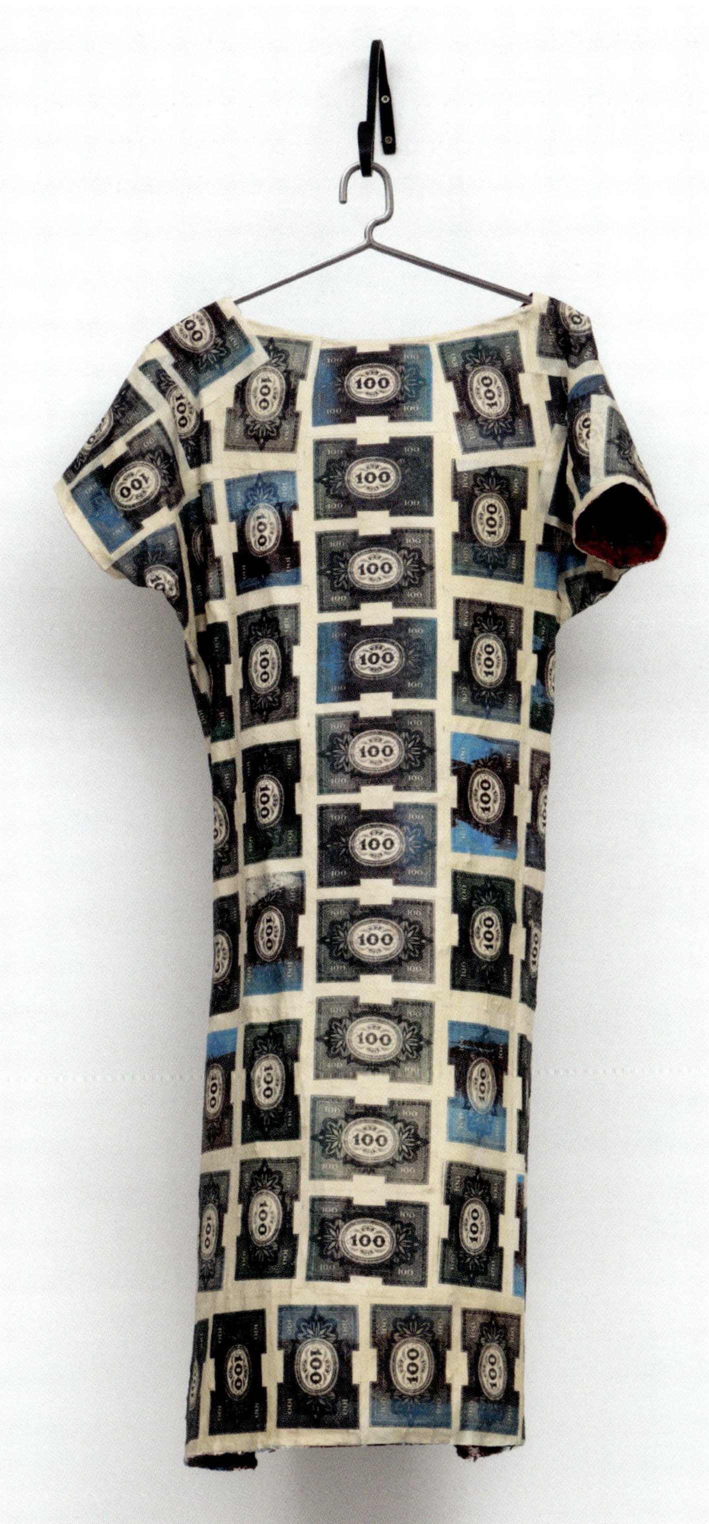

In the winter of 2020, the Danish artist Jens Haaning (b. 1965) was commissioned by the Kunsten Museum of Modern Art in Aalborg, Denmark, to recreate two of his earlier artworks for an upcoming exhibition entitled 'Work it Out' about the future of employment. In the pieces — *An Average Danish Annual Income* (2010) and *An Average Austrian Annual Income* (2007) — large amounts of cash were arranged in grids and displayed in frames as a physical representation of the respective salaries. The museum loaned Haaning 534,000 Danish kroner but, two days before the exhibition was due to open, the artist delivered a pair of seemingly empty frames, with backing boards that appeared as though previously-attached banknotes had been hurriedly removed, leaving behind scraps of torn paper and glue residue across their surfaces. Haaning stated he had instead created a new work: *Take the Money and Run*. Although the artist's contract included a fee and reimbursement for expenses, Haaning claimed that remaking his older works would result in him suffering a loss. The new piece, he said, was a statement about the working conditions of artists, tapping into a broader debate relating to deficient employment contracts, low fees and lack of financial support in the Danish art sector. 'It's not theft', he told Danish radio. 'It is breach of contract, and breach of contract is part of the work'. The museum put the new artwork on display, but when Haaning declined to return the money, it took legal action, and in 2023 a court in Copenhagen ordered him to pay back 492,549 kroner, representing the sum of money originally loaned minus a fee for his participation in the exhibition.

 Jens Haaning

Take the Money and Run (detail), 2021
Framed paperwork
173 × 334 cm (68⅛ × 131½ in.) and
not pictured: 92 × 112 cm (36¼ × 44⅛ in.)
installation view, 'Work It Out', Kunsten
Museum of Modern Art, Aalborg, Denmark

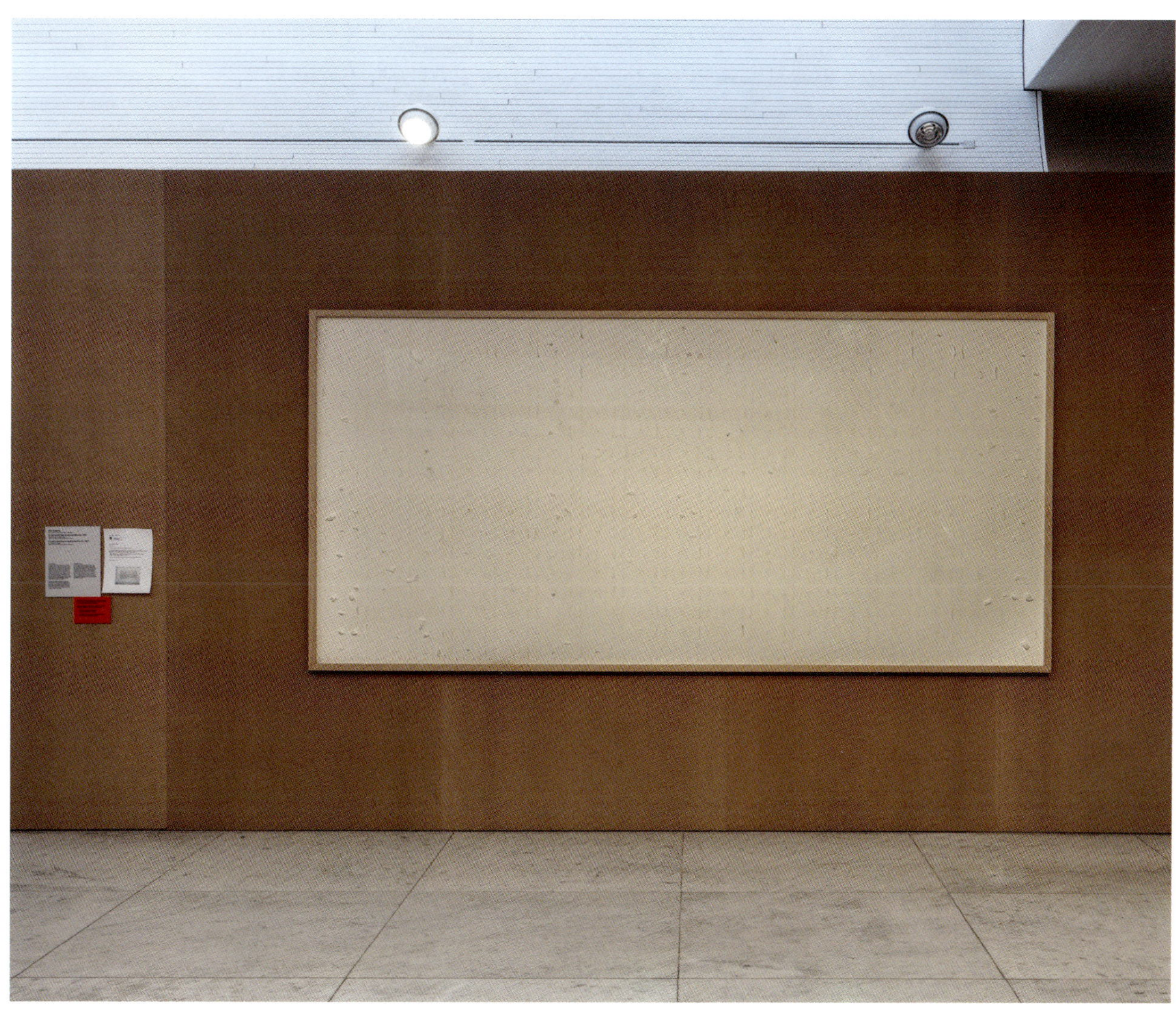

The term 'Bitcoin' was first introduced to the world in a 2008 white paper entitled 'Bitcoin: A Peer-to-Peer Electronic Cash System' that was posted to an obscure cryptography mailing list by a person or group of people using the pseudonym Satoshi Nakamoto. The document laid out the concept and technical details of an entirely new kind of money, a digital currency that was decentralised, secured by cryptography and that operated outside the control of governments and banks. Nakamoto's innovation was revealed 60 years after the term 'bit' was first used in the field of computing. This term, a contraction of 'binary digit', represents the smallest unit of data that a computer can process and is represented by a single binary value, usually a 0 or 1. In the English language, 'bit' is also the past tense of the verb 'to bite' and it is this homonym that British artist and designer Lucie Davis (b.1993) playfully riffs on in *Bit Coin*, where cartoonish bite marks have been hand-carved in 50 one-euro coins. Looking as if they have been chomped on like biscuits, the final ten of Davis's humorous coins were minted as carbon neutral NFTs in which each one rotates slowly to show both faces. (The image shown here is the Italian euro featuring Leonardo da Vinci's *Vitruvian Man*). The price of each NFT was calculated at one tenth of a Bitcoin at the moment it was minted, linking the whole edition to the wider economy of cryptocurrency.

     Lucie Davis

Bit Coin (physical and digital NFT), 2021/2022
Hand-carved 'bite mark' into a physical one euro
coin / digital animation of rotating 'Bit coin'
2.3 × 2 × 0.2 cm (⅞ × ¾ × ⅛ in.) / video MP4

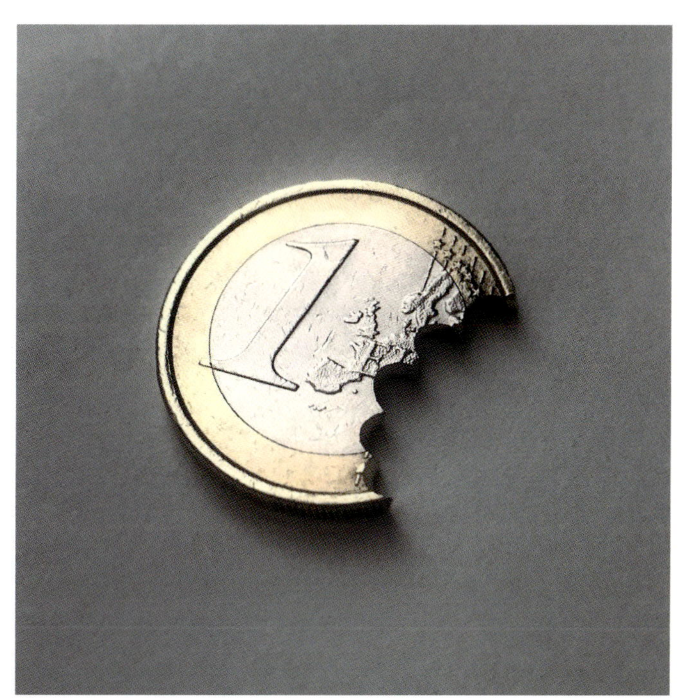

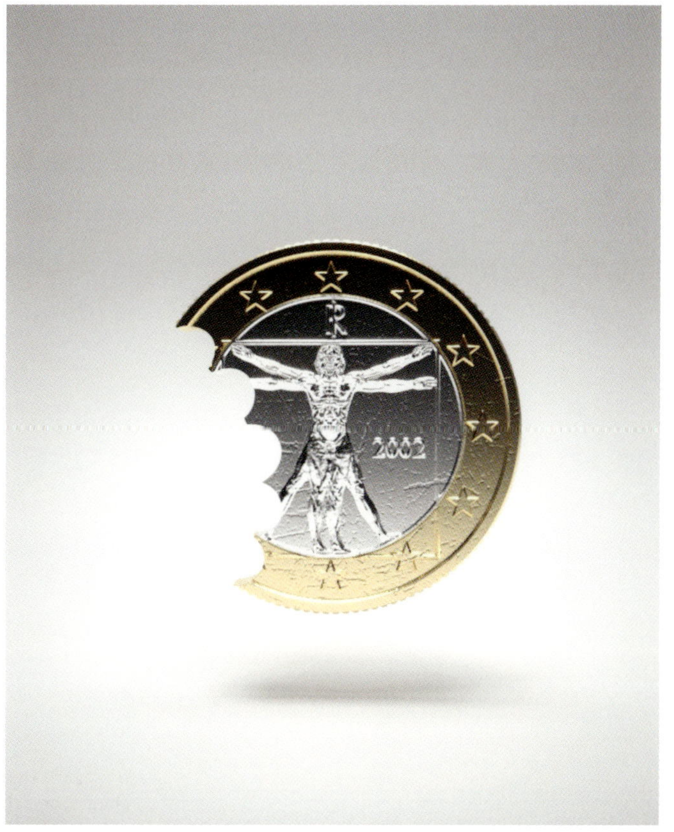

Colourful banknotes from the world's wealthiest countries are cut into letterforms and neatly arranged into repeating variations of the ominous phrase 'I WILL DIE'. Emphasising the value of this material, each letter is held in place by gold pins and the whole work is presented in a gilded frame of the purest gold leaf. At once a prognostication regarding the future of physical forms of money and a statement about human mortality, it is one of many works by Spanish artist Carlos Aires (b. 1974) that manipulate legal tender to interrogate the function of money in contemporary society. Aires's videos, installations, collages and objects start from his belief that money runs the world and causes many of humanity's problems. His 'Disasters' series (2014) is a set of banknotes featuring mass-media images relating to calamities and unrest in each bill's country of origin, while in *I Only Have Eyes For You* (2023), eyes isolated from banknote portraits are printed onto porcelain dinner plates to suggest the pervasive influence of money in daily life. For Aires, capitalism is a failing system that brings more pain than it alleviates. *I will die* is a poignant reminder that no matter how much wealth we accumulate, none can be taken to the grave.

I will die, 2022
Original banknotes (Legal tender currency) from the 30 richest countries in the world (based on the GDP), golden pins, cardboard and walnut pine wooden frame with stucco, 24 karat polished gold leaf and anti-reflective museum glass
153 × 186 × 10 cm (60¼ × 73¼ × 3⅞ in.)

     Carlos Aires

I WILL DIE, I WILL DIE, YOU WILL DIE, WE WILL DIE, YOU WILL DIE, I WILL DIE, SHE WILL DIE, I WILL DIE, WE WILL DIE, I WILL DIE, I WILL DIE, WE WILL DIE, YOU WILL DIE, I WILL DIE, I WILL DIE, I WILL DIE, I WILL DIE, YOU WILL DIE, I WILL DIE, THEY WILL DIE, I WILL DIE, SHE WILL DIE, I WILL DIE, WE WILL DIE, I WILL DIE, I WILL DIE, THEY WILL DIE, YOU WILL DIE, I WILL DIE, I WILL DIE, WE WILL DIE, I WILL DIE, SHE WILL DIE, I WILL DIE, THEY WILL DIE, I WILL DIE, SHE WILL DIE, I WILL DIE, I WILL DIE, I WILL DIE, I WILL DIE, YOU WILL DIE, YOU WILL DIE, I WILL DIE, I WILL DIE.

In late 2020, the subversive American art collective MSCHF (founded 2016) listed a product in its web store that appeared to be a stack of US 20-dollar bills. The image was blurred, as though its true nature would only be revealed to the customer upon purchase. In fact, it turned out to be exactly as it looked online: a three-dimensional solid object resembling a pile of blurry banknotes. Despite being out of focus, its printed imagery remains entirely recognisable. MSCHF have since added several variations to the 'Blur' series, including Japanese yen, Australian dollars and, as here, US one hundred-dollar bills. Each listing is accompanied by a product description stating 'all money, from its inception, has been an exercise in trust; a communal suspension of disbelief', pointing to the human tendency to ascribe value to intrinsically functionless objects — including the sheets of paper we call money. Since 2016, the Brooklyn-based artists have created an array of mischievous products critiquing consumer culture and revealing the absurdities of late capitalism. They have sold paintings of people's medical bills and used the profits to pay off the debts and created 'Birkinstock' sandals from destroyed designer 'Birkin bags'. The collective has also tackled the subject of wealth in relation to the art world, installing a functional cash machine at the Art Basel Miami art fair in 2022. The installation displayed the bank balance of anyone who inserted their card, creating a leader board that ranked participants from the wealthiest — $9.5m being the highest amount — to those with considerably less.

     MSCHF

BLUR $100 USD, 2022
Resin, rubber and acrylic
6.4 × 15.7 × 4.4 cm (2 ½ × 6⅛ × 1¾ in.)

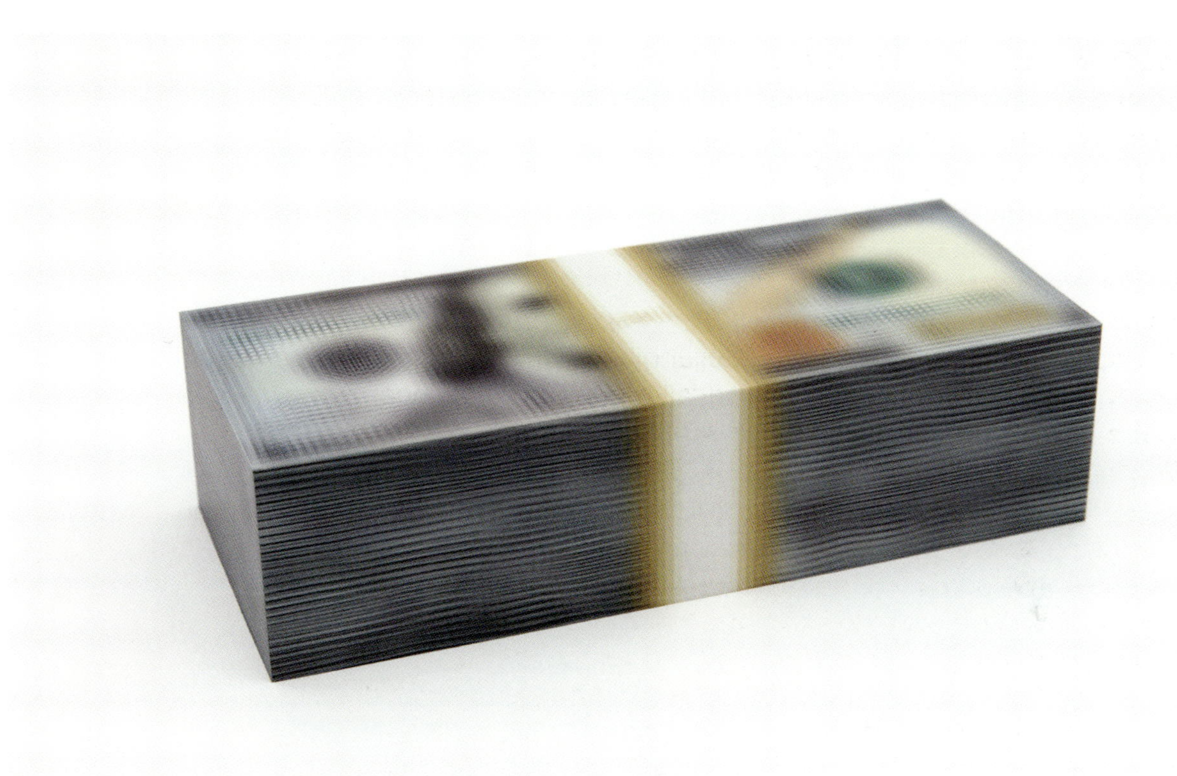

This sculpture reimagines the personal credit card of Mexican artist Gabriel Kuri (b.1970), whose conceptually-driven works in diverse media frequently address themes of finance, consumption and value. Here, the familiar design — in this case of the brand Mastercard, as revealed by the overlapping red and yellow circles — is fragmented, enlarged and reconfigured to suggest the precarious nature of the financial credit system. Plastic payment cards connect their users to a world of desire and fulfilment, allowing people to access funds even when their bank accounts are dwindling. They also, however, contain the risk of falling into problem debt if full repayment cannot be achieved, and many have historically charged notoriously high rates of interest. Such tensions are reflected in this work by the presence of padding blankets that appear to be swallowing an oversized credit card, at once pointing to the comfort and risk associated with using them. Above these, the card's shape is replicated by a sheet of stainless steel with curved corners that is disrupted by a sharp kink in its middle. At one end, an enlarged replica of the gold smart chip used to securely manage transactions is embedded in a clump of black concrete. Through the juxtaposition of materials with opposing properties — hard and soft, flexible and rigid, smooth and rough — Kuri gives form to the complex and contradictory nature of credit, which despite functioning as a means of empowerment remains a type of debt with the potential for dispossession.

card eating tongue, 2022
Stainless steel, padding blankets, composite concrete and vacuum formed plastic
22.5 × 90 × 181 cm (8 ⅞ × 35 ⅜ × 71 ¼ in.)
Installation view, 'motion in acceptance of an impending crash', Sadie Coles HQ, Bury St, London, 11 March — 23 April 2022

     Gabriel Kuri

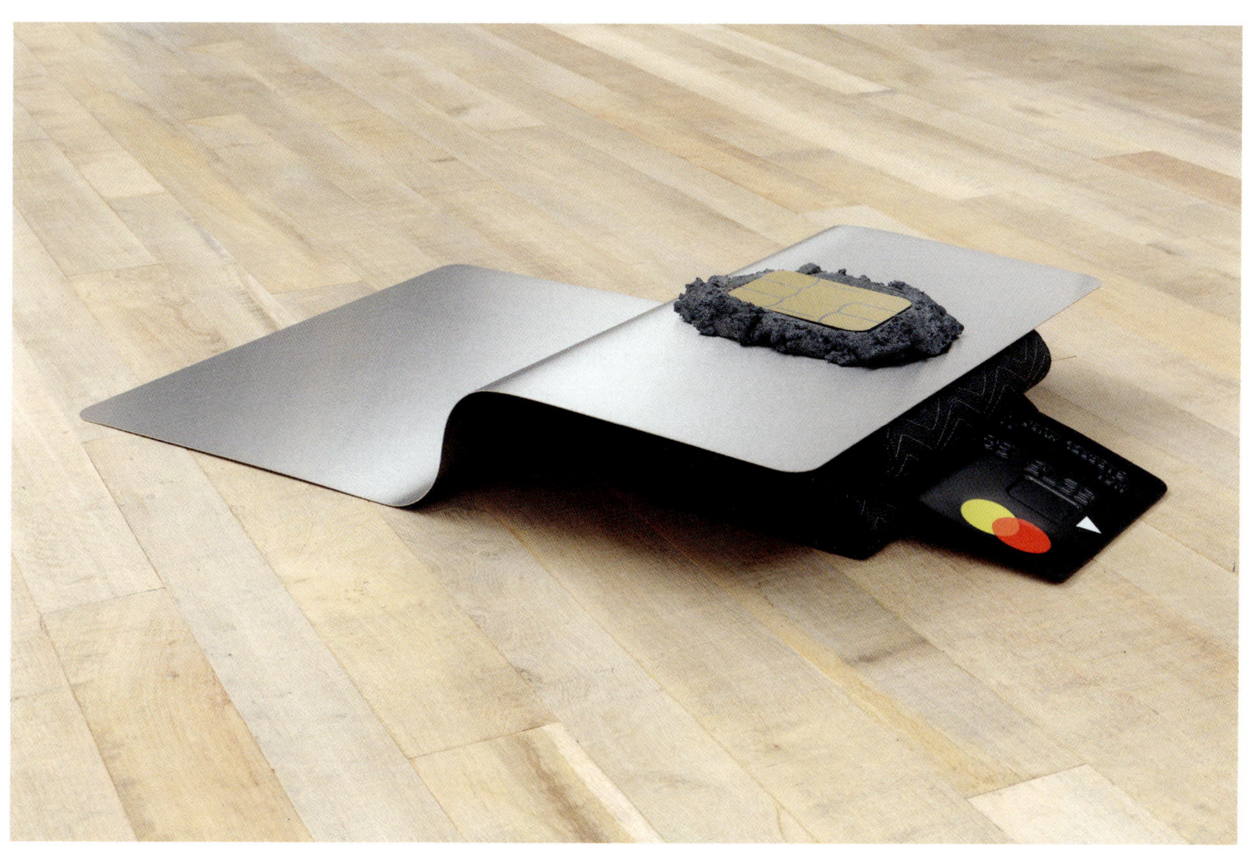

On 14 July 2021, Damien Hirst (b. 1965) in collaboration with HENI released *The Currency*, a collection of 10,000 digital NFTs that corresponded to 10,000 physical paintings comprising brightly coloured daubs of enamel paint arranged in busy patterns on handmade paper. As with all of Hirst's 'Spot Paintings', no colour is repeated twice and each piece, despite looking extremely similar, is totally unique. As an experiment in belief and speculation, *The Currency* forced each participant to confront their own perception of value. Buyers paying $2,000 had one year to decide whether they would exchange their NFT for the physical artwork or keep its digital on-chain representation. A total of 4,851 people decided to keep the digital artwork with the remaining 5,149 opting for the physical. The unwanted paper artworks were burnt in a furnace at Hirst's Newport Street Gallery in October 2022, while the superfluous electronic tokens were destroyed by digital burning, a process that involves sending them to an address on the blockchain that no one has access to. In this way, the artist ensured that each piece exists exclusively in either the digital or the physical realm, and while their status as unique artworks was not lost, only time will reveal which asset represents the better investment and whether owners will hold or sell.

8483. *May I stay like this?*, 2021
Enamel paint on handmade paper,
a unique variant from a series of 5,149
21 × 29.7 cm (8¼ × 11¾ in.)
Private collection

Detail of *The Currency* artworks, 2021

Currency Burn, Newport Street Gallery,
London, 11 October 2022

   Damien Hirst

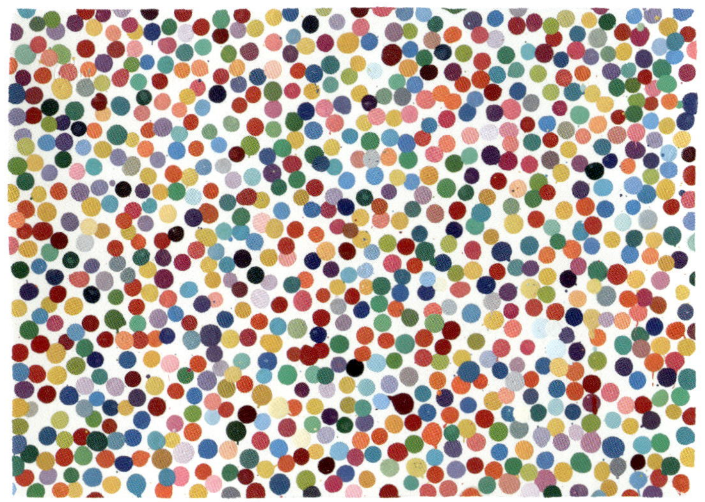

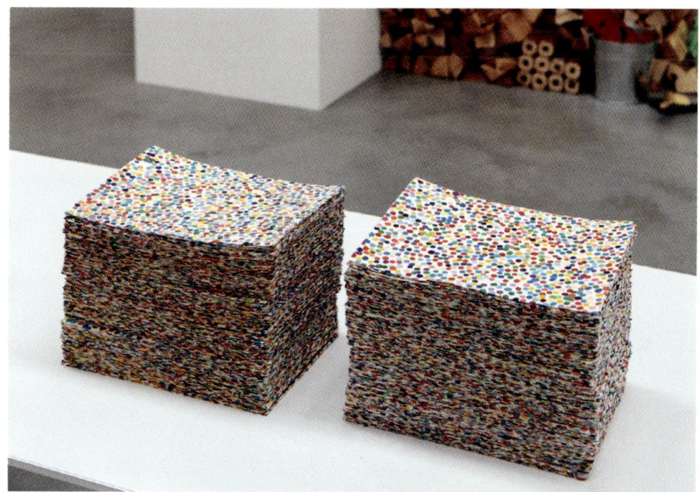

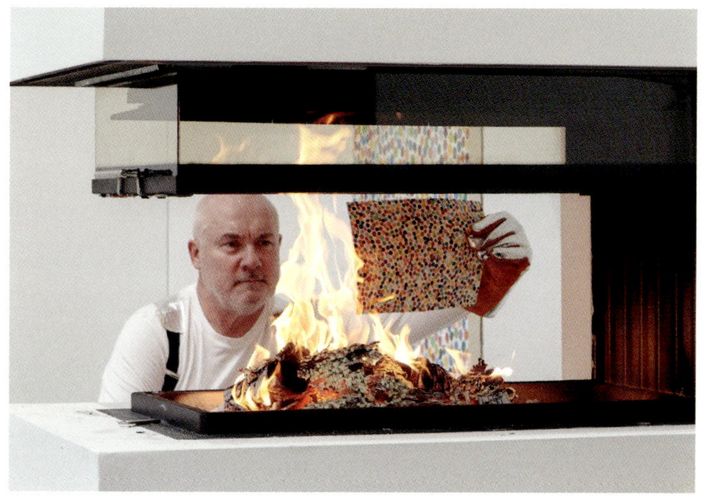

This sparkling, mosaic-like wall relief by Ghanaian artist Yaw Owusu (b.1992) comprises hundreds of pesewa coins (Ghana's smallest denomination coin) juxtaposed with strips of steel, canvas fabric and wood in a dynamic interplay of colour, texture and pattern. With its abstract geometric forms evoking kente — a traditional Ghanaian woven cloth famed for its bright colours and intricate repeating patterns — the work points to the interconnected histories of trade, exchange and capital across the African continent. The Ghanaian pesewa was first introduced in 2007 as part of an attempt to cure the country's rampant inflation. Today, they are virtually worthless and, though still legal tender, are not accepted by most traders. After extensive negotiations with the Central Bank of Ghana, Owusu was able to acquire thousands of the coins to use in his work. Utilising water, vinegar, salt and other substances, Owusu submits the copper coated steel coinage to various chemical processes, which produces a wide range of different patinas. The variegated pennies are then carefully arranged onto metal sheets or wood panels, always face down so that the national coat of arms remains visible. Upon researching the history of his material, Owusu was shocked to learn that the coins are not minted in Ghana but in Canada by the Royal Canadian Mint (a former outpost of the Royal Mint of Britain, Ghana's former colonial rulers). As with Owusu's other works, *The Glories of our Past* is a testimony to the economic challenges facing post-colonial African countries because of global capitalism and the enduring legacies of colonialism.

The Glories of our Past, 2023
Ghanaian pesewas, steel, canvas and wood
168 × 158 × 9.5 cm (66⅛ × 62¼ × 3¾ in.)

     Yaw Owusu

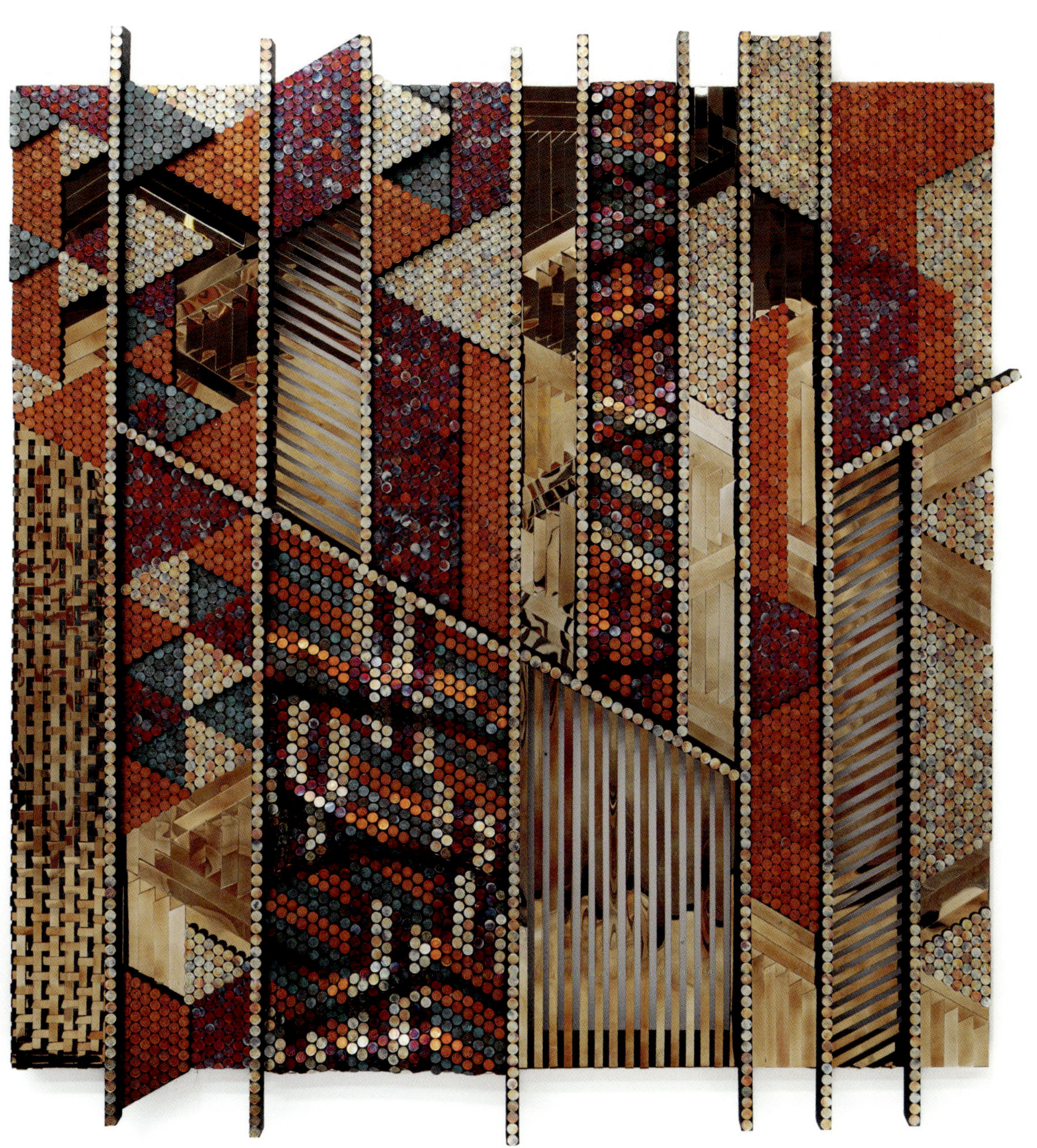

In this immersive collaged painting by Mandy El-Sayegh (b. 1985), Venezuelan and English banknotes appear alongside screenprinted-fragments of US dollar bills, erotic imagery from the pages of Penthouse magazine, and assorted gestural marks. Covering its surface is a hand-painted grid, that brings a sense of order and unity to the chaotic composition while simultaneously acting as a barrier that frustrates the viewer's reading of the imagery. The intricate work is part of the Malaysian-born, London-based artist's ongoing series 'Net-Grid', in which painting, drawing, screenprinting and accumulations of printed ephemera (often including scraps of recognisably pink newsprint from the *Financial Times*) are combined to interrogate the prevalent circulation of information and images in society, as well as the structures that contain them. In view here is the complex relationship between money and sex; the pornographic material speaks to the objectification of the female body, while the Venezuelan bolívar fuerte notes — worthless today because of hyperinflation — are a spectre of economic instability. In 2014, political and financial unrest saw the South American country's inflation rate reach sixty-nine per cent: the highest in the world. Continuing to increase, it reached two million per cent in 2018. The ensuing social problems have included an increase in sex trafficking, with women and girls from the poorest communities being subjected to exploitation around the world. While the complex interrelations of sexuality and commerce are alluded to in this work, El-Sayegh is never overly prescriptive. Welcoming the construction of new narratives, she provides space for viewers to form their own interpretations.

Net-Grid (Venezuelan thousands), 2023
Oil and acrylic on canvas with collaged
and silkscreened elements
235 × 225 cm (92 ½ × 88 ⅝ in.)

     Mandy El-Sayegh

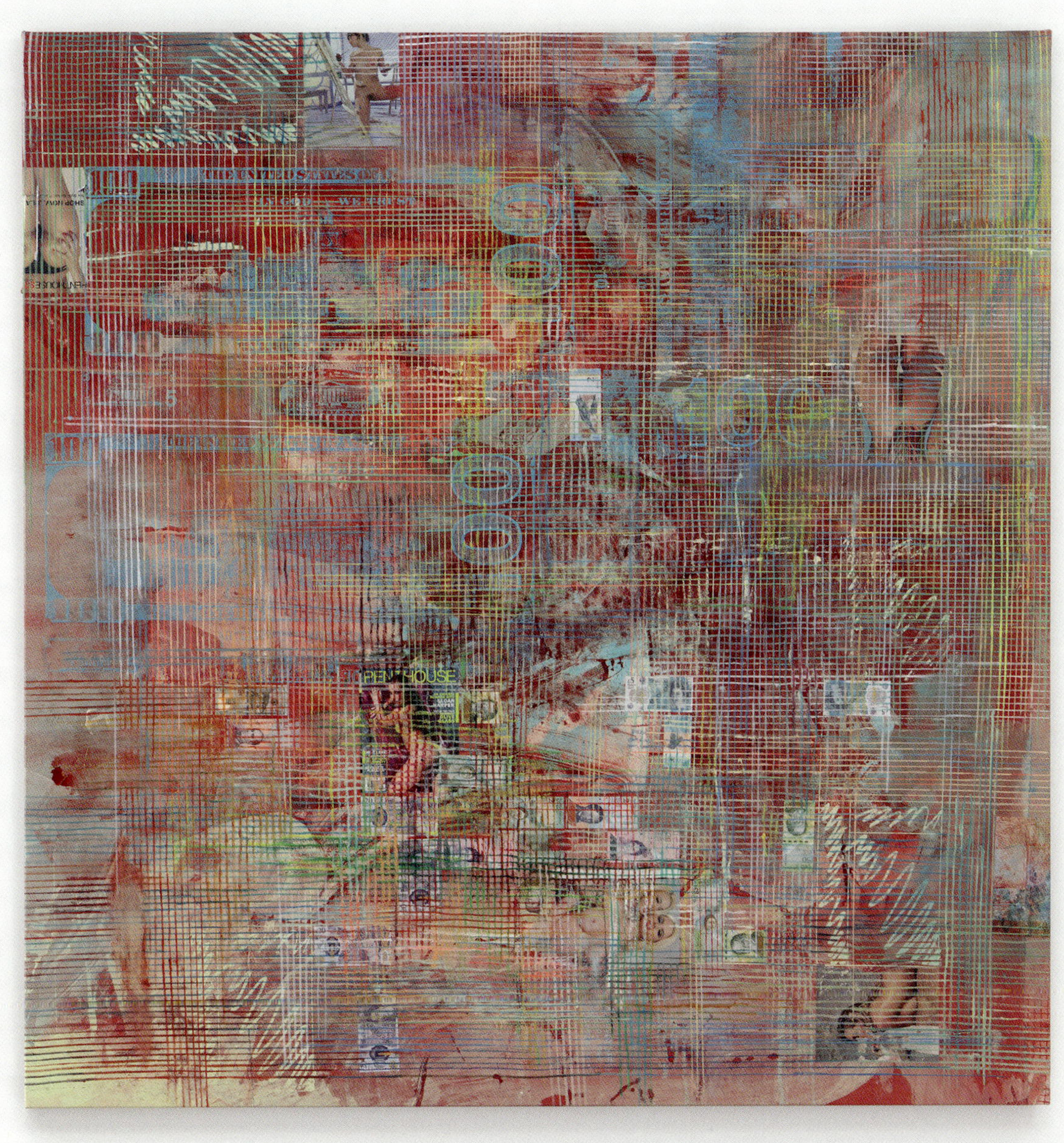

This forlorn and decrepit ATM (Automatic Teller Machine), situated on one of Liverpool's major party streets, has been the victim of sustained abuse and neglect. Covered in grime and graffiti, parts of the machine have been ripped away and it appears as if someone has even attempted to prise it from the wall. No wonder its electronic display reads 'sorry, out of service'. The sad specimen was photographed by British artist Leo Fitzmaurice (b. 1963) for his ongoing series 'The Way Things Appear'. In it, he documents striking or unusual urban sights that record and reveal aspects of contemporary life in the UK. That this cash machine has been allowed to fall into such a state of disrepair in an area packed with pubs, bars and restaurants, implies that the demand for physical money is not what it was. Indeed, as contactless cards and mobile payments have become commonplace, notes and coinage are increasingly perceived as an unnecessary encumbrance. This has led to a year-on-year decrease in ATMs in the UK, which will likely accelerate in the future. For those that still rely on cash transactions, many of them elderly, there is a risk that they will be excluded from participating in the economy. To that end, the UK government has legally protected 3,000 cash machines, within at least 1 km (0.62 miles) of each other, against closure. Nevertheless, as Fitzmaurice's photograph suggests, such technology, which revolutionised how money could be accessed when it was first introduced in 1967, may one day be consigned to history.

   Leo Fitzmaurice

Slater Street ATM, Nov 2023, 2023, from the series 'The Way Things Appear', 2011–ongoing
Digital photograph

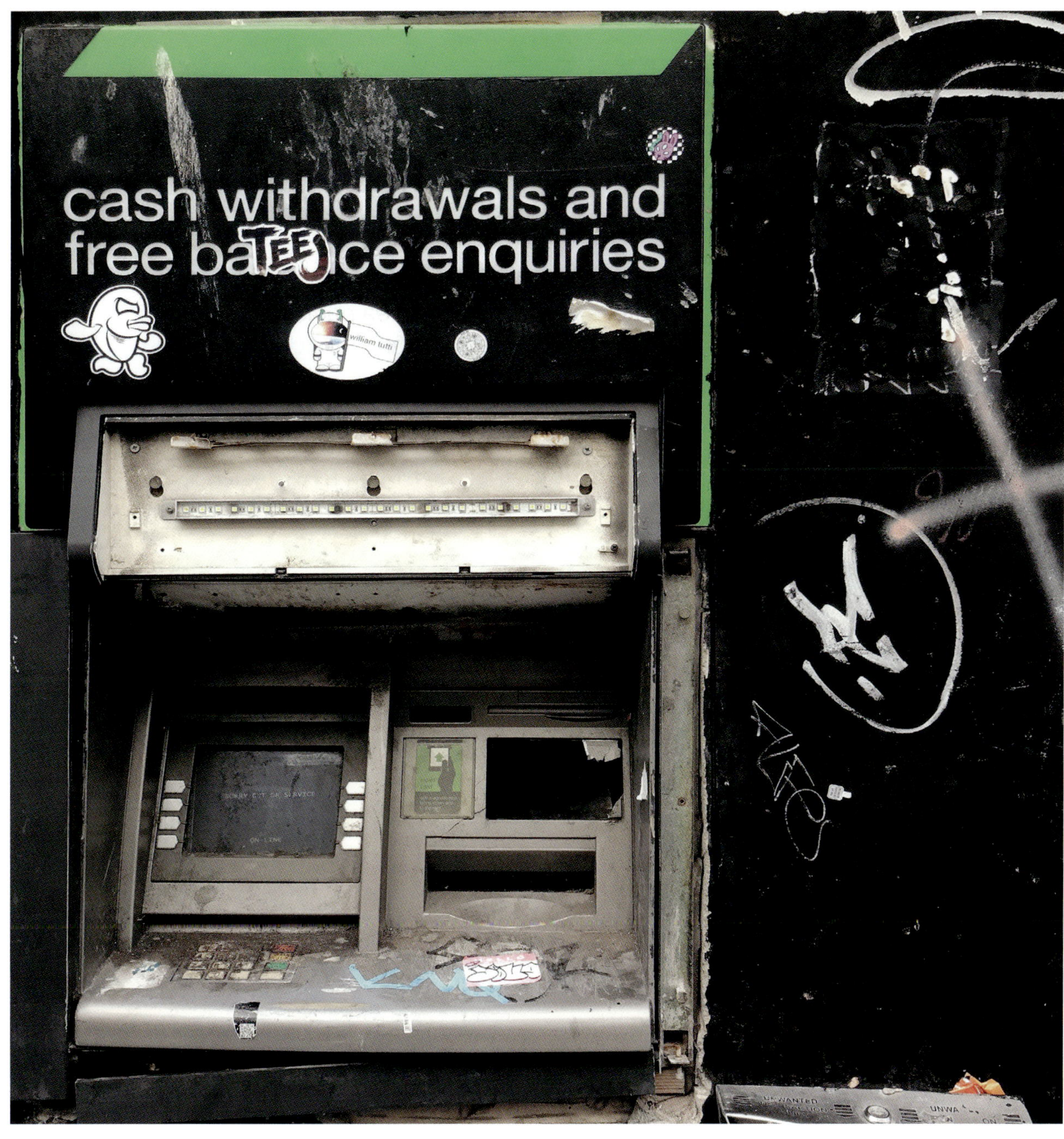
cash withdrawals and
free balance enquiries
william tutti

Communism 21, 76, 92
Conceptual art 88
Costa Rica 96
Counter Reformation 14
COVID-19 pandemic 22, 163, 166
Croatia 102
Crosby, Bing 8
cruzeiro, Brazilian 66, *67*
cryptocurrencies 23, 56, 136, 156, 170
Cuba 72, *73*, 74, 82, *83*, 149
Cytter, Keren, *Che Guevara (banknote)* 149, *149*

D
Dada 8, 20, 28, 36, 38
Daesh (Islamic State) 154
Danaë 8–10
Davis, Lucie, *Bit Coin* 170, *171*
de Andrade, Jonathas, *Voyeuristico* 152, *153*
Dean, Michael, *United Kingdom poverty line for two adults …* 144, *145*
Deller, Jeremy, *Brixton Pound* 132, *133*
denarius 13
Deng, Luol 132
Deng Xiaoping 92
Denmark 112, 168
Depeche Mode 150
d'Este, Alfonso I, Duke of Ferrara 13
deutsche mark, German 48, *48*, 81
Deutscher and Hackett 120
dime, US 124, *125*
dinar, Iraqi 86
Dine, Jim 28

dollars:
    Australian 120, *121*, 162, *162*, 174
    Taiwanese 134
    US 18–20, *18*, 22, 26–7, *26–7*, 30, *31*, 32, 36, *37*, 38, *39*, 42, 46, 50, *51*, 58, 72–6, *75*, 86, 96, 100, *101*, 104–8, *105*, *107*, *109*, 114, *114*, 128, *129*, 134, 140, *141* , 148–150, *148*, 174, *175*, 182
    Zimbabwean 122, 146, *147*
dong, Vietnamese 86
drachma, Greek 9, 102, *115*, 115
Drummond, Bill 60
Dubreuil, Victor 18, 19
    Money to Burn 19, *19*

E
Einstein, Albert 164
El-Sayegh, Mandy 182, *183*
    Net-Grid (Venezuelan thousands) 182
Elford, William 160
Elizabeth II, Queen 78, *79*, 96
Ethereum 136
euro 81, 98, *99*, 102, 112, *113*, 115, 130, *131*, 170, *171*
European Union (EU) 81, 102, 112

F
Federal Reserve (US) 46, 116, 140
Feigen (Richard L.) Gallery, Chicago 36
Feldmann, Hans-Peter, *The Hugo Boss Prize* 108, *109*
financial crisis (2007–8) 22, 70, 74, 104, *104*, 140, 142, 158

Financial Times 182
Fine, Jud 86
Finland 102
Finn-Kelcey, Rose, *Bureau de Change* 52, *53*
First World War 20, 166
Fitzmaurice, Leo: *Slater Street ATM* 184, *185*
    'The Way Things Appear' 184, *185*
Fluxus 27
Fonseca, Diana, *Pasatiempo (dinero)* 82, *83*
France 81, 102
francs:
    Communauté Financière Africaine (CFA) 146
    French 81, 102
Fraser Muggeridge studio, *Brixton Pound* 132, *133*
Friedman, Tom: *Untitled (Dollar Bill)* 114
    Untitled (Dollar Bill, Back) 114, *114*
Frieze Art Fair, London (2011) 110
Fust, Johann 34

G
Gaba, Meschac, *Bank or Economy: Inflation* 146, *147*
Galleria Schwarz, Milan 27
Gander, Ryan, *We never had a lot of € around here* 112, *113*
Gandhi, Mahatma 96, 164
Gentileschi, Artemisia, *Danaë* 9, *9*
Gentileschi, Orazio, *Danaë and the Shower of Gold* 9, *9*
Germany 48, 68, 81, 130, 166

PICTURE CREDITS

Every effort has been made to contact copyright holders. The publisher will be pleased to amend in future printings any errors or omissions brought to their attention.

p.8: RMN-Grand Palais / Hervè Lewandowski / RMN-GP / Dist. Foto SCALA, Florence. p.11, fig.7: Gift of The Print Club of Cleveland. p.11, fig.8: Harris Brisbane Dick Fund, 1926. p.14, fig.15: Gift of Andrew W. Johnson, Mrs. J. Russell Forgan, and Mrs. Bradford Shinkle in memory of Mrs. Jackson Johnson. p.18, fig.23: The Alex Simpson, Jr., Collection, 1943. p.19, fig.26: © the artist. Courtesy Private Collection. p.20: © ADAGP, Paris, and DACS, London 2024. p.21, fig.28: Kurt Schwitters Archive, Sprengel Museum Hannover. p.21, fig.19: The Vera and Arturo Schwarz Collection of Dada and Surrealist Art. p.22, fig.30: © The Heartfield Community of Heirs / DACS 2024. p.26: © Estate of Roy Lichtenstein / DACS 2024. p.27: Courtesy and © Robert Watts Estate, NY, 1962 / 2024. p.29: © The Estate of Claes Oldenburg. Image courtesy Specific Object / David Platzker, New York, 2023. p.31: © 2024 The Andy Warhol Foundation for the Visual Arts, Inc. / Licensed by DACS, London. Photo courtesy Sotheby's. p.33: © Morgan Art Foundation Ltd. / Artists Rights Society (ARS), New York, DACS, London 2024. p.35: © Genpei Akasegawa / Courtesy SCAI THE BATHHOUSE. p.37: © Ray Johnson Estate, New York. p.39: © ADAGP, Paris, and DACS, London, 2024. Photo courtesy Sotheby's. p.40: Courtesy Ateliê Cildo Meireles. p.41: Courtesy Hotwire Productions LLC. © Lynn Hershman Leeson. p.43: © Estate of Nancy Reddin Kienholz. Courtesy L.A. Louver, Venice, CA. p.45: © Chris Burden. Licensed by The Chris Burden Estate and DACS 2024. p.47: Courtesy BorzoGallery, Amsterdam. p.48: © DACS 2024. p.49: Courtesy the artist and Sprüth Magers. p.51: © Guerrilla Girls. Courtesy guerrillagirls.com. p.53: © the Estate of Rose Finn-Kelcey. Courtesy the Estate and Kate MacGarry. p.55: Courtesy Ann Hamilton Studio. Photo: Ben Blackwell. p.57: Archives of J.S.G. Boggs. Courtesy J.S.G. Boggs Art, LLC. p.59: Courtesy LEE Studio. p.61: © the artists. Courtesy L-13 Light Industrial Workshop. p.63: Courtesy the artist and Frith Street Gallery, London. Special thanks to the Royal Mint.

p.65: Courtesy Thaddaeus Ropac Gallery, London, Paris, Salzburg and Seoul. p.67: Courtesy the artist and Fortes D'Aloia & Gabriel, São Paulo/Rio de Janeiro. Photo: Eduardo Ortega. p.69: Courtesy the artist. p.71: Courtesy Lauren Greenfield / Institute. p.73: Courtesy the artist. p.75: Courtesy Annet Gelink Gallery, Amsterdam. p.77: Courtesy Yanagi Studio. p.79: Courtesy Live Stock Market Ltd & Gavin Turk. © the artist. p.80: Photo Germaine Koh p.81: Courtesy the artist. p.83: Courtesy Galeria Max Estrella. p.85: © ARS, NY and DACS, London 2024. Alessandra Pezzotta / Alamy Stock Photo. p.87: Courtesy the artists and Ronald Feldman Gallery, New York. p.89: Courtesy the artist and Peter Freeman, Inc. p.91: © Jonathan Horowitz. Courtesy the artist and Sadie Coles HQ, London. p.93: © Hong Hao. Courtesy Pace Gallery. p.95: Courtesy the artist and Galerie Neu, Berlin. p.97: Courtesy the artist. p.99: Courtesy the artist and Esther Schipper, Berlin, Paris and Seoul. p.101: Courtesy Mark Moore Fine Art, Los Angeles. Photo: Chris Bliss Photography. p.103: Courtesy the artist. p.105: Courtesy the artist. Photo © Renato Ghiazza. p.107: Courtesy Migrosmuseum für Gegenwartskunst Zürich and Gianni Motti. Photo: Stefan Altenburger. p.109: © Michael Landy. All rights reserved, DACS 2024. Courtesy the artist and Thomas Dane Gallery. Photo: Natalia Tsoukala. Courtesy NEON. p.111: © DACS 2024. Courtesy Hans-Peter Feldmann Estate, Düsseldorf and VG-Bild Kunst, Bonn. © Solomon R. Guggenheim Foundation, New York. Photo: David Heald. p.113: © Ryan Gander. Courtesy Annet Gelink Gallery, Amsterdam. p.114: © Tom Friedman. Courtesy the artist; Stephen Friedman Gallery, London and New York; and Lehmann Maupin, New York, Hong Kong, Seoul and London. p.115: Courtesy the artist. p.117: Courtesy Artists Space, New York. p.119: © Lubaina Himid. Courtesy the artist and Hollybush Gardens, London. p.121: Copyright and © Denis Beaubois. p.123: © Gerald Machona, Courtesy Goodman Gallery. p.125: © Kerry James Marshall. Courtesy the artist and Jack Shainman Gallery, New York. p.127: Courtesy Halycon Art International. p.129: Courtesy and © Shan Goshorn Estate, p.131: Courtesy the artist and i8 Gallery, Reykjavík. p.133: Courtesy the artist, Fraser Muggeridge studio and The Modern Institute, Glasgow. p.135: Courtesy the artist

and Almine Rech. Photo: Sven Laurent. p.137: © Sarah Meyohas. Courtesy the artist and Marianne Boesky Gallery, New York and Aspen. p.139: Art Collection of the free state of Thuringia. Courtesy Philipp Valenta. p.141: Courtesy the artist. p.143: © Grayson Perry. Courtesy the artist and Victoria Miro. p.145: Courtesy the artist; Herald St, London; Andrew Kreps Gallery, New York; and Mendes Wood DM, São Paulo, Brussels, New York and Paris. Photo: M. Dean. p.147: © Meschac Gaba. Courtesy Stevenson, Cape Town, Johannesburg and Amsterdam. p.148: © the artist and kurimanzutto, Mexico City / New York. Photo: Estudio Michel Zabé. p.149: © Keren Cytter. Courtesy the artist & Pilar Corrias, London. Photo: Damian Griffiths. p.151: Courtesy the artist and Octavia Art Gallery, New Orleans. p.153: Camera: Jonathas de Andrade. Edition: Tita e Pedro Melo. Sound: Maurício D'Orey. Courtesy the artist and Galleria Continua. p.155: © ADAGP, Paris and DACS, London, 2024. © Thomas Hirschhorn / ADAGP, Paris (2023). Courtesy the artist and Galerie Chantal Crousel, Paris. Photo: Florian Kleinefenn. p.157: Courtesy Christos J. Palios. p.159: © Hew Locke. All rights reserved, DACS 2024. Image courtesy the artist; Hales, London and New York, and P·P·O·W, New York. p.161: © Hank Willis Thomas. Courtesy the artist & Jack Shainman Gallery, New York. p.162: Courtesy the artist and Milani Gallery. Photo: Carl Warner. p.163: Courtesy the artist, Creative Time, New York, and LABOR, Mexico City. p.165: © the artist. Courtesy the artist and Aicon Contemporary, NYC. Photo: Document Photography, Sydney, Australia. p.167: Courtesy the artist and Vielmetter Los Angeles. Photo: Brica Wilcox. p.169: Courtesy Atelier Jens Haaning. Photo: Niels Fabæk / Kunsten Museum of Modern Art Aalborg. p.171: Courtesy the artist. p.173: Courtesy Carlos Aires studio and Sabrina Amrani Gallery. Photo: Oak Taylor-Smith. p.175: Courtesy the artists & Perrotin. Photo: Guillaume Ziccarelli. p.177: © Gabriel Kuri. Courtesy the artist and Sadie Coles HQ, London. Photo: Eva Herzog. p.179: © Damien Hirst and Science Ltd. All rights reserved, DACS 2024. Photo: Prudence Cuming Associates Ltd. p.181: Courtesy the artist and Gallery 1957. p.183: Courtesy Mandy El-Sayegh and Thaddaeus Ropac gallery London, Paris, Salzburg, Seoul. Photo: Ulrich Ghezzi. p.185: © Leo Fitzmaurice. Courtesy Sunday Painter.